St Vrain Valley Pioneers:

An Annotated Index

Compiled by Dina C. Carson

St Vrain Valley Pioneers:

An Annotated Index

Indexed by Dina C. Carson

Published by:
Iron Gate Publishing
P.O. Box 999
Niwot, CO 80544
www.irongate.com

All rights reserved. No part of this book may be reproduced or transmitted in any form or by any means, electronic or mechanical, including photocopying, recording or any information storage and retrieval system without written permission from the author, except for the inclusion of brief quotations in a review.

The Publisher of this index makes no representation that it is absolutely accurate or complete. Errors and omissions, whether typographical, clerical or otherwise do sometimes occur and may occur anywhere within the body of this publication. The Publisher does not assume and hereby disclaims any liability to any party for loss or damage by errors or omissions in this publication, whether such errors or omissions result from negligence, accident or any other cause.

Iron Gate Publishing has used its best efforts in collecting and preparing material for inclusion in the *St Vrain Valley Pioneers* but does not warrant that the information herein is complete or accurate, and does not assume, and hereby disclaims, any liability to any person for any loss or damage caused by errors or omissions in the *St Vrain Valley Pioneers,* whether such errors or omissions result from negligence, accident or any other cause.

Copyright © 2025 by Dina C. Carson, Iron Gate Publishing

Printed in the United States of America

ISBN 978-1-68224-197-4

Introduction

The *St Vrain Valley Pioneers* is an annotated index of the people who settled in the St Vrain Valley before 1880 and their descendants. It was compiled for the 120th Annual Meeting of the St Vrain Valley Pioneers Association. This information was compiled from many different source records.

The "St Vrain Pioneers Association Arrival Date" is taken from the "blue book" that the association produced in 1940. There are some people in the blue book who are listed by name but do not have an arrival date. There are others who are listed as Mr. and Mrs. so-and-so and family. They are all recorded in this book, but oftentimes, their first names are not known ... at least not yet.

The "St Vrain Land Club M687" is a copy of a document kept in the Greeley County Commissioners office. Th version I used to add this information is a copy from the Denver Public Library in the archives there.

The "Franklin Township Land Club Date" comes from one of three St Vrain area land clubs whose records have survived and are at the Carnegie Library for Local History. The other two are the "Troy District Land Club" and another "St Vrain Land Club." The St Vrain Land Club record that is archived at the Carnegie Library for Local History is distinct and contains different names than the one in the archives at the Denver Public Library.

The "St Vrain Ditch Owners" came from the 1883 Coffin vs. Left Hand Ditch Company lawsuit which resulted in a change in the way water was dispersed in the West. In the East, landowners along the ditch first could pull whatever as much water as they wanted leaving the last land along the ditch with little water. The Coffin vs. Left Hand Ditch Company lawsuit brought a change to first-in, first-rights which meant establishing a Water Court to establish who had been there the longest. All of the ditch owners listed here had ditches that came from St Vrain Creek. Boulder County was in Water Districts 5 and 6. The affidavits in the water cases are held in the Carnegie Library for Local History (not indexed or listed here), and he dispositions of the cases (ditch owners and their date of origination, listed here) are held in the Colorado State Archives.

In the 1860 United States Census, there were two places that fell within the St Vrain Valley Pioneers description of the area covered by the Association; both were in Nebraska Territory: Altona and the Platte River Settlements.

In the 1870 United States Census, there were three districts that fit the criteria: 1870 US Census, Colorado Territory, Boulder County, Left Hand; 1870 US Census, Colorado Territory, Boulder County, St Vrain District; and 1870 US Census, Colorado Territory, Weld County, St Vrain District.

The St Vrain Valley Pioneers Association Minute Book was indexed, but only the names of those who were recorded as being deceased are included here. The Minute Book began in 1904 when the Association was established, and the names of those memorialized were included in the early years of the Minute Book, but around 1931, the names were recorded instead in a Memorial Book. The names were also often printed in the newspaper. Unfortunately, the Memorial Books have disappeared, and do not seem to exist at this time, although efforts continue to recover them. There was not enough time to include the names of those who appeared in the book so they will appear in a separate index later.

Spelling is taken directly from the source record, and spelling of names in the 1860s and 1870s was "creative" some times.

Women are listed by their most recent married names. For example: Blackburn, Mary Jane Harding Burke. Mary Jane Harding is her maiden name. Mary Jane Harding Burke is the name she used while married to her first husband, and Mary Jane Harding Burke Blackburn is the name she used when married to her second husband.

Dates are often written with the year followed by the month followed by the day (e.g. 1861 May 21). This is because when the information was extracted from the original records, it was done in Microsoft Excel and that is one of the only ways to keep Excel from altering the date into another form, often an incorrect form.

South Boulder Cemetery is the earliest name of that cemetery which is also called Sacred Heart of Mary Cemetery. They are one and the same.

Mountain View Memorial Park Cemetery is along Iris Street in Boulder, whereas Mountain View Cemetery is in Longmont along Main Street.

A

Adair, Stephen Turrel
b. 2 Sept 1840, Moniteau Co, MO
d. 27 Jan 1909, Erie, Weld, CO
bd. Green Mountain, Boulder
spouse: Elizabeth Jane Fisher Adair; Concusion Susannah Smith Adair
father: Trustan Adair
mother: Elizabeth Jane Davis Adair
St Vrain Pioneers Assn Arrival Date: 1867

Adams, J Q
b. abt 1844
spouse: Angie Adams
St Vrain Pioneers Assn Arrival Date: 1865

Adams, R D
b. abt 1821, PA
Franklin Township Land Club Claim Date: 1860 June 25
St Vrain Land Club Date: 1860 June 26

Affolter, Albert
b. abt 1867, Colorado Territory
father: Jacob Affolter
mother: Martha Ann Jeffers Affolter
1870 US Census, Colorado Territory, Boulder County, Left Hand

Affolter, Anne E
b. 3 Mar 1880, CO
d. 26 Mar 1968
bd. Burlington Cemetery, Longmont, Boulder, CO
father: Frederick Affolter
mother: Elizabeth Ruch Affolter

Affolter, Eliza
b. abt 1866, Colorado Territory
father: Jacob Affolter
mother: Martha Ann Jeffers Affolter
1870 US Census, Colorado Territory, Boulder County, Left Hand

Affolter, Elizabeth Ruch
b. 11 Dec 1841, Sumiswald, Switzerland
d. 11 Oct 1926, Longmont, Boulder, CO
bd. Burlington Cemetery, Longmont, Boulder, CO
spouse: Frederick Affolter
St Vrain Pioneers Assn Arrival Date: [not recorded]
1870 US Census, Colorado Territory, Boulder County, Left Hand

Affolter, Frederick
b. 10 July 1832, Koppigen, Bern, Switzerland
d. 17 June 1895
bd. Burlington Cemetery, Longmont, Boulder, CO
spouse: Elisabeth Ruch Affolter
father: Jakob Affolter
mother: Elizabeth Baumberger Affolter
St Vrain Pioneers Assn Arrival Date: 1861
St Vrain Land Club Date: 1861 Feb 18
St Vrain Ditch Owner: Beckwith Ditch No 5, 8 Mar 1861
1870 US Census, Colorado Territory, Boulder County, Left Hand

Affolter, Jacob
b. abt 1830, Switzerland
d. 1 May 1903, Phelps, MO
spouse: Martha Ann Jeffers Affolter
1870 US Census, Colorado Territory, Boulder County, Left Hand

Affolter, Martha Ann Jeffers
b. 15 Aug 1840, Clark, IL
d. 15 Dec 1892, Rolla, Phelps, MO
spouse: Jacob Affolter
father: James Jeffers
mother: Catherine Jeffers
1870 US Census, Colorado Territory, Boulder County, Left Hand

Affolter, Oscar
b. 30 Jan 1871, Colorado Territory
d. 13 Feb 1933, Phelps, MO
father: Jacob Affolter
mother: Martha Ann Jeffers Affolter
1870 US Census, Colorado Territory, Boulder County, Left Hand

Akins, Samuel James
b. 16 Dec 1835, Bloomington, McLean, IL
d. 16 Sept 1916, Enterprise, Wallowa, OR
bd. Enterprise Cemetery, Enterprise, Wallowa, OR
spouse: Mary Ann Burns Akins
father: Charles Brookins Akins
mother: Phebe Brentlinger Akins
St Vrain Pioneers Assn Arrival Date: 1858

St Vrain Valley Pioneers

Akins, Thomas Avery
b. 8 Aug 1808, MD
d. 16 Apr 1878, Valmont, Boulder, CO
bd. Valmont Cemetery, Boulder, CO
spouse: Margaret Skerrit Ross Akins
father: James Akins
mother: Margaret Brookins Mathews Akins
St Vrain Pioneers Assn Arrival Date: 1858

Allebaugh, Charles Christian
b. Jan 1846, IN
d. 1937, Gilpin, CO
spouse: Emma Davis Allebaugh
father: Noah Sangston Allebaugh
mother: Sarah A Allebaugh
1870 US Census, Colorado Territory, Boulder County, St Vrain District

Allen, Alexander Pope
b. 22 May 1816, Auburn, Cayuga, NY
d. 12 Apr 1880, Valmont, Boulder, CO
bd. Valmont Cemetery, Boulder, CO
spouse: Cornelia Marie Hayden Allen
father: Abner Allen
mother: Martha Smith Allen
Franklin Township Land Club Claim Date: 1860 June 25
St Vrain Land Club Date: 1861 Apr 7

Allen, Alonzo Harris
b. 8 Feb 1860, Columbia, WI
d. 21 Feb 1951, Mendocino, CA
bd. Mountain View Cemetery, Longmont, Boulder, CO
spouse: Margaret Ann Ross Allen
father: Alonzo Nelson Allen
mother: Mary Ann Harris Allen
St Vrain Pioneers Assn Arrival Date: 1863
1870 US Census, Colorado Territory, Boulder County, St Vrain District

Allen, Alonzo Nelson
b. 1 Mar 1819, Wolcott, Wayne, NY
d. 27 July 1894, Pueblo, CO
bd. Burlington Cemetery, Longmont, Boulder, CO
spouse: Mary Ann Harris Allen
father: John L Allen
mother: Anna Greenleaf Allen
St Vrain Pioneers Assn Arrival Date: 1859
Troy District Land Club Claim Date: 1860 July 5
1870 US Census, Colorado Territory, Boulder County, St Vrain District

Allen, Anne Elizabeth Scoville
b. 6 July 1846, Washington, WI
d. 10 Nov 1929, Basin, WY
spouse: James D Allen
father: Samuel Yates Scoville
mother: Celia Littlefield Sample
1870 US Census, Colorado Territory, Boulder County, St Vrain District

Allen, Caroline
b. abt 1854, IL
1860 US Census, Nebraska Territory, Platte River

Allen, Charles F
b. July 1856, WI
d. 31 Mar 1937, Longmont, CO
bd. Mountain View Cemetery, Longmont, Boulder, CO
spouse: Margaret M
father: Alonzo Nelson Allen
mother: Mary Harris Allen
St Vrain Pioneers Assn Arrival Date: 1863
1870 US Census, Colorado Territory, Boulder County, St Vrain District

Allen, Claude Bridges
b. 25 Apr 1880, Slater, Saline, MO
d. 16 Oct 1959, Longmont, Boulder, CO
bd. Mountain View Cemetery, Longmont, Boulder, CO
spouse: Elizabeth Bell Allen
father: John Henry Allen
mother: Sarah Frances Bridges Allen

Allen, Elizabeth Bell Dodd
b. 9 Apr 1897, Niwot, Boulder, CO
d. 3 Feb 1982, Longmont, Boulder, CO
bd. Mountain View Cemetery, Longmont, Boulder, CO
spouse: C B Allen
father: A M Dodd
mother: Della Gould Dodd

Allen, F M
b. abt 1852, IL
1860 US Census, Nebraska Territory, Platte River

St Vrain Valley Pioneers

Allen, G B
b. abt 1859, IA
1860 US Census, Nebraska Territory, Platte River

Allen, George
b. Feb 1854, Columbia, WI
father: Alonzo Nelson Allen
mother: Mary Ann Harris Allen
St Vrain Pioneers Assn Arrival Date: 1863
1870 US Census, Colorado Territory, Boulder County, St Vrain District

Allen, Hattie Louis August
b. 1880
d. 22 June 1967
bd. Green Mountain Cemetery, Boulder, CO
spouse: Jacob Max Allen
father: Anthony Joseph August

Allen, Henly Wheaton
b. 28 Dec 1838, Oswego, Kane Cty, IL
d. 14 Feb 1920, Boulder, CO
bd. Columbia Cemetery, Boulder, CO
spouse: Meldred McNeel Allen
father: Alexander Pope Allen
mother: Cornelia Marie Hayden Allen
St Vrain Pioneers Assn Arrival Date: 1865

Allen, J B
b. abt 1840, IA
1860 US Census, Nebraska Territory, Platte River

Allen, James D
b. 9 Dec 1844, Washington, WI
d. 3 Dec 1910, Basin, WY
spouse: Annie E Scoville Allen
father: Daniel Allen
mother: Ann Coates Allen
1870 US Census, Colorado Territory, Boulder County, St Vrain District

Allen, Jane
b. abt 1836, OH
1860 US Census, Nebraska Territory, Platte River

Allen, King
b. abt 1800, PA
1860 US Census, Nebraska Territory, Platte River

Allen, Maria Tourtellot Knowles
b. 20 May 1870, Boulder, Colorado Territory
d. 27 May 1949, Pullman, Whitman, WA
bd. Greenwood Memorial Trace, Spokane, WA
spouse: Frank Knowles; Arthur Henley Allen
father: James Buchanan Tourtellot
mother: Sarah Ann Smith Tourtellot
1870 US Census, Colorado Territory, Boulder County, Left Hand

Allen, Martha J
b. Mar 1870, Colorado Territory
father: James D Allen
mother: Annie E Scoville Allen
1870 US Census, Colorado Territory, Boulder County, St Vrain District

Allen, Mary Ann Harris Dickens
b. June 1818, Leicestershire, England
d. 16 June 1905, Longmont, Boulder, CO
bd. Mountain View Cemetery, Longmont, Boulder, CO
spouse: William Henry Dickens; Alonzo Nelson Allen
father: John Harris
mother: Mary Jerome Harris
St Vrain Pioneers Assn Arrival Date: 1863
1870 US Census, Colorado Territory, Boulder County, St Vrain District

Allen, Meldred McNeel
b. 2 Oct 1843, Potsdam, NY
d. 8 July 1916, Boulder, CO
bd. Columbia Cemetery, Boulder, CO
spouse: Henley Wheaton Allen, MD
father: James Taylor McNeel
mother: Betsey E Norton McNeel
St Vrain Pioneers Assn Arrival Date: 1865

Allen, Nelson
St Vrain Land Club (M687) Date: 1861 Jan 27

Allen, Rhine E
b. abt 1846, OH
1860 US Census, Nebraska Territory, Platte River

Allen, Rudolphus N
b. 7 Apr 1850, Columbia, WI
d. 24 Nov 1886, Boulder, CO
bd. Mountain View Cemetery, Longmont, Boulder, CO
spouse: Jennie R Peasce Allen
father: Alonzo Nelson Allen
mother: Mary Harris Allen
St Vrain Pioneers Assn Arrival Date: 1863

St Vrain Valley Pioneers

1870 US Census, Colorado Territory, Boulder County, St Vrain District

Allman, Charles
b. abt 1839, England
1870 US Census, Colorado Territory, Boulder County, St Vrain District

Anderson, Erick J
b. 18 Aug 1840, Javela, Sweden
d. 13 Sept 1925, Marysville, Snohomish, WA
bd. Marysville Cemetery, Marysville, WA
spouse: Fidelia Russell Anderson
father: Jonas Anderson, Sr
mother: Christine Anderson
St Vrain Pioneers Assn Arrival Date: 1860

Anderson, Hugo
St Vrain Ditch Owner: Ullery Ditch No. 66, 1 July 1874

Anderson, Jonas
b. abt 1813, Sweden
d. 1 Aug 1894, Boulder, CO
bd. Columbia Cemetery, Boulder, CO
St Vrain Pioneers Assn Arrival Date: [not recorded]
Troy District Land Club Claim Date: 1861 Jan 29

Anderson, Jonas A
b. 1 Oct 1844, Sweden
d. 25 Mar 1919, Boulder, CO
bd. Columbia Cemetery, Boulder, CO
spouse: Sarah Nyberg Anderson
father: Jonas Anderson, Sr
mother: Christine Anderson

Anderson, Swan
spouse: Hilda Ernburg Anderson
St Vrain Ditch Owner: Ullery Ditch No. 66, 1 July 1874

Andrew, James
St Vrain Pioneers Assn Arrival Date: 1863

Andrew, Margaret Wain
b. 15 July 1834, Hurdsville, Cheshire, England
d. 13 Aug 1899, Longmont, Boulder, CO
spouse: James Andrews
father: William Wain
mother: Sarah Roylance Wain
St Vrain Pioneers Assn Arrival Date: 1863

1870 US Census, Colorado Territory, Boulder County, St Vrain District

Andrew, William B
b. 3 Nov 1859, Grant, WI
d. 2 Feb 1914, Galveston, TX
bd. Riverside Cemetery, Denver, CO
spouse: Eva Eunice Starbird Andrew
father: James Andrew
mother: Margaret Wain Andrew

Andrews, Bertha
b. abt 1842, WI/NY
d. abt 21 Jan 1891, Niwot, Boulder, CO
bd. Niwot Cemetery, Niwot, Boulder, CO
1870 US Census, Colorado Territory, Boulder County, St Vrain District

Andrews, Elijah H
b. abt 1836, Syracuse, Onondaga, NY
d. 6 Jan 1905, Leadville, Lake, CO
spouse: Mary A Lockhart Andrews
1870 US Census, Colorado Territory, Boulder County, St Vrain District

Andrews, Emma Luella
b. abt 1868, Colorado Territory
d. bef 1880?
father: James Andrews
mother: Margaret Andrews
1870 US Census, Colorado Territory, Boulder County, St Vrain District

Andrews, James
b. abt 1833, England
d. 3 Mar 1920, Boulder, CO?
spouse: Margaret Wain Andrews
1870 US Census, Colorado Territory, Boulder County, St Vrain District

Andrews, Wilber F
b. abt 1844, NY
1870 US Census, Colorado Territory, Boulder County, St Vrain District

Andrews, William A
b. abt 1859, CO/WI
father: James Andrews
mother: Margaret Wain Andrews
1870 US Census, Colorado Territory, Boulder County, St Vrain District

St Vrain Valley Pioneers

Andrus, James A S
b. 10 Nov 1856, Richland, WI
d. 16 Mar 1934, Seymour, Warren, MO
bd. Columbia Cemetery, Boulder, CO
spouse: Nellie Yockey Andrus, Bertha Harrell Andrus
father: Horace Andrus
mother: Mary Lucinda Slaughter Andrus

Arbacht, Fenands
b. abt 1847, France
1870 US Census, Colorado Territory, Boulder County, St Vrain District

Arbuthnot, Carson William
b. 2 May 1804, Pine Township, Allegheny Cty, PA
d. 1 Jan 1873, Boulder Cty, Colorado Territory
bd. Haystack Mountain?
spouse: Frances Jones Arbuthnot

Arbuthnot, Fredrick William
b. 30 Nov 1869, Haystack Mountain, Boulder Cty, CO
d. 10 Nov 1957, Boulder, CO
bd. Niwot Cemetery, Niwot, Boulder, CO
spouse: Margie Ann Coe Arbuthnot
father: William Arbuthnot
mother: Mary Elizabeth Bader Arbuthnot
1870 US Census, Colorado Territory, Boulder County, Left Hand

Arbuthnot, James A
b. 2 Nov 1841, Pine Township, Allegheny Cty, PA
d. 25 Nov 1886, Niwot, Boulder Cty, CO
bd. Niwot Cemetery, Niwot, Boulder, CO
spouse: Phoebe Ann Evans Steele Arbuthnot
father: Carson William Arbuthnot
mother: Frances Jones Arbuthnot
St Vrain Pioneers Assn Arrival Date: 1859

Arbuthnot, Mary Elizabeth Bader
b. 17 June 1848, Baden-Baden, Germany
d. 22 June 1923, Niwot, Boulder Cty, CO
bd. Hygiene Cemetery, Hygiene, Boulder, CO
spouse: William Arbuthnot
father: John George Bader
mother: Mary Messinger Bader
St Vrain Pioneers Assn Arrival Date: 1866
1870 US Census, Colorado Territory, Boulder County, Left Hand

Arbuthnot, Mary Rachel Johnson
b. 4 June 1851, Kendellville, Winneshiek, IA
d. 1 July 1925, Boulder, CO
bd. Niwot Cemetery, Niwot, Boulder, CO
spouse: Samuel Cristy Arbuthnot
father: Joshua P Johnson
mother: Christina Jeffers Johnson
St Vrain Pioneers Assn Arrival Date: 1863
1870 US Census, Colorado Territory, Boulder County, Left Hand

Arbuthnot, Phoebe Ann Evans Steele
b. 27 Jan 1835, Lehigh, PA
d. 15 Sept 1919, Boulder, CO
bd. Niwot Cemetery, Niwot, Boulder, CO
spouse: Edward Dunsha Steele; James A Arbuthnot
father: Jonathan P Evans
mother: Sarah Chesley Thompson Evans
St Vrain Pioneers Assn Arrival Date: 1864
1870 US Census, Colorado Territory, Boulder County, Left Hand

Arbuthnot, Ray Elon
b. 5 Mar 1889, Boulder, CO
d. 21 Mar 1967, Boulder, CO
bd. Mountain View Cemetery, Longmont, Boulder, CO
father: Samuel Christy Arbuthnot
mother: Mary Rachel Johnson Arbuthnot

Arbuthnot, Samuel Cristy
b. 17 Aug 1833, Pine Township, Allegheny Cty, PA
d. 21 Mar 1915, Niwot, Boulder Cty, CO
bd. Niwot Cemetery, Niwot, Boulder, CO
spouse: Mary Rachel Johnson Arbuthnot
father: Carson W Arbuthnot
mother: Mary Frances Jones Arbuthnot
St Vrain Pioneers Assn Arrival Date: 1859
1870 US Census, Colorado Territory, Boulder County, Left Hand

Arbuthnot, William Carson
b. 30 Aug 1835, Pine Township, Allegheny Cty, PA
d. 21 Apr 1882, Haystack Mountain, Boulder Cty, CO
bd. Hygiene Cemetery, Hygiene, Boulder, CO
spouse: Mary Elizabeth Bader Arbuthnot
father: Carson William Arbuthnot
mother: Frances Jones Arbuthnot

St Vrain Valley Pioneers

St Vrain Pioneers Assn Arrival Date: 1859
1870 US Census, Colorado Territory, Boulder County, Left Hand

Armitage, J
b. abt 1838, England
1860 US Census, Nebraska Territory, Platte River

Armstrong, Charles Harvey
b. abt 1870, Colorado Territory
d. 22 Aug 1871, Colorado Territory
bd. Burlington Cemetery, Longmont, Boulder, CO
father: Thomas G W Armstrong
mother: Isabel Agnes Honaker Miller Armstrong
1870 US Census, Colorado Territory, Boulder County, St Vrain District

Armstrong, Harvey
b. 2 Mar 1875, Colorado Territory
d. 1967, Longmont, Boulder, CO
bd. Mountain View Cemetery, Longmont, Boulder, CO
spouse: Hattie Gregg Armstrong
father: John M Armstrong
mother: Sarah E Rannells Armstrong

Armstrong, Isabella Agnes Honaker Miller
b. 29 June 1833, Monroe, WV
d. 29 Dec 1900, Denver, CO
bd. Lakeview, Loveland, CO
spouse: Michael Christ Miller, m2 Thomas G W Armstrong
father: John Honaker
mother: Margaret A Sams Honaker
St Vrain Pioneers Assn Arrival Date: 1866
1870 US Census, Colorado Territory, Boulder County, St Vrain District

Armstrong, John M
b. 26 Nov 1846, VA
d. 23 Apr 1917, Boulder, CO
bd. Mountain View Cemetery, Longmont, Boulder, CO
spouse: Sarah E Rannells Armstrong
St Vrain Pioneers Assn Arrival Date: 1867
1870 US Census, Colorado Territory, Boulder County, St Vrain District

Armstrong, Robert Lee
b. 4 Feb 1868, Colorado Territory
d. 9 Nov 1880, Boulder, CO
bd. Burlington Cemetery, Longmont, Boulder, CO
father: Thomas G W Armstrong
mother: Isabella Agnes Honaker MillerArmstrong
1870 US Census, Colorado Territory, Boulder County, St Vrain District

Armstrong, Samuel
b. 9 Nov 1832, Bedford, PA
d. 6 May 1908, Garden Plain, Whiteside, IL
bd. Mountain View Cemetery, Longmont, Boulder, CO
spouse: Sarah E Davis Armstrong; Jemima Maddux Armstrong
St Vrain Pioneers Assn Arrival Date: 1866

Armstrong, Samuel Frederick
b. 9 June 1881
d. 27 Feb 1927, Longmont, Boulder, CO
bd. Mountain View Cemetery, Longmont, Boulder, CO
spouse: Wilda Jane Dodd Armstrong Cosslett
father: John M Armstrong
mother: Sarah Elizabeth Rannells Armstrong

Armstrong, Sarah Elizabeth Rannells
b. 7 June 1853, Caldwell, MO
d. 21 Apr 1903, Longmont, Boulder, CO
bd. Mountain View Cemetery, Longmont, Boulder, CO
spouse: John M Armstrong
father: Samuel Flemming Rannells
mother: Sarah Bay Rannells
St Vrain Pioneers Assn Arrival Date: 1864

Armstrong, Thomas G W
b. 20 June 1823, Lewisburg, Greenbrier, VA
d. 25 Nov 1894, Loeland, Larimer, CO
bd. Lakeview Cemetery, Loveland, CO
spouse: Martha Ann Honaker Armstrong; Isabella Agnes Honaker Miller Armstrong
St Vrain Pioneers Assn Arrival Date: 1866
1870 US Census, Colorado Territory, Boulder County, St Vrain District

Armstrong, William
b. abt 1818, OH
1860 US Census, Nebraska Territory, Platte River

Arnett, Anthony
b. 7 July 1819, Reichstaff, Alsace-Lorraine, France
d. 11 June 1903, La Jolla, CA

bd. Columbia Cemetery, Boulder, CO
spouse: Mary Rose Graham Arnett
father: Francois Louis Arnett
mother: Marie Claire Schetty Arnett
St Vrain Pioneers Assn Arrival Date: 1859

Arnett, Eugene
b. abt 1871, Colorado Territory
d. Sept 1917, Los Angeles, CA
spouse: Lucy B Clayton
father: Anthony Arnett
mother: Mary Rose Graham Arnett

Arnett, Mary Rose Graham
b. abt 1832, Monagham, Ulster, Ireland
d. 9 May 1903, La Jolla, CA
bd. Columbia Cemetery, Boulder, CO
spouse: Anthony Arnett
father: William Graham
mother: Rose Murphy Graham
St Vrain Pioneers Assn Arrival Date: 1859

Arnett, Robert Emmett
b. 7 June 1861, Geneseo, Henry Co, IL
d. 27 Oct 1944, Boulder, CO
bd. Columbia Cemetery, Boulder, CO
spouse: Ida Drumm Arnett
father: Anthony Arnett
mother: Mary Rose Graham Arnett

Arnett, Williamette H
b. 1848, Portland, IL
d. bef 9 Apr 1901, Dawson, Yukon, Canada
spouse: Lucy Katie Spencer Arnett, Ella P Armstrong Arnett
father: Anthony Arnett
mother: Mary Rose Graham Arnett

Ashcroft, Samuel
St Vrain Pioneers Assn Arrival Date: 1865

Atwood, Addie McCaslin
b. abt 1867
d. 1922
spouse: Joseph Atwood
father: Matthew L McCaslin
mother: Miranda McCaslin

Atwood, family Newton J
St Vrain Pioneers Assn Arrival Date: 1859

Atwood, George Nicholas
b. May 1850, ME
d. 8 Oct 1926, Santa Ana, Orange, CA
bd. cremated
spouse: Hannah May Gregg Atwood

Atwood, Mrs Newton J
b. 1864
spouse: Newton John Atwood
St Vrain Pioneers Assn Arrival Date: 1859

Atwood, Newton John
b. 8 Jan 1832, Morgador, Summit, OH
d. 7 Apr 1915, Longmont, Boulder, CO
bd. Mountain View Cemetery, Longmont, Boulder, CO
spouse: Ida M Taylor Atwood
father: Philo Atwood
mother: Margaret Hall Atwood
St Vrain Pioneers Assn Arrival Date: 1859

Austan, J B
St Vrain Land Club Date: [not recorded]

Austin, James
b. abt 1850, MO
1870 US Census, Colorado Territory, Weld County, St Vrain District

Austin, Julia Ellen
b. 28 Apr 1843, Lockport, Will Co, IL
d. 10 May 1922, Boulder, CO
bd. Columbia Cemetery, Boulder, CO
father: Ira Austin
mother: Harriett Benjamin Austin

Autrey, John Joseph
b. 11 Aug 1891
d. 27 Mar 1968
bd. Lafayette Cemetery, Lafayette, Boulder, CO
spouse: Carrie Ann Cobb Autrey; Mary Wagner Autrey
father: George Kenison Autrey

St Vrain Valley Pioneers

B

Bacon, Andrew
b. 27 May 1835
d. 8 Feb 1932, Golden, CO
bd. Golden Cemetery, Golden, Jefferson, CO
spouse: Emmaline Margaret Atwood Bacon
father: William A Bacon
mother: Malinda Foote Bacon

Bacon, Cora A
d. abt 1967
bd. Mountain View Cemetery, Longmont, Boulder, CO

Bacon, Emmaline Margaret Atwood
b. 15 May 1835
d. 2 Jan 1921, Golden, CO
bd. Golden Cemetery, Golden, Jefferson, CO
spouse: Andrew Bacon

Bacon, Harold W
b. 1 Jan 1904
d. 18 June 1967
bd. Mountain View Cemetery, Longmont, Boulder, CO
spouse: Clara A Augustine Bacon
father: Laren F Bacon
mother: Gussie Bacon

Bacon, John W
b. abt 1838, OH
d. 1916, Denver, CO
St Vrain Pioneers Assn Arrival Date: 1861
St Vrain Ditch Owner: Bacon's Ditch No. 7, 1 June 1861
1870 US Census, Colorado Territory, Weld County, St Vrain District

Bacon, Lauren F
b. abt 1876, Longmont, CO
d. 19 Mar 1920
father: J W Bacon

Bader, Elizy
bd. Burlington Cemetery?, Longmont, Boulder, CO

Bader, Friedrich Wilhelm
b. abt 1851, Baden-Baden, Germany
d. 27 Sept 1927, San Jose, Santa Clara, CA
spouse: Ada Boot Bader
father: John George Bader
mother: Mary Messinger Bader
St Vrain Pioneers Assn Arrival Date: 1866
1870 US Census, Colorado Territory, Boulder County, Left Hand

Bader, George Nicholas
b. 21 Jan 1873, Niwot, Boulder, CO
d. 26 Oct 1926, Boulder, CO
bd. Green Mountain Cemetery, Boulder, CO
spouse: Ivy May Burch Bader
father: Nicholas Ernest Bader
mother: Eliza A Greub Bader Knaus

Bader, Hazel Ruth Strain
b. 29 Dec 1894, Mount Ayr, Ringgold, IA
d. 24 July 1982, Loveland, Larimer, CO
bd. Loveland Burial Park, Loveland, Larimer, CO
spouse: Ivan E Bader
father: Samuel George Strain
mother: Sarah E Andrews Strain

Bader, John George
b. 9 Dec 1825, Baden-Baden, Germany
d. 8 Dec 1895, Boulder, CO
bd. Columbia Cemetery, Boulder, CO
spouse: Mary Bader; Susan Bader, m3. Mary F Roberts Bader
father: Konrad Bader
mother: Maria Kreuter Bader
St Vrain Pioneers Assn Arrival Date: 1866
1870 US Census, Colorado Territory, Boulder County, Left Hand

Bader, Nicholas Ernest
b. 13 Mar 1828, Baden-Baden, Germany
d. 5 Dec 1873, Left Hand District, Boulder, Colorado Territory
bd. Burlington Cemetery, Longmont, Boulder, Colorado Territory
spouse: Eliza A Greub Bader
father: Konrad Bader
mother: Maria Kreuter Bader
St Vrain Pioneers Assn Arrival Date: 1860
1870 US Census, Colorado Territory, Boulder County, Left Hand

Bader, William Ernest
b. 28 Nov 1868, Niwot, Boulder, CO
d. 23 Feb 1931, Loveland, Larimer, CO

spouse: Sarah Elizabeth Welty
father: Nicholas Ernest Bader
mother: Eliza Alice Greub Bader Knaus
1870 US Census, Colorado Territory, Boulder County, Left Hand

Bailey, Elias
b. 1844, Ashland, OH
d. 5 Oct 1911, Longmont, Boulder, CO
father: John Campbell Bailey
mother: Elizabeth Platt Bailey
St Vrain Pioneers Assn Arrival Date: 1866
1870 US Census, Colorado Territory, Weld County, St Vrain District

Bailey, Elizabeth Platt
b. Jan 1823, Tuscarawas, OH
d. 25 July 1884, Longmont, Boulder, CO
bd. Mountain View Cemetery, Longmont, Boulder, CO
spouse: John Campbell Bailey
father: Richard Platt
mother: Margaret Dickson Platt
St Vrain Pioneers Assn Arrival Date: 1860
1870 US Census, Colorado Territory, Weld County, St Vrain District

Bailey, John Campbell
b. 11 Jan 1821, Clearcreek Twp, Ashland, OH
d. 2 Sept 1906, Longmont, Boulder, CO
bd. Mountain View Cemetery, Longmont, Boulder, CO
spouse: Elizabeth Platt Bailey
father: Nathaniel Elias Bailey
mother: Mary Magdelina Pollock Shriver Bailey
St Vrain Pioneers Assn Arrival Date: 1860
1870 US Census, Colorado Territory, Weld County, St Vrain District

Bailey, Joseph
b. June 1850, IA
d. CA?
father: John Campbell Bailey
mother: Elizabeth A Platt Bailey
St Vrain Pioneers Assn Arrival Date: 1860
1870 US Census, Colorado Territory, Weld County, St Vrain District

Bailey, L L
St Vrain Land Club (M687) Date: 1861 Jan 25

Baker, Albert Clark
b. 26 Aug 1858, Juneau, Dodge, WI
d. 21 Nov 1933, Larimer, CO
bd. Grandview Cemetery, Fort Collins, Larimer, CO
spouse: Nancy C Baker
father: Alexander Kendrick Baker
mother: Helen Maria Butler Baker
1870 US Census, Colorado Territory, Boulder County, Left Hand

Baker, Alexander Kendrick
b. 28 Apr 1818, Oswego, NY
d. 10 Oct 1909, Fort Collins, Larimer, CO
spouse: Hellen Maria Baker
father: Edward Baker
mother: Patience Allen Baker
1870 US Census, Colorado Territory, Boulder County, Left Hand

Baker, Charles Henry
b. 20 Nov 1846, Providence, RI
d. 13 Oct 1937, Longmont, Boulder, CO
bd. Mountain View Cemetery, Longmont, Boulder, CO
spouse: Mary Jane Entwistle Baker
father: Alexander Kendrick Baker
mother: Helen Marie Butler Baker
St Vrain Pioneers Assn Arrival Date: 1865
1870 US Census, Colorado Territory, Boulder County, Left Hand

Baker, Helen Maria Butler
b. 15 July 1823, NY
d. 20 May 1912, Fort Collins, Larimer, CO
bd. Grandview Cemetery, Fort Collins, Larimer, CO
spouse: Alexander Kendrick Baker
father: Linus Butler
mother: Polly Landon Butler
St Vrain Pioneers Assn Arrival Date: 1866
1870 US Census, Colorado Territory, Boulder County, Left Hand

Baker, Imogene Dailey
b. abt 1869, Boulder Creek, Boulder, CO
spouse: Fred Baker
father: Dennis Dailey
mother: Juliette McDonald Green Dailey

St Vrain Valley Pioneers

1870 US Census, Colorado Territory, Weld County, St Vrain District

Baker, J J
b. abt 1832, MO
1860 US Census, Nebraska Territory, Platte River

Baker, Larkin
St Vrain Pioneers Assn Arrival Date: 1859

Baker, Mary Jane Entwistle
b. July 1854, Blackburn, Lancashire, England
d. 18 Nov 1919, Longmont, Boulder, CO
bd. Mountain View Cemetery, Longmont, Boulder, CO
spouse: Charles Henry Baker
father: James Entwistle
mother: Sarah Harwood Entwistle
St Vrain Pioneers Assn Arrival Date: 1865

Baker, Mrs Larkin
spouse: Larkin Baker
St Vrain Pioneers Assn Arrival Date: 1859

Baker, Pamela Jane Smart Franklin
b. 1827, Dresden, Weakly, TN
d. 9 Nov 1921, Twin Falls, ID
spouse: Benjamin A Franklin, William Samuel Baker
St Vrain Pioneers Assn Arrival Date: 1859

Baker, Priscilla
b. abt 1830, TN
d. 6 Sept 1904, Hygiene, Boulder, CO
bd. Hygiene Cemetery, Hygiene, Boulder, CO
spouse: William Samuel Baker
1870 US Census, Colorado Territory, Boulder County, St Vrain District

Baker, S H
b. abt 1830, MO
1860 US Census, Nebraska Territory, Platte River

Baker, William Samuel
b. 1826, TN
d. 6 Apr 1907, Hygiene, Boulder, CO
bd. Hygiene Cemetery, Hygiene, Boulder, CO
spouse: Pamelia Jane Smart Baker
St Vrain Pioneers Assn Arrival Date: 1859
Franklin Township Land Club Claim Date: 1860 Feb 11
St Vrain Land Club Date: 1860 Feb 11

1870 US Census, Colorado Territory, Boulder County, St Vrain District

Baldwin, Charles G
b. abt 1820
d. 28 Sept 1885, Longmont, Boulder, CO
bd. Mountain View Cemetery, Longmont, Boulder, CO
St Vrain Pioneers Assn Arrival Date: [not recorded]

Baller, Anna Larson
b. 27 July 1829
d. 28 Oct 1887, Longmont, Boulder, CO
bd. Mountain View Cemetery, Longmont, Boulder, CO
spouse: Nils Baller
St Vrain Pioneers Assn Arrival Date: 1868

Baller, Nils
b. 7 Sept 1844, Sweden
d. 16 Dec 1915, Longmont, Boulder, CO
bd. Mountain View Cemetery, Longmont, Boulder, CO
spouse: Anna Larson Baller, Maria Larson Baller
St Vrain Pioneers Assn Arrival Date: 1868

Ballinger, Andrew J
b. abt 1863, IA
father: Harmon Ballinger
mother: Mary J Ballinger
St Vrain Pioneers Assn Arrival Date: 1863

Ballinger, Benjamin
b. abt 1858, IA
father: Harmon Ballinger
mother: Mary J Ballinger
St Vrain Pioneers Assn Arrival Date: 1863

Ballinger, David
b. abt 1856, OH
father: Harmon Ballinger
mother: Mary J Ballinger
St Vrain Pioneers Assn Arrival Date: 1863

Ballinger, Harmon
b. abt 1832, Hesse-Darmstadt, Germany
spouse: Mary J Ballinger
St Vrain Pioneers Assn Arrival Date: 1860

Ballinger, Isaac
b. abt 1853, IA

father: Harmon Ballinger
mother: Mary J Ballinger
St Vrain Pioneers Assn Arrival Date: 1863

Ballinger, James L
b. abt 1861, OH
father: Harmon Ballinger
mother: Mary J Ballinger
St Vrain Pioneers Assn Arrival Date: 1863

Ballinger, Laura Curtis
b. 18 May 1864, Pleasant Hll, Pike, IL
d. 31 July 1929, Mead, Weld, CO
bd. Mountain View Cemetery, Longmont, Boulder, CO
spouse: James L Ballinger
father: Henry Amos Curtis
mother: Patience "Pink" Cannon Curtis Quinn

Ballinger, Mary J
b. abt 1833, OH
spouse: Harmon Ballinger
St Vrain Pioneers Assn Arrival Date: 1863

Baner, James
b. abt 1812, PA
1860 US Census, Nebraska Territory, Platte River

Banner, George W
b. abt 1845, PA
1870 US Census, Colorado Territory, Weld County, St Vrain District

Bannock, G M
b. abt 1845, DE
1870 US Census, Colorado Territory, Weld County, St Vrain District

Barber, Joseph Steven
b. 23 July 1820, Tioga, NY
d. 11 Feb 1894, Boulder, CO
bd. Columbia Cemetery, Boulder, CO
spouse: Harriet Lucinda Conklin Barber
St Vrain Pioneers Assn Arrival Date: 1862
St Vrain Land Club (M687) Date: 1861 Mar 21

Barber, O F
b. abt 1843, IL
1860 US Census, Nebraska Territory, Platte River

Barber, T H
b. abt 1830, NY
1860 US Census, Nebraska Territory, Platte River

Barclay, Joseph B
b. 19 Mar 1819, PA
d. 27 Sept 1896
bd. Mountain View Cemetery, Longmont, Boulder, CO
spouse: Jane E Cooper Barclay

Barker, Ezra
b. abt 1797, ME
d. 5 Feb 1878, Boulder, CO
bd. Columbia Cemetery, Boulder, CO
father: Ezra Barker
St Vrain Pioneers Assn Arrival Date: 1860

Barkhurst, Ira C
b. abt 1850, IA
1870 US Census, Colorado Territory, Boulder County, St Vrain District

Barkley, Joseph B
St Vrain Pioneers Assn Arrival Date: 1870

Barnes, Lafayette
b. abt 1836
1870 US Census, Colorado Territory, Weld County, St Vrain District

Barney, baby girl
b. abt 1870, Colorado Territory
bd. Burlington Cemetery?, Longmont, Boulder, CO
father: William Miles Barney
mother: Malissa J Rannels Willson Barney
1870 US Census, Colorado Territory, Boulder County, St Vrain District

Barney, Daniel H
b. abt 1827, PA
1870 US Census, Colorado Territory, Boulder County, St Vrain District

Barney, Malissa Jane Rannells Wilson
b. 18 Dec 1835, Morgan, OH
d. 17 Feb 1879, Longmont, Boulder, CO
spouse: James Wilson; William Miles Barney
father: Samuel Flemming Rannells
mother: Sarah Bay Rannells
St Vrain Pioneers Assn Arrival Date: 1864
1870 US Census, Colorado Territory, Boulder County, St Vrain District

St Vrain Valley Pioneers

Barney, William Julius
b. 14 Aug 1868, Colorado Territory
d. 1898
spouse: Sadie?
father: William Miles Barney
mother: Malissa Jane Rannells Wilson Barney
1870 US Census, Colorado Territory, Boulder County, St Vrain District

Barney, William Miles
b. 8 July 1823, Herron Cty, OH
d. 26 Oct 1905, Longmont, CO
bd. Mountain View Cemetery, Longmont, Boulder, CO
spouse: Malissa J Rannells Wilson Barney; Helen Barclay Barney
father: Henry Barney
mother: Jane Ackley Barney
1870 US Census, Colorado Territory, Boulder County, St Vrain District

Barnoby, Robert
b. abt 1821, KY
1870 US Census, Colorado Territory, Boulder County, St Vrain District

Barre, Anne
b. abt 1862, IL
father: George Barre
mother: Ellen Barre
1870 US Census, Colorado Territory, Boulder County, St Vrain District

Barre, Ella
b. abt 1858, IL
father: George Barre
mother: Ellen Barre
1870 US Census, Colorado Territory, Boulder County, St Vrain District

Barre, Ellen
b. abt 1834, England
spouse: George Barre
1870 US Census, Colorado Territory, Boulder County, St Vrain District

Barre, Fred
b. abt 1865, Colorado Territory
father: George Barre
mother: Ellen Barre
1870 US Census, Colorado Territory, Boulder County, St Vrain District

Barre, George
b. abt 1826, England
spouse: Ellen Barre
1870 US Census, Colorado Territory, Boulder County, St Vrain District

Barre, George
b. abt 1870, Colorado Territory
father: George Barre
mother: Ellen Barre
1870 US Census, Colorado Territory, Boulder County, St Vrain District

Barre, John
b. abt 1860, IL
father: George Barre
mother: Ellen Barre
1870 US Census, Colorado Territory, Boulder County, St Vrain District

Barre, Mattie
b. abt 1867, Colorado Territory
father: George Barre
mother: Ellen Barre
1870 US Census, Colorado Territory, Boulder County, St Vrain District

Barrons, Antone
b. abt 1832, Canada
1870 US Census, Colorado Territory, Boulder County, St Vrain District

Bartley, William
b. abt 1839, NY
1860 US Census, Nebraska Territory, Platte River

Barto, boy
b. May 1870, Colorado Territory
father: Peter Barto
mother: Mary Barto
1870 US Census, Colorado Territory, Boulder County, Left Hand

Barto, John
b. abt 1867, Colorado Territory
father: Peter Barto
mother: Mary Barto
1870 US Census, Colorado Territory, Boulder County, Left Hand

St Vrain Valley Pioneers

Barto, Kate
b. abt 1865, Colorado Territory
father: Peter Barto
mother: Mary Barto
1870 US Census, Colorado Territory, Boulder County, Left Hand

Barto, Martin
b. abt 1869, Colorado Territory
father: Peter Barto
mother: Mary Barto
1870 US Census, Colorado Territory, Boulder County, Left Hand

Barto, Mary
b. abt 1844, NY
spouse: Peter Barto
1870 US Census, Colorado Territory, Boulder County, Left Hand

Barto, Peter
b. abt 1824, Prussia
spouse: Mary Barto
1870 US Census, Colorado Territory, Boulder County, Left Hand

Bashor, Albert D
b. 19 Apr 1882
d. 20 Oct 1966
bd. Hygiene Cemetery, Hygiene, Boulder, CO

Bass, P H
St Vrain Land Club Date: 1861 May 6

Bassett, Alonzo D
b. abt 1831, NY
spouse: Harriet Bassett
St Vrain Pioneers Assn Arrival Date: 1864
1870 US Census, Colorado Territory, Boulder County, St Vrain District

Bassett, Clara
b. abt 1861, WI
father: Alonzo Bassett
mother: Harriet Bassett
1870 US Census, Colorado Territory, Boulder County, St Vrain District

Bassett, Edwin
b. abt 1865, Colorado Territory
father: Alonzo Bassett
mother: Harriet Bassett
1870 US Census, Colorado Territory, Boulder County, St Vrain District

Bassett, Elmer
b. abt 1863, WI
father: Alonzo Bassett
mother: Harriet Bassett
1870 US Census, Colorado Territory, Boulder County, St Vrain District

Bassett, Estella
b. abt 1867, Colorado Territory
father: Alonzo Bassett
mother: Harriet Bassett
1870 US Census, Colorado Territory, Boulder County, St Vrain District

Bassett, H E
St Vrain Pioneers Assn Arrival Date: 1864

Bassett, Harriet
b. abt 1836, NY
spouse: Alonzo Bassett
1870 US Census, Colorado Territory, Boulder County, St Vrain District

Bassett, Kenneth
b. abt 1869, Colorado Territory
father: Alonzo Bassett
mother: Harriet Bassett
1870 US Census, Colorado Territory, Boulder County, St Vrain District

Bassett, Willis
b. abt 1859, IL
father: Alonzo Bassett
mother: Harriet Bassett
1870 US Census, Colorado Territory, Boulder County, St Vrain District

Batchelder, George Culyer
b. 17 June 1813, Fort Ann, Washington, NY
d. 9 Sept 1906, Boulder, CO
bd. Columbia Cemetery, Boulder, CO
spouse: Melvina Fitzland Stevens Batcheldor
St Vrain Pioneers Assn Arrival Date: [not recorded]

Batchelder, George H
St Vrain Pioneers Assn Arrival Date: [not recorded]

St Vrain Valley Pioneers

Batchelder, William Walter
b. 16 Dec 1858, Jasper Co, IA
d. 14 Dec 1929, Boulder, CO
bd. Columbia Cemetery, Boulder, CO
spouse: Lura Effie Berkley Batchelder
father: George Cuyler Batchelder
mother: Melvina Fitzland Stevens Batchelder
St Vrain Pioneers Assn Arrival Date: [not recorded]

Baumert, David
b. abt 1838, PA
St Vrain Pioneers Assn Arrival Date: 1860

Baumert, Iciminda Harper
b. 12 Aug 1855, What Cheer, Keokuk, IA
d. 20 Dec 1890, Longmont, Boulder, CO
bd. Mountain View Cemetery, Longmont, Boulder, CO
spouse: David Baumert
father: Joseph H Harper
St Vrain Pioneers Assn Arrival Date: 1860

Beach, David Watson
b. 19 June 1834, Delaware Co, NY
d. 11 May 1920, Boulder, CO
bd. Columbia Cemetery, Boulder, CO
spouse: Margaret Lawler Beach
father: Alfred Beach
mother: Rebekah Henderson Beach
1870 US Census, Colorado Territory, Boulder County, St Vrain District

Beadle, James O
b. abt 1842, PA
d. 19 Feb 1897, Longmont, CO
bd. Mountain View Cemetery, Longmont, Boulder, CO
spouse: Olive Beadle
St Vrain Pioneers Assn Arrival Date: 1870

Bean, Mary Catherine DuBois
b. Oct 1844, OH
d. 29 Mar 1914, IN
spouse: William Avery Bean
father: Ebenezer Collins Dubois
mother: Sarah Ann Cahoon Dubois
St Vrain Pioneers Assn Arrival Date: [not recorded]
1860 US Census, Nebraska Territory, Altona

Bean, William Avery
b. June 1836, Oswego, NY
d. 29 Feb 1912, Nederland, Boulder, CO
spouse: Mary Catherine DuBois Bean
father: Josiah Bean
mother: Bathsheba Benson Bumpas Bean
St Vrain Pioneers Assn Arrival Date: 1860

Bear, George E
b. abt 1825, England
St Vrain Pioneers Assn Arrival Date: 1864

Bearman, James
St Vrain Land Club Date: 1861

Beasley, Alice
b. abt 1859
father: James Jackson Beasley
mother: Eliza Jones Beasley
St Vrain Pioneers Assn Arrival Date: 1863

Beasley, Clara A Forsyth
b. 1871
d. 1952
bd. Burlington Cemetery, Longmont, Boulder, CO

Beasley, Eliza Jones
b. 20 Mar 1833, Johnson, IN
d. 30 Aug 1903, Longmont, Boulder, CO
bd. Burlington Cemetery, Longmont, Boulder, CO
spouse: James Jackson Beasley
St Vrain Pioneers Assn Arrival Date: 1863

Beasley, Isaac Lee
b. 2 July 1864, Lancaster, Schuyler, MO
d. 6 Dec 1912, Groveland, Bingham, ID
spouse: Elsa M Beasley
father: James Jackson Beasley
mother: Eliza Jones Beasley
St Vrain Pioneers Assn Arrival Date: 1863

Beasley, James Jackson
b. 20 Oct 1831, Morgan, IL
d. 20 Jan 1907, Longmont, Boulder, CO
bd. Burlington Cemetery, Longmont, Boulder, CO
spouse: Eliza Jones Beasley
father: William J Beasley
mother: Dulcena Westrope Beasley
St Vrain Pioneers Assn Arrival Date: 1860

Beasley, John William
b. 12 Aug 1852, MO
d. 22 July 1928, Stanislaus, CA

spouse: Elizabeth Emma Beasley
father: James Jackson Beasley
mother: Eliza Jones Beasley
St Vrain Pioneers Assn Arrival Date: 1863

Beasley, Maude Blanche Eshelman
b. 4 Apr 1895, Fontanelle, Adair, IA
d. 10 May 1986, Denver, CO
bd. Mountain View Cemetery, Longmont, Boulder, CO
spouse: William Lee Beasley, Sr
father: Christian Eshelman
mother: Anna Myrah Tobias Eshelman

Beasley, Richard Milton
b. 2 Oct 1866, Boulder, Colorado Territory
d. 1 Oct 1940
bd. Burlington Cemetery, Longmont, Boulder, CO
spouse: Clara A Forsyth Beasley
father: James Jackson Beasley
mother: Eliza Jones Beasley

Beasley, William Lee
b. 1893
d. 1981
bd. Mountain View Cemetery, Longmont, Boulder, CO
spouse: Maude Blanche Eshelman Beasley
father: Richard Milton Beasley
mother: Clara A Forsyth Beasley

Beckwith, Eleanor Fenton
b. abt 1818, NH
d. 3 Dec 1910, Boulder, CO
spouse: Lawson Beckwith
1870 US Census, Colorado Territory, Boulder County, Left Hand

Beckwith, Elmer Francis
b. 17 Feb 1849, Swanzey, Cheshire, NH
d. 7 Nov 1929, Longmont, Boulder, CO
spouse: Terrasena S Merrill Beckwith
father: Lawson Beckwith
mother: Eleanor Fenton Beckwith
1870 US Census, Colorado Territory, Boulder County, St Vrain District

Beckwith, family of Henry Clark
St Vrain Pioneers Assn Arrival Date: 1862

Beckwith, Francis
b. 30 Jan 1875, Longmont, Boulder, Colorado Territory
d. 24 Apr 1968

Beckwith, Frederick Clark
b. abt 1840, Swanzey, Cheshire, NH
d. bef 1895, WI
spouse: Louisa P Beckwith
father: Lawson Beckwith
mother: Eleanor Fenton Beckwith
St Vrain Pioneers Assn Arrival Date: 1859
St Vrain Land Club Date: 1861 Feb 24
1870 US Census, Colorado Territory, Boulder County, St Vrain District

Beckwith, George C
St Vrain Pioneers Assn Arrival Date: 1864
St Vrain Ditch Owner: Beckwith Ditch No 5, 8 Mar 1861

Beckwith, George F
b. abt 1885
d. 28 Aug 1920, Longmont, Boulder, CO
father: George L Beckwith
mother: Emily F Dodge Beckwith

Beckwith, George Lawson
b. 20 Jan 1842, Unity, NY
d. 22 Mar 1931
bd. Mountain View Cemetery, Longmont, Boulder, CO
spouse: Emily F Dodge Beckwith
father: Lawson Beckwith
mother: Eleanor Fenton Beckwith
St Vrain Pioneers Assn Arrival Date: 1864
St Vrain Land Club Date: 1861 Apr 7
St Vrain Ditch Owner: Beckwith Ditch No 5, 8 Mar 1861
1870 US Census, Colorado Territory, Boulder County, Left Hand

Beckwith, Lawson
b. 10 July 1811, Lempster, Cheshire, NH
d. 9 Sept 1880, Longmont, Boulder, CO
spouse: Eleanor Fenton Beckwith
father: Nathaniel Beckwith
mother: Eunice Parkhurst Beckwith
St Vrain Land Club Date: 1861 Apr 7

St Vrain Valley Pioneers

1870 US Census, Colorado Territory, Boulder County, Left Hand

Beckwith, Louise Patten Fisher
b. Jan 1837, ME
d. 1925, Brodhead City, Green, WI
spouse: Frederick Clark Beckwith
mother: Penelope Fisher
St Vrain Pioneers Assn Arrival Date: 1862
1870 US Census, Colorado Territory, Boulder County, St Vrain District

Beckwith, Oscar F
b. 31 May 1859, MA
d. 23 Apr 1929, Longmont, Boulder, CO
spouse: Jennie Adelia Howe Beckwith
father: Lawson Beckwith
mother: Elenor Fenton Beckwith
1870 US Census, Colorado Territory, Boulder County, Left Hand

Behrung, Emma G
b. 12 Aug 1870, Colorado Springs, El Paso, Colorado Territory
d. 24 Nov 1966

Belan, Oliver
b. abt 1841, Canada
1860 US Census, Nebraska Territory, Platte River

Belcher, Freeman
b. 12 Nov 1833, IL/NY
d. 29 Apr 1913, Boulder, CO
bd. Burlington Cemetery, Longmont, Boulder, CO
spouse: Malissa Sophia Corwin Greenly Belcher
father: John Belcher
mother: Rachel Ann Collier Belcher
St Vrain Pioneers Assn Arrival Date: 1859
Troy District Land Club Claim Date: 1860 May 6
St Vrain Ditch Owner: Bonus Ditch No. 6, 30 Mar 1861
1870 US Census, Colorado Territory, Weld County, St Vrain District

Belcher, Malissa Sophia Corwin Greenly
b. 22 July 1833, IN
d. 19 May 1909, Boulder, CO
bd. Burlington Cemetery, Longmont, Boulder, CO
spouse: Jesse Hamilton Greenly; Freeman Belcher
father: Nathan Clinton Corwin
mother: Sophia Jewell Corwin
St Vrain Pioneers Assn Arrival Date: 1859
1870 US Census, Colorado Territory, Boulder County, St Vrain District

Bell, J W
Franklin Township Land Club Claim Date: 1860 July 6

Bellman, Emma Frances Bailey
b. 24 Apr 1846, England
d. 21 Mar 1880, Boulder, CO
bd. Mountain View Cemetery, Longmont, Boulder, CO
spouse: John Bellman
St Vrain Pioneers Assn Arrival Date: [not recorded]

Bellman, John
b. 10 June 1841, PA
d. 18 May 1890, Boulder, CO
bd. Mountain View Cemetery, Longmont, Boulder, CO
spouse: Emma Bailey Bellman; Elizabeth Hetzel Bellman
St Vrain Pioneers Assn Arrival Date: [not recorded]

Benham
b. abt 1834, NY
1860 US Census, Nebraska Territory, Platte River

Bennett, Charles
b. abt 1842, WI
1870 US Census, Colorado Territory, Boulder County, St Vrain District

Benson, Israel
b. 10 July 1845, PA
d. 18 Nov 1914, Boulder, CO
bd. Green Mountain Cemetery, Boulder, CO
spouse: Esther A Fleck Benson
father: William Benson
mother: Rose Ann Benson
1870 US Census, Colorado Territory, Boulder County, St Vrain District

Benton, Harry
b. abt 1847, OH
spouse: Jane Benton
1870 US Census, Colorado Territory, Boulder County, St Vrain District

Benton, Jane
   b. abt 1845, Canada
   spouse: Harry Benton
   1870 US Census, Colorado Territory, Boulder County, St Vrain District

Berkey, Amanda
   b. abt 1866, Colorado Territory
   father: Orange Grove Berkey
   mother: Margaret Berkey
   1870 US Census, Colorado Territory, Boulder County, Left Hand

Berkey, George
   b. abt 1861, IA
   father: Orange Grove Berkey
   mother: Margaret Berkey
   1870 US Census, Colorado Territory, Boulder County, Left Hand

Berkey, Margaret
   b. abt 1839, Darmstadt, Hesse, Germany
   spouse: Orange Grove Berkey
   1870 US Census, Colorado Territory, Boulder County, Left Hand

Berkey, Mary
   b. abt 1863, IA
   father: Orange Grove Berkey
   mother: Margaret Berkey
   1870 US Census, Colorado Territory, Boulder County, Left Hand

Berkey, Orange Grove
   b. Apr 1826, Tiscarawas, OH
   d. 9 June 1910, Belpre, Edwards, KS
   spouse: Margaret Berkey
   father: William Berkey
   mother: Elizabeth Grove Berkey
   1870 US Census, Colorado Territory, Boulder County, Left Hand

Berkey, Orange H
   b. abt 1865, IA
   father: Orange Grove Berkey
   mother: Margaret Berkey
   1870 US Census, Colorado Territory, Boulder County, Left Hand

Berkey, Sonora
   b. abt 1860, IA
   father: Orange Grove Berkey
   mother: Margaret Berkey
   1870 US Census, Colorado Territory, Boulder County, Left Hand

Berkey, Virgil
   b. abt 1858, IA
   d. 7 July 1896, Sunshine, Boulder, CO
   bd. Columbia Cemetery, Boulder, CO
   spouse: Mary E Berkey
   father: Orange Grove Berkey
   mother: Margaret Berkey
   1870 US Census, Colorado Territory, Boulder County, Left Hand

Berkey, William
   b. abt 1869, Colorado Territory
   father: Orange Grove Berkey
   mother: Margaret Berkey
   1870 US Census, Colorado Territory, Boulder County, Left Hand

Berkley, Annie Lefforts Mason
   b. 1 Dec 1827, New York City, NY
   d. 27 Aug 1880, Boulder, Boulder, CO
   bd. Columbia Cemetery, Boulder, CO
   spouse: Granville Berkley, Sr
   father: A Mason
   mother: Elizabeth Potts Weir Mason
   St Vrain Pioneers Assn Arrival Date: 1863

Berkley, Clarissa Cordelia White
   b. July 1850, OH
   d. 5 Sept 1924, Boulder, CO
   bd. Green Mountain Cemetery, Boulder, CO
   spouse: Granville Berkley, Jr
   father: Perry White
   mother: Rachel Irene Barlow White
   1870 US Census, Colorado Territory, Boulder County, St Vrain District

Berkley, Granville
   b. 11 Feb 1846, Sisterville, Tyler, VA
   d. 11 May 1931, Boulder, CO
   bd. Green Mountain Cemetery, Boulder, CO
   spouse: Clarissa Cordelia White Berkley
   father: Granville Berkley, Sr
   mother: Lydia Hough Nicklin Berkley
   1870 US Census, Colorado Territory, Boulder County, St Vrain District

St Vrain Valley Pioneers

Berkley, Granville
b. 22 Feb 1820, Berkeley, VA
d. 2 July 1884, Boulder, CO
bd. Columbia Cemetery, Boulder, CO
spouse: Lydia Hough Nicklin Berkley; Zipparah Jane Meserve Berkley, m3. Anna Lefferts Mason Berkley
father: James Berkley
mother: Margaretta Hawthorne Berkley
St Vrain Pioneers Assn Arrival Date: 1863

Berry, R
St Vrain Land Club (M687) Date: 1860 Apr 7

Bestle, Christian Gotlieb
b. 1832
d. 22 Apr 1912
bd. Hygiene Cemetery, Hygiene, Boulder, CO
St Vrain Pioneers Assn Arrival Date: 1864
1870 US Census, Colorado Territory, Boulder County, St Vrain District

Bestle, David
b. abt 1821, Wurtemburg, Germany
d. 15 Apr 1892
bd. Hygiene Cemetery, Hygiene, Boulder, CO
1870 US Census, Colorado Territory, Boulder County, St Vrain District

Bestle, Joseph D
b. 1884
d. 1967
bd. Foothills Gardens of Memory, Longmont, Boulder, CO
spouse: Elsie Mae Walter Bestle
father: David Friedrich Bestle

Bestler, David
St Vrain Ditch Owner: Zweck & Turner Ditch No. 21, 30 June 1864

Biederman, Julia Eve Terry
b. 26 Jan 1869, Horton, IN
d. 8 July 1929, Longmont, Boulder, CO
bd. Mountain View Cemetery, Longmont, Boulder, CO
spouse: Gus Biederman
father: James M Terry
mother: Sarah Ellen Clements Terry Mayfield

Bigalow, J E
St Vrain Land Club (M687) Date: 1859 Oct 13

Bigsby, Amiza
b. abt 1825, ME
1870 US Census, Colorado Territory, Boulder County, St Vrain District

Billings, George
b. abt 1843, MA
spouse: Henrietta Billings
1870 US Census, Colorado Territory, Boulder County, St Vrain District

Billingsley, John
b. abt 1839, NY
1860 US Census, Nebraska Territory, Platte River

Bills, Bertie
b. abt 1870, MI
father: Charles E Bills
mother: Jennie Bills
1870 US Census, Colorado Territory, Boulder County, Left Hand

Bills, Charles E
b. abt 1845, OH
spouse: Jennie Bills
1870 US Census, Colorado Territory, Boulder County, Left Hand

Bills, Jennie
b. abt 1846, IN
spouse: Charles E Bills
1870 US Census, Colorado Territory, Boulder County, Left Hand

Birdsill, Ebenezer
b. 1 Jan 1833, Eaton, Luzerne, PA
d. 8 Apr 1911, Hygiene, Boulder, CO
bd. Hygiene Cemetery, Hygiene, Boulder, CO
spouse: Sarah Elizabeth Strock Birdsill
father: Isaac Birdsill
mother: Anna Thurston Birdsill
St Vrain Pioneers Assn Arrival Date: 1859

Birdsill, Maude R
b. 1886
d. 1966
bd. Foothills Garden of Memory, Longmont, CO
father: Henry Alpheus Birdsill
mother: Sarah E Alpa Birdsill

Birdsill, Raymond E
b. 1884
d. 1968

bd. Foothills Gardens of Memory, Longmont, Boulder, CO
father: Henry Alpheus Birdsill
mother: Sarah E Alps Birdsill

Birdsill, Roy H
b. 1886
d. 1968
bd. Mountain View Cemetery, Longmont, Boulder, CO
spouse: Alida Birdsill
father: Henry Alpheus Birdsill
mother: Sarah E Alps Birdsill

Birkle, David
b. 1838, Hohenzollern, Germany
spouse: Johanna Bruner Birkle
St Vrain Pioneers Assn Arrival Date: 1860

Black, Joseph
b. abt 1848, KY
1870 US Census, Colorado Territory, Weld County, St Vrain District

Blackburn, Mary Jane Harding Burke
b. 10 Apr 1842, IL
d. 19 June 1919, Boulder, CO
bd. Columbia Cemetery, Boulder, CO
spouse: August G Burke; Joseph L Blackburn
father: Silas Harding
mother: Catherine Hartman Harding
1870 US Census, Colorado Territory, Boulder County, Left Hand

Blackwell, Mrs William
St Vrain Pioneers Assn Arrival Date: 1869

Blackwell, William N
St Vrain Pioneers Assn Arrival Date: 1869

Blair, C
b. abt 1833, NY
1860 US Census, Nebraska Territory, Platte River

Blair, James M
b. abt 1844, OH
1870 US Census, Colorado Territory, Boulder County, St Vrain District

Blake, Karle
b. 1808, Belgium
d. 14 Oct 1873, Boulder, CO
bd. South Boulder Cemetery, Boulder, CO
spouse: Clementine Margaret DeBacker Blake McGinn
father: Johannes Franciscus DeBlieck
St Vrain Pioneers Assn Arrival Date: 1864

Bland, J F
b. abt 1825, MO
1860 US Census, Nebraska Territory, Platte River

Blevin, William R
b. abt 1833, NY
1870 US Census, Colorado Territory, Boulder County, St Vrain District

Bliven, Andrew J
b. 6 May 1835, Mystic, New London, CT
d. 24 Nov 1897, Boulder, CO
bd. Niwot Cemetery, Niwot, Boulder, CO
spouse: Sarah W Hempstead Bliven
father: Russell Bliven
mother: Lucy Main Crumb Bliven
1870 US Census, Colorado Territory, Boulder County, St Vrain District

Bliven, George E
b. 14 May 1865, CT
d. 3 Feb 1917, Niwot, Boulder, CO
bd. Niwot Cemetery, Niwot, Boulder, CO
spouse: Mary Sophia Tower Bliven
father: Andrew J Bliven
mother: Sarah W Hempstead Bliven
1870 US Census, Colorado Territory, Boulder County, St Vrain District

Bliven, Horace
St Vrain Pioneers Assn Arrival Date: 1869

Bliven, Horace R
b. May 1859, CT
d. 12 Aug 1936, Jackson, OR
spouse: Emma Phileva Spackman Bliven
father: Andrew J Bliven
mother: Sarah W Hempstead Bliven
1870 US Census, Colorado Territory, Boulder County, St Vrain District

Bliven, Mrs Horace
spouse: Horace Bliven
St Vrain Pioneers Assn Arrival Date: 1869

Bliven, Sarah W Hempstead
b. 27 June 1835, Groton, New London, CT
d. 6 Oct 1913, Niwot, Boulder, CO

St Vrain Valley Pioneers

bd. Niwot Cemetery?, Niwot, Boulder, CO
spouse: Andrew J Bliven
1870 US Census, Colorado Territory, Boulder County, St Vrain District

Block, Augusta Ernestine Hauck
b. 9 Feb 1872, Boulder, Colorado Territory
d. 6 Nov 1967, Lakewood, Jefferson, CO
bd. Crown Hill Cemetery, Wheatridge, Jefferson, CO
spouse: Joseph H Block Jr
father: Robert August Hauck
mother: Ernestine Lange Hauck

Block, Joseph
b. 1830, France
St Vrain Pioneers Assn Arrival Date: 1859

Bloodworth, Jesse
St Vrain Land Club Date: 1861 Feb 16

Blore, William H
b. 23 Oct 1876, CO
d. June 1929, Denver, CO
bd. Crown Hill Cemetery, Wheat Ridge, Jefferson, CO
spouse: Ray Smithee Blore
father: William Richard Blore
mother: Elizabeth Lettise Manners Blore

Blore, William Richard
b. 27 July 1832, PA
d. 16 Jan 1902, Denver, CO
bd. Mountain View Cemetery, Longmont, Boulder, CO
spouse: Elizabeth Lettice Manners Blore
St Vrain Pioneers Assn Arrival Date: 1858
St Vrain Land Club Date: 1861 Sep 3

Blum, Robert
b. abt 1844, Austria
spouse: Louisa Krueger Blum
St Vrain Pioneers Assn Arrival Date: 1870

Bochiler, George
b. abt 1844, IA
1870 US Census, Colorado Territory, Boulder County, St Vrain District

Bond, Fred
St Vrain Pioneers Assn Arrival Date: 1859

Bond, Mrs Fred
spouse: Fred Bond
St Vrain Pioneers Assn Arrival Date: 1859

Boot, Henry
b. abt 1818, England
d. 19 Dec 1880, Left Hand, Boulder, CO
bd. Jamestown Cemetery, Jamestown, Boulder, CO
spouse: Sarah Boot
St Vrain Pioneers Assn Arrival Date: [not recorded]

Boot, William H
St Vrain Pioneers Assn Arrival Date: [not recorded]

Botts, Burrel Bryan
b. 22 Oct 1895, IA
d. 1 Jan 1982, Longmont, Boulder, CO
bd. Mountain View Cemetery, Longmont, Boulder, CO
spouse: Emeline Mumford Botts
father: John William Botts
mother: Mary Louise McCullough Botts

Botts, Emeline Mumford
b. 7 Feb 1898, Longmont, Boulder, CO
d. 7 Sept 1982, Lafayette, Boulder, CO
bd. Mountain View Cemetery, Longmont, Boulder, CO
spouse: Burrell Bryan Botts
father: Joseph Chandler Mumford
mother: Cora Electa Meeker Mumford

Boughton, M B
St Vrain Land Club (M687) Date: 1861 July 4

Boughton, Martin V B
St Vrain Pioneers Assn Arrival Date: 1860
St Vrain Land Club (M687) Date: 1860 Apr 25

Boutwell, James L
b. 27 Oct 1829, NY
d. 21 Oct 1913, Denver, CO
St Vrain Pioneers Assn Arrival Date: 1860

Boyd, John
b. abt 1820
1870 US Census, Colorado Territory, Boulder County, St Vrain District

St Vrain Valley Pioneers

Boyer, Peter
b. abt 1838, PA
1870 US Census, Colorado Territory, Boulder County, St Vrain District

Boylan, Robert
b. 2 Jan 1841
spouse: Alice Allen Boylan
St Vrain Pioneers Assn Arrival Date: 1860

Brackett, Levi
b. 1821, TN
d. 7 Oct 1898, Hygiene, Boulder, CO
bd. Hygiene Cemetery, Hygiene, Boulder, CO
spouse: Permelia Brackett
1870 US Census, Colorado Territory, Boulder County, St Vrain District

Bradford, Charles
b. 7 June 1844, NY
d. 13 Jan 1929, Lyons, Boulder, CO
bd. Lyons Cemetery, Lyons, Boulder, CO
spouse: Sarah S Bradford
St Vrain Pioneers Assn Arrival Date: 1866
1870 US Census, Colorado Territory, Boulder County, St Vrain District

Bradford, Sarah S
b. abt 1844, IL
spouse: Charles Bradford
St Vrain Pioneers Assn Arrival Date: 1866
1870 US Census, Colorado Territory, Boulder County, St Vrain District

Brainard, E
b. abt 1839, NY
1860 US Census, Nebraska Territory, Platte River

Bran, S
St Vrain Land Club Date: 1861 Nov 8

Breath, Amanda M Goss Barker
b. 4 Nov 1832, Lower Waterford, Caledonia, VT
d. 8 Dec 1907, Boulder, CO
bd. Green Mountain Cemetery, Boulder, CO
spouse: Jerome B Barker, Samuel M Breath
father: Abel Goss
mother: Amanda Hebard Goss
1870 US Census, Colorado Territory, Boulder County, St Vrain District

Breath, Edward
b. abt 1866, Boulder, Colorado Territory
d. 13 Dec 1881, Nederland, Boulder, CO
bd. Green Mountain Cemetery, Boulder, CO
father: Samuel M Breath
mother: Amanda M Goss Barker Breath
1870 US Census, Colorado Territory, Boulder County, St Vrain District

Breath, Samuel M
b. 5 Oct 1817, New York City, NY
d. 15 Nov 1901, Boulder, CO
bd. Green Mountain Cemetery, Boulder, CO
spouse: Amanda M Goss Barker Breath
father: James Breath
mother: Elizabeth Leggett Breath
1870 US Census, Colorado Territory, Boulder County, St Vrain District

Briggs, David
d. bef 6 Jan 1886 CO
bd. Mount Pleasant Cemetery?, Erie, Weld, CO
St Vrain Pioneers Assn Arrival Date: 1869

Briggs, George W
spouse: Emily Gutches Briggs
St Vrain Pioneers Assn Arrival Date: 1858

Briggs, Henry
b. 3 Oct 1827, NY
St Vrain Pioneers Assn Arrival Date: 1869

Brill, Albredine
b. abt 1869, Colorado Territory
father: Edward P Brill
mother: Elisabeth Brill
1870 US Census, Colorado Territory, Boulder County, St Vrain District

Brill, Edward P
b. abt 1842, Bavaria
spouse: Elisabeth Brill
1870 US Census, Colorado Territory, Boulder County, St Vrain District

Brill, Elisabeth
b. abt 1848, IL
spouse: Edward Brill
1870 US Census, Colorado Territory, Boulder County, St Vrain District

St Vrain Valley Pioneers

Brinkerhoff, family of James
St Vrain Pioneers Assn Arrival Date: 1866

Brinkerhoff, James
St Vrain Pioneers Assn Arrival Date: 1866

Brinkerhoff, Mrs James
spouse: James Brinkerhoff
St Vrain Pioneers Assn Arrival Date: 1866

Brinkerhuff, Jennie
b. 23 May 1888
d. 4 May 1966
bd. Mountain View Cemetery, Longmont, Boulder, CO
father: Samuel W Brinkerhuff
mother: Lavina N Ballinger Brunkerhuff

Brinkerhuff, Lavina N Ballinger
b. 29 Sept 1865, Jefferson, Colorado Territory
d. 20 Aug 1936, Longmont, Boulder, CO
spouse: Samuel W Brinkerhuff
father: Harmon Ballinger
mother: Mary Jane Patterson Ballinger

Brinkerhuff, Samuel W
b. 1858
d. 5 July 1929, Longmont, Boulder, CO
bd. Mountain View Cemetery, Longmont, Boulder, CO
spouse: Lavina N Ballinger Brinherkuff
father: James W Brinkerhuff
mother: Isabella Anne Slater Brinkerhuff

Brock, Louise Plumb
b. abt 1832, NY
d. 25 July 1908, Longmont, Boulder, CO
spouse: Sylvester J Plumb, Lewis Brock
St Vrain Pioneers Assn Arrival Date: 1859
1870 US Census, Colorado Territory, Weld County, St Vrain District

Brookfield, Alfred Augustus
b. 31 Jan 1830, Morristown, Morris, NJ
d. 8 Mar 1897, Boulder, CO
bd. Green Mountain Cemetery, Boulder, CO
spouse: Emma Lorton Brookfield
father: Moses Allen Brookfield
mother: Catherine Archer Douglas Brookfield
St Vrain Pioneers Assn Arrival Date: 1858
1870 US Census, Colorado Territory, Boulder County, St Vrain District

Brookfield, Emily Lorton
b. 21 June 1821, IL
d. 3 Aug 1914, Boulder, CO
bd. Green Mountain Cemetery, Boulder, CO
spouse: Alfred A Brookfield
father: John Robert Lorton
mother: Martha Lorton
1870 US Census, Colorado Territory, Boulder County, St Vrain District

Brooks, Charles
b. abt 1834, MA
1870 US Census, Colorado Territory, Boulder County, St Vrain District

Broughton, Henrietta Burch
b. 7 Nov 1868, Hygiene, Colorado Territory
d. 25 Feb 1939, Hygiene, Boulder, CO
bd. Hygiene Cemetery, Hygiene, Boulder, CO
spouse: Charles James Broughton
father: William Wallace Burch
mother: Roxie Jane Carter Burch
1870 US Census, Colorado Territory, Boulder County, St Vrain District

Brown, Abner Roe
b. 29 June 1829, Ireland/CT
d. 2 Sept 1922, Canon City, Fremont, CO
bd. Lakeside Cemetery, Fremont, Canon City
spouse: Jennie A Batchelder Brown

Brown, Carrie A Sawyer
b. 4 Dec 1869, Fitchburg, Worcester, MA
d. 10 Aug 1927, Longmont, Boulder, CO
bd. Mountain View Cemetery, Longmont, Boulder, CO
spouse: George William Brown

Brown, Clark R
Troy District Land Club Claim Date: 1861 Jan 28

Brown, family of Samuel
St Vrain Pioneers Assn Arrival Date: 1862

Brown, G P
St Vrain Land Club Date: 1861 Aug 14

Brown, George
b. abt 1841, MA
1870 US Census, Colorado Territory, Weld County, St Vrain District

St Vrain Valley Pioneers

Brown, George A
St Vrain Land Club Date: 1861 Aug 18

Brown, George William
b. 29 Mar 1840, Leominster, Worcester, MA
d. 4 June 1928, Longmont, Boulder, CO
bd. Mountain View Cemetery, Longmont, Boulder, CO
spouse: Carrie A Sawyer Brown
father: Mark Kendall Brown
mother: Sarah Ann May Brown
St Vrain Pioneers Assn Arrival Date: 1865

Brown, James H
b. abt 1830, Ireland
1870 US Census, Colorado Territory, Boulder County, St Vrain District

Brown, Joseph
b. abt 1826, Canada
1860 US Census, Nebraska Territory, Platte River

Brown, La Castus
b. 1866, Colorado Territory
d. 1872
bd. Nederland Cemetery?, Nederland, Boulder, CO
father: Nathaniel W Brown
mother: Caroline E Brown Hill
1870 US Census, Colorado Territory, Boulder County, St Vrain District

Brown, Lilly L
b. 1861, Colorado Territory
d. 1872
bd. Nederland Cemetery?, Nederland, Boulder, CO
father: Nathaniel W Brown
mother: Caroline E Brown Hill
1870 US Census, Colorado Territory, Boulder County, St Vrain District

Brown, Mrs Samuel
spouse: Samuel Brown
St Vrain Pioneers Assn Arrival Date: 1866

Brown, Nathaniel W
b. 15 Oct 1818, Meadville, Crawford, PA
d. 28 Dec 1898, Boulder, CO
bd. Nederland Cemetery, Nederland, Boulder, CO
spouse: Caroline E Leach Brown Hill Leahy, Virginia J Nossman Brown
1870 US Census, Colorado Territory, Boulder County, St Vrain District

Brown, Samuel E
St Vrain Pioneers Assn Arrival Date: 1862

Brown, Susan Savanah
b. 19 Nov 1882
d. 26 Apr 1967
bd. Lyons Cemetery, Lyons, Boulder, CO
spouse: William H Noyes, Harry Earl Brown

Brown, William
b. abt 1843, NY
1870 US Census, Colorado Territory, Boulder County, St Vrain District

Browne, Hiram T
Troy District Land Club Claim Date: 1861 Jan 11

Bruce, Jacob
St Vrain Land Club Date: 1861 Aug 22

Brush, Jared
St Vrain Pioneers Assn Arrival Date: 1860

Brush, John
St Vrain Pioneers Assn Arrival Date: 1860

Brush, Minnebell
b. abt 1868, Colorado Territory
mother: Martha Brush Matthews
1870 US Census, Colorado Territory, Boulder County, Left Hand

Brush, Mrs Jared
spouse: Jared Brush
St Vrain Pioneers Assn Arrival Date: 1860

Brush, Mrs John
spouse: John Brush
St Vrain Pioneers Assn Arrival Date: 1864

Brush, Mrs William
spouse: William Brush
St Vrain Pioneers Assn Arrival Date: 1864

Brush, William
St Vrain Pioneers Assn Arrival Date: 1860

Bryan, William
b. abt 1812, PA
1870 US Census, Colorado Territory, Boulder County, St Vrain District

St Vrain Valley Pioneers

Bucherdee, Fred C
  b. 17 Nov 1848, IN
  d. 28 Sept 1909, Lyons, Boulder, CO
  bd. Lyons Cemetery, Lyons, Boulder, CO
  spouse: Sarah Eunice Hutchinson Bucherdee
  1870 US Census, Colorado Territory, Weld County, St Vrain District

Buck, Hiram
  b. abt 1838, OH
  spouse: Mary J Buck
  father: William Buck
  mother: Jerusha L Rose Buck
  St Vrain Pioneers Assn Arrival Date: 1859

Buck, Mary J Jay
  b. abt 1840, NY
  spouse: Hiram Buck
  St Vrain Pioneers Assn Arrival Date: 1863

Buck, Oskar
  b. abt 1864, Colorado Territory
  mother: Cynthia S Buck
  1870 US Census, Colorado Territory, Boulder County, St Vrain District

Buckingham, Nellie
  b. 12 May 1876, Longmont, Boulder, Colorado Territory
  d. 25 May 1967, Denver, CO
  bd. Green Mountain Cemetery, Boulder, CO
  father: Walter Alva Buckingham
  mother: Mary E Emerson Buckingham

Budd, Sylvanus
  b. 5 Feb 1835, Allen Cty, OH
  d. 23 Feb 1910, Boulder, CO
  bd. Niwot Cemetery, Niwot, Boulder, CO
  spouse: Samantha Rebecca Severns Budd; Lucy Budd
  father: Andrew Budd
  mother: Asenath Nancy Hasson Budd
  St Vrain Pioneers Assn Arrival Date: 1860
  1870 US Census, Colorado Territory, Boulder County, Left Hand

Buell, Ida Wilhelmina Johnson
  b. 28 Aug 1869, Left Hand, Boulder, CO
  d. 9 Apr 1956, Longmont, Boulder, CO
  bd. Hygiene Cemetery, Hygiene, Boulder, CO
  spouse: Henry B Buell
  father: Carl August Johnson
  mother: Anna Sophia Jonsdotter Johnson
  1870 US Census, Colorado Territory, Boulder County, Left Hand

Buford, family of William
  St Vrain Pioneers Assn Arrival Date: 1860

Buford, Mrs William
  spouse: William Buford
  St Vrain Pioneers Assn Arrival Date: 1860

Buford, William
  St Vrain Pioneers Assn Arrival Date: 1860

Bull, Isaac S
  St Vrain Pioneers Assn Arrival Date: 1859

Burbridge, Charles William
  b. 19 Mar 1843, Galena, Jo Daviess, IL
  d. 31 July 1936, Platteville, Weld, CO
  bd. Mountain View Cemetery, Longmont, Boulder, CO
  spouse: Harriet Clarinda Thatcher
  father: Thomas Burbridge
  mother: Anna S M Hathaway Burbridge
  St Vrain Land Club (M687) Date: 1864, Dec 1
  1870 US Census, Colorado Territory, Weld County, St Vrain District

Burbridge, Thomas P
  b. 1 Sept 1804, Butler, PA
  d. 16 May 1875, Gowanda, Weld, CO
  bd. Burbridge Cemetery, Weld, CO
  spouse: Anna Sophia M Hathaway Burbridge
  father: William Burbridge
  mother: Elizabeth Burkhart Burbridge
  St Vrain Pioneers Assn Arrival Date: 1860
  1870 US Census, Colorado Territory, Weld County, St Vrain District

Burch, Ann E
  b. abt 1845, RI
  spouse: Richard Burch
  1870 US Census, Colorado Territory, Boulder County, Left Hand

Burch, baby girl
  b. abt 1870, Colorado Territory
  bd. Hygiene Cemetery?, Hygiene, Boulder, CO
  father: William W Burch
  mother: Roxie Jane Carter Burch

1870 US Census, Colorado Territory, Boulder County, St Vrain District

Burch, Henry Hoopman
b. 19 Dec 1840, Van Buren, IA
d. 7 Jan 1917, Longmont, Boulder, CO
bd. Niwot Cemetery, Niwot, Boulder, CO
spouse: Louisa Maria Frederick Burch
father: William David Burch
mother: Nancy Elliott Burch
St Vrain Pioneers Assn Arrival Date: 1860
1870 US Census, Colorado Territory, Boulder County, Left Hand

Burch, John T
Franklin Township Land Club Claim Date: 1860 June 26
St Vrain Land Club Date: 1860 June 26

Burch, Louisa Maria Frederick
b. Mar 1841, Pike, IN
d. 5 Oct 1916, CO
bd. Niwot Cemetery, Niwot, Boulder, CO
spouse: Henry Hoopman Burch
father: Daniel Frederick
mother: Iva Mary Elizabeth Decker Frederick
St Vrain Pioneers Assn Arrival Date: 1865
1870 US Census, Colorado Territory, Boulder County, Left Hand

Burch, Maria E
b. abt 1870, Colorado Territory
father: Henry Hoopman Burch
mother: Louisa Maria Frederick Burch
1870 US Census, Colorado Territory, Boulder County, Left Hand

Burch, Richard
b. abt 1831, KY
spouse: Ann E Burch
father: Robert Benham Burch
mother: Annie Nichols Burch
1870 US Census, Colorado Territory, Boulder County, Left Hand

Burch, Robert A
b. abt 1869, Colorado Territory
father: Richard Burch
mother: Anne E Burch
1870 US Census, Colorado Territory, Boulder County, Left Hand

Burch, Roxey Jane Carter
b. 13 Dec 1851, OH
d. 2 Feb 1908
bd. Hygiene Cemetery, Hygiene, Boulder, CO
spouse: William W Burch
father: John Henry Clay Carter
mother: Sarah Ann Dovener Carter
St Vrain Pioneers Assn Arrival Date: 1864
1870 US Census, Colorado Territory, Boulder County, St Vrain District

Burch, William Daniel
b. abt 1869, Colorado Territory
father: Henry Hoopman Burch
mother: Louisa Maria Frederick Burch
1870 US Census, Colorado Territory, Boulder County, Left Hand

Burch, William Wallace
b. 31 July 1844, Van Buren, IA
d. 31 July 1910, Hygiene, Boulder, CO
bd. Hygiene Cemetery, Hygiene, Boulder, CO
spouse: Roxey Jane Carter Burch
father: William D Burch
mother: Nancy Elliott Burch
St Vrain Pioneers Assn Arrival Date: 1864
1870 US Census, Colorado Territory, Boulder County, St Vrain District

Burgus, John
b. abt 1840, Mexico
1860 US Census, Nebraska Territory, Platte River

Burk, E
b. abt 1836, NY
1860 US Census, Nebraska Territory, Platte River

Burke, August Gustaf
b. 14 Dec 1834, Stockholm, Sweden
d. 14 Feb 1914, Boulder, CO
bd. Columbia Cemetery, Boulder, CO
spouse: Mary Jane Harding Burke; Jennie Dorsy Burke
father: August G Burke
mother: Anna Stiener Burke
1870 US Census, Colorado Territory, Boulder County, Left Hand

Burke, Carl William
b. Nov 1861, Boulder, Colorado Territory
d. 1941, Bent, CO

St Vrain Valley Pioneers

bd. Wiley Cemetery, Bent, CO
spouse: Allie Florence McIntosh Burke
father: August Gustaf Burke
mother: Mary Jane Harding Burke Blackburn
1870 US Census, Colorado Territory, Boulder County, Left Hand

Burke, Frank Peter
b. 22 Mar 1865, Omaha, Douglas, NE
d. 5 May 1936, Boulder, CO
bd. Columbia Cemetery, Boulder, CO
spouse: Emma Boland Burke
father: August Gustaf Burke
mother: Mary Jane Harding Burke Blackburn
1870 US Census, Colorado Territory, Boulder County, Left Hand

Burke, Oscar A
b. 2 June 1863, Colorado Territory
d. 1933, Boulder, CO
bd. Green Mountain Cemetery, Boulder, CO
father: August G Burke
mother: Mary Jane Harding Burke Blackburn
1870 US Census, Colorado Territory, Boulder County, Left Hand

Burkey, Joseph
b. abt 1852
d. 23 Oct 1936
bd. South Boulder Cemetery, Boulder, CO
St Vrain Pioneers Assn Arrival Date: [not recorded]

Burnett, William
b. abt 1843, MO
spouse: Delia Milne Burnett
1870 US Census, Colorado Territory, Boulder County, St Vrain District

Busby, Albert
b. abt 1835, NY
1870 US Census, Colorado Territory, Boulder County, St Vrain District

Buster, William Louden
b. June 1839, MO
d. 4 Dec 1904, Weld, CO
bd. Pleasant View Ridge Cemetery, Weld, CO
spouse: Emma C Buster
St Vrain Pioneers Assn Arrival Date: 1862

Butler, Benjamin
b. abt 1843, MA
1870 US Census, Colorado Territory, Boulder County, St Vrain District

Butler, Helen
spouse: William E Butler
Vrain Land Club Date: 1861 May 29

Butler, William E
b. 2 Sept 1841, England
d. 31 Oct 1928, Longmont, CO
bd. Mountain View Cemetery, Longmont, Boulder, CO
spouse: Helen Butler
father: William Elijah Butler
St Vrain Pioneers Assn Arrival Date: 1859
St Vrain Land Club Date: 1861 Apr 7

Butterson, Eric
b. abt 1832, OH
1870 US Census, Colorado Territory, Boulder County, St Vrain District

Byers, William T
St Vrain Land Club (M687) Date: 1859 Oct 12

C

Cain, David
b. abt 1845, OH
1870 US Census, Colorado Territory, Boulder County, St Vrain District

Calderbank, William
Troy District Land Club Claim Date: 1861 July 29

Calhuen, C B
St Vrain Land Club Date: 1861 Aug 18

Calhuen, W W
St Vrain Land Club Date: 1861 Aug 18

Calton, William
b. abt 1835, Germany
1860 US Census, Nebraska Territory, Platte River

Camenisch, Eugene D
b. 13 May 1904
d. 9 Nov 1966
bd. Arvada Cemetery, Arvada, Jefferson, CO
spouse: Alice E Bates Camenisch
father: David Camenisch
mother: Eugenia Camenisch

St Vrain Valley Pioneers

Campbell, Inez B Clawson
b. Feb 1868, MN
d. 26 July 1964, Omaha, Douglas, NE
spouse: Jacob Campbell MD
father: Abraham Clawson
mother: Olive Garrett Richards Clawson
1870 US Census, Colorado Territory, Boulder County, Left Hand

Canaday, Caron H
b. abt 1812, TN
spouse: Thomas Canaday
1870 US Census, Colorado Territory, Weld County, St Vrain District

Canaday, Elisobeth
b. abt 1832, IN
1870 US Census, Colorado Territory, Weld County, St Vrain District

Canaday, Ira
b. abt 1833, IN
father: Thomas Canaday
mother: Karen Happuck Mills Canaday
1870 US Census, Colorado Territory, Weld County, St Vrain District

Canaday, Irene
b. abt 1847, IL
1870 US Census, Colorado Territory, Weld County, St Vrain District

Canaday, Judith
b. abt 1852, IL
1870 US Census, Colorado Territory, Weld County, St Vrain District

Canaday, Sarah E
b. abt 1848, IL
1870 US Census, Colorado Territory, Weld County, St Vrain District

Canaday, Thomas
b. abt 1814, TN
spouse: Caron H Canaday
St Vrain Pioneers Assn Arrival Date: 1860
1870 US Census, Colorado Territory, Weld County, St Vrain District

Canger, Saul
b. abt 1832, OH
1870 US Census, Colorado Territory, Boulder County, St Vrain District

Carden, John
Franklin Township Land Club Claim Date: 1860 June 26

Carl, James
b. abt 1846, AL
1870 US Census, Colorado Territory, Boulder County, St Vrain District

Carl, James H
b. abt 1832, NY
spouse: Lucy J Carl
1870 US Census, Colorado Territory, Boulder County, St Vrain District

Carl, Lucy J
b. abt 1834, NY
spouse: James H Carl
1870 US Census, Colorado Territory, Boulder County, St Vrain District

Carless, C
b. abt 1830, PA
1860 US Census, Nebraska Territory, Platte River

Carmigle, John
b. abt 1844, IA
1870 US Census, Colorado Territory, Weld County, St Vrain District

Carnahan, family of James
St Vrain Pioneers Assn Arrival Date: 1870

Carnahan, James
St Vrain Pioneers Assn Arrival Date: 1870

Carnahan, Mrs James
spouse: James Carnahan
St Vrain Pioneers Assn Arrival Date: 1870

Carpe, Lincoln
St Vrain Land Club (M687) Date: 1860 Oct 23

Carpe, Simeon
St Vrain Land Club (M687) Date: 1860 Dec 6

Carr, Mary Elizabeth "Lizzie" Oliphant
b. abt 1840, PA
d. 21 May 1904, Longmont, CO
bd. Mountain View Cemetery, Longmont, Boulder, CO
spouse: Stephen H Carr
St Vrain Pioneers Assn Arrival Date: 1859
1870 US Census, Colorado Territory, Weld County, St Vrain District

St Vrain Valley Pioneers

Carr, Lucinde
b. abt 1865, Colorado Territory
father: Stephen H Carr
mother: Lizzie Oliphant Carr
1870 US Census, Colorado Territory, Weld County, St Vrain District

Carr, Stephen Hadley
b. 23 Jan 1825, Belknap, NH
d. 21 May 1904, Longmont, CO
spouse: Lizzie Oliphant Carr
St Vrain Pioneers Assn Arrival Date: 1859
1870 US Census, Colorado Territory, Weld County, St Vrain District

Carroll, Ada
b. abt 1838, CT
1860 US Census, Nebraska Territory, Platte River

Carson, Ethel J
b. 1885
d. 1966
bd. Mountain View Cemetery, Longmont, Boulder, CO
spouse: Clyde J Carson

Carter, Andrew
b. abt 1855, IA
1870 US Census, Colorado Territory, Boulder County, St Vrain District

Carter, Catherine
b. abt 1867, IA
1870 US Census, Colorado Territory, Boulder County, St Vrain District

Carter, John C
St Vrain Land Club Date: 1861 Apr 7

Carter, John Henry Clay
b. 31 Aug 1829, Gallia, OH
d. 18 Jan 1879, Boulder, CO
bd. Hygiene Cemetery, Hygiene, Boulder, CO
spouse: Sarah Ann Dovener Carter
father: John Carter, Jr
mother: Jane Swindler Carter
St Vrain Pioneers Assn Arrival Date: 1861
1870 US Census, Colorado Territory, Boulder County, St Vrain District

Carter, John Lewis
b. 1849, OH
d. 21 Nov 1918, Hygiene, CO
bd. Hygiene Cemetery, Hygiene, Boulder, CO
spouse: Cora G Weisner Carter; Martha Nichols Carter
father: John Henry Clay Carter
mother: Sarah Ann Dovener Carter
1870 US Census, Colorado Territory, Boulder County, St Vrain District

Carter, Laura A
b. abt 1863, IA
father: John Hhenry Clay Carter
mother: Sarah Ann Dovener Carter
1870 US Census, Colorado Territory, Boulder County, St Vrain District

Carter, Lydia
b. abt 1857, IA
father: John Henry Clay Carter
mother: Sarah Ann Dovener Carter
1870 US Census, Colorado Territory, Boulder County, St Vrain District

Carter, Miranda McCaslin Coulehan
b. 10 Aug 1860, Gold Hill, Boulder, NE Terr
d. 24 May 1936, Loveland, CO
bd. Columbia Cemetery, Boulder, CO
spouse: James Carroll Couleham; William B Carter
father: Matthew L McCaslin
mother: Miranda Haggerty McCaslin
1870 US Census, Colorado Territory, Boulder County, St Vrain District

Carter, Robert A
b. 21 Apr 1862, Union, Floyd, IA
d. 24 Dec 1927, Tungsten, Boulder, CO
bd. Columbia Cemetery, Boulder, CO
spouse: Mary Jane Waterman Brown
father: John Henry Clay Carter
mother: Sarah Ann Dovener Carter
1870 US Census, Colorado Territory, Boulder County, St Vrain District

Carter, Sarah Ann Dovener
b. 27 Feb 1829, Gallia, OH
d. 30 July 1907, Jamestown, Boulder, CO
bd. Hygiene Cemetery, Hygiene, Boulder, CO
spouse: John Henry Clay Carter
father: John H Dovener
mother: Roxalina Ripley Dovener

St Vrain Pioneers Assn Arrival Date: [not recorded]
1870 US Census, Colorado Territory, Boulder County, St Vrain District

Cartright
St Vrain Land Club Date: 1860 Feb 1

Case, Asenth
b. abt 1846, IL
spouse: Willis Case
1870 US Census, Colorado Territory, Weld County, St Vrain District

Case, Eliza A
b. abt 1858, NE Terr
father: Melton B Case
mother: Elizabeth H Case
St Vrain Pioneers Assn Arrival Date: 1862

Case, Elizabeth H
b. abt 1835, NC
spouse: Melton B Case
St Vrain Pioneers Assn Arrival Date: 1862

Case, Lester Sylvanus
b. abt 1838, NY
1870 US Census, Colorado Territory, Boulder County, St Vrain District

Case, Martha C
b. abt 1857, NE Terr
father: Melton B Case
mother: Elizabeth H Case
St Vrain Pioneers Assn Arrival Date: 1862

Case, Melton B
b. abt 1818, OH
spouse: Elizabeth Case
father: Samuel Youngs Case
mother: Jane Akwrght Case
St Vrain Pioneers Assn Arrival Date: 1860

Case, Phila Vivian
b. abt 1869, MO
father: Willis Case
mother: Asenth Case
1870 US Census, Colorado Territory, Weld County, St Vrain District

Case, Willis
b. abt 1840, DeKalb, IL
d. 12 Sept 1925, Arlington, VA
spouse: Asenth Case
father: Willis Case
mother: Ann Dean Case
1870 US Census, Colorado Territory, Weld County, St Vrain District

Case, Winfield S
b. abt 1848, IA
father: Melton B Case
mother: Elizabeth H Case
St Vrain Pioneers Assn Arrival Date: 1862

Cassity, John
St Vrain Land Club (M687) Date: 1860 May 10

Castle, W W
St Vrain Land Club (M687) Date: 1859 Oct 12

Cavey, Emilia
b. abt 1833, England
spouse: Thomas Cavey
1870 US Census, Colorado Territory, Boulder County, Left Hand

Cavey, Stephen E
b. abt 1813
d. 22 Dec 1886
bd. Burlington Cemetery, Longmont, Boulder, CO
spouse: Mary Cavey
St Vrain Pioneers Assn Arrival Date: 1862

Cavey, Stephen E
b. abt 1841
d. 17 Dec 1923, St Joseph, MO?

Cavey, Thomas
b. abt 1833, England
spouse: Emelia Cavey, Rebecca Cavey
St Vrain Pioneers Assn Arrival Date: 1861
1870 US Census, Colorado Territory, Boulder County, Left Hand

Caywood, Frances Mary
b. abt 1866, Colorado Territory
father: Samuel M Caywood
mother: Sarah Caywood
1870 US Census, Colorado Territory, Boulder County, Left Hand

Caywood, Iatha
b. 1854, IN
d. bef 1870, IA or CO
father: William Wesley Caywood

St Vrain Valley Pioneers

mother: Katharine Donovan Newman Caywood
St Vrain Pioneers Assn Arrival Date: 1864

Caywood, James Arthur
b. 13 May 1863, Wapello, IA
d. 21 June 1930, Delta, CO
spouse: Anna Grossclose Caywood
father: William Wesley Caywood
mother: Katharine Donovan Newman Caywood
St Vrain Pioneers Assn Arrival Date: 1864
1870 US Census, Colorado Territory, Boulder
  County, Left Hand

Caywood, John Thomas
b. 3 Apr 1846, KY
d. 24 Dec 1900, CO
bd. Burlington Cemetery, Longmont, Boulder, CO
father: William Wesley Caywood
mother: Katharine Donovan Newman Caywood
St Vrain Pioneers Assn Arrival Date: 1864

Caywood, Katharine Donovan Newman
b. 7 Oct 1819, Fleming, KY
d. 30 Jan 1907, Boulder, CO
bd. Burlington Cemetery, Longmont, Boulder, CO
spouse: William Wesley Caywood
father: John Dudley Newman
mother: Nancy Donovan Newman
St Vrain Pioneers Assn Arrival Date: 1864
1870 US Census, Colorado Territory, Boulder
  County, Left Hand

Caywood, Luther Delgreen
b. 9 July 1854, Danville, Hendricks, IN
d. 29 Dec 1933, Boulder, CO
bd. Green Mountain Cemetery, Boulder, CO
spouse: Elizabeth Crain Caywood
father: William Wesley Caywood
mother: Katharine Donovan Newman Caywood
St Vrain Pioneers Assn Arrival Date: 1864
1870 US Census, Colorado Territory, Boulder
  County, Left Hand

Caywood, M
b. abt 1851, KY
father: William Wesley Caywood
mother: Katharine Donovan Newman Caywood
St Vrain Pioneers Assn Arrival Date: 1864

Caywood, Nathaniel
b. abt 1863, IA
father: Samuel M Caywood
mother: Sarah N Caywood
1870 US Census, Colorado Territory, Boulder
  County, Left Hand

Caywood, Richard French
b. 2 Sept 1847, KY
d. 18 Mar 1880, CO
bd. Burlington Cemetery, Longmont, Boulder, CO
spouse: Ada Myers Doggett Myers Caywood
father: William Wesley Caywood
mother: Katharine Donovan Newman Caywood
St Vrain Pioneers Assn Arrival Date: 1864

Caywood, Samuel M
b. Oct 1842, Fleming, KY
d. 11 Feb 1925, Fort Lupton, Weld, CO
bd. Mizpah Cemetery, Platteville, Weld, CO
spouse: Sarah Williamson Caywood
father: William Wesley Caywood
mother: Katharine Donovan Newman Caywood
St Vrain Pioneers Assn Arrival Date: 1864
1870 US Census, Colorado Territory, Boulder
  County, Left Hand

Caywood, Sarah N Williamson
b. abt 1840, IL
spouse: Samuel M Caywood
father: Thomas Williamson
mother: Lumira Newman Williamson
1870 US Census, Colorado Territory, Boulder
  County, Left Hand

Caywood, William A
b. 8 Sept 1852
d. 1853
father: William Wesley Caywood
mother: Katharine Donovan Newman Caywood
St Vrain Pioneers Assn Arrival Date: 1864

Caywood, William H
b. abt 1868, Colorado Territory
father: Samuel M Caywood
mother: Sarah Caywood
1870 US Census, Colorado Territory, Boulder
  County, Left Hand

Caywood, William Wesley
b. 4 Sept 1815, Fleming, KY
d. 28 June 1889, Longmont, Boulder, CO
bd. Burlington Cemetery, Longmont, Boulder, CO
spouse: Katharine Donovan Newman Caywood
father: Asa Caywood
mother: Margaret Foster Caywood
St Vrain Pioneers Assn Arrival Date: 1864
1870 US Census, Colorado Territory, Boulder County, Left Hand

Ceenan, Jeremiah
St Vrain Land Club (M687) Date: 1860 Oct 23

Chamberlain, John
b. abt 1828, WI
1870 US Census, Colorado Territory, Boulder County, Left Hand

Chambers, George Washington
b. 9 May 1826, Westmoreland, PA
d. 1901, Boulder, CO
bd. Valmont Cemetery, Boulder, CO
spouse: Eliza Jones Chambers
father: Benjamn M Chambers
mother: Mary Ralston Chambers
St Vrain Pioneers Assn Arrival Date: 1859

Chambers, John
b. abt 1830, MO
spouse: Martha Chambers
1870 US Census, Colorado Territory, Boulder County, St Vrain District

Chambers, Martha
b. abt 1835, NC
spouse: John Chambers
1870 US Census, Colorado Territory, Boulder County, St Vrain District

Chapman, Adelbert
b. abt 1862, IA
father: Eri W Chapman
mother: Maria Thankful Richardson Chapman
1870 US Census, Colorado Territory, Boulder County, St Vrain District

Chapman, Clara E
b. abt 1862, IA
father: Joshua Ewing Chapman
mother: Martha Diantha Richardson Chapman
1870 US Census, Colorado Territory, Boulder County, St Vrain District

Chapman, Clarence J
b. 1858, IA
d. 1909
bd. Hygiene Cemetery, Hygiene, Boulder, CO
father: Joshua Ewing Chapman
mother: Martha Diantha Richardson Chapman
1870 US Census, Colorado Territory, Boulder County, St Vrain District

Chapman, Emma
b. abt 1868, Colorado Territory
father: Eri W Chapman
mother: Maria Thnkful Richardson Chapman
1870 US Census, Colorado Territory, Boulder County, St Vrain District

Chapman Eri W
b. abt 1837 OH
spouse: Maria Thankful Richardson Chapman
father: David Chapman
mother: Mary Jamison Ewing Chapman
St Vrain Pioneers Assn Arrival Date: 1863
1870 US Census, Colorado Territory, Boulder County, St Vrain District

Chapman Herbert
b. abt 1866, Colorado Territory
father: Eri W Chapman
mother: Maria Thankful Richardson Chapman
1870 US Census, Colorado Territory, Boulder County, St Vrain District

Chapman Isabel
b. abt 1864, Colorado Territory
father: Eri W Chapman
mother: Maria Thankful Richardson Chapman
1870 US Census, Colorado Territory, Boulder County, St Vrain District

Chapman, Joshua Ewing
b. 23 Sept 1826, Madison, OH
d. 3 Nov 1894, Longmont, Boulder, CO
bd. Hygiene Cemetery, Hygiene, Boulder, CO
spouse: Martha Diantha Richardson Chapman
father: David Chapman
mother: Mary Jameson Ewing Chapman
St Vrain Pioneers Assn Arrival Date: 1863

St Vrain Valley Pioneers

1870 US Census, Colorado Territory, Boulder County, St Vrain District

Chapman, Maria Thankful Richardson
b. abt 1842, OH
d. 1907, Marion, OR
spouse: Eri W Chapman
father: Frederick Richardson
mother: Laura Campbell Brown Richardson
St Vrain Pioneers Assn Arrival Date: 1863
1870 US Census, Colorado Territory, Boulder County, St Vrain District

Chapman, Martha Diantha Richardson
b. 9 Feb 1834, Waterford, Caledonia, VT
d. 18 July 1905, Longmont, Boulder, CO
bd. Hygiene Cemetery, Hygiene, Boulder, CO
spouse: Joshua Ewing Chapman
father: Frederick Richardson
mother: [Sophia] Laura Campbell Brown Richardson
St Vrain Pioneers Assn Arrival Date: 1863
1870 US Census, Colorado Territory, Boulder County, St Vrain District

Chapman, Viola
b. Nov 1859, IA
father: Eri W Chapman
mother: Maria Thankful Richardson Chapman
1870 US Census, Colorado Territory, Boulder County, St Vrain District

Charles, John Q
Troy District Land Club Claim Date: 1860 Oct 4

Charles, Richard
b. abt 1820, KY
1870 US Census, Colorado Territory, Weld County, St Vrain District

Chrisman, G S
b. abt 1835, SC
1860 US Census, Nebraska Territory, Platte River

Christensen, Hans
St Vrain Ditch Owner: Renner Ditch No. 60, 1 May 1874

Christie, Augustus
b. abt 1838, Canada
1860 US Census, Nebraska Territory, Platte River

Church, family of George Henry
father: George Henry Church
St Vrain Pioneers Assn Arrival Date: 1860

Church, George Henry
b. 11 Dec 1830, Rochester, Monroe, NY
d. 7 Jan 1918, Broomfield, Jefferson, CO
bd. Fairmount Cemetery, Denver, CO
spouse: Sarah Henderson Miller Church
St Vrain Pioneers Assn Arrival Date: 1860

Church, Sarah Henderson Miller
b. Oct 1838, Stark, IL
d. 9 Feb 1920, Broomfield, Boulder, CO
spouse: George Henry Church
father: John Miller
mother: Mary Ann D Able Miller
St Vrain Pioneers Assn Arrival Date: 1860

Churches, Henry G
b. 11 Sept 1852, England
spouse: Belle Haslip Churches
St Vrain Pioneers Assn Arrival Date: 1862
1870 US Census, Colorado Territory, Weld County, St Vrain District

Churches, V J
b. abt 1846, England
1870 US Census, Colorado Territory, Weld County, St Vrain District

Clark, Cora A
b. 1959
d. Aug 1929, Johnstown, Weld, CO
bd. Johnstown Cemetery, Elwell, Weld, CO
spouse: William Clark

Clark, William
b. abt 1845, Ireland
1870 US Census, Colorado Territory, Weld County, St Vrain District

Clarke, Jennie Smith
b. 3 June 1850, Waukesha, WI
d. 4 Oct 1930, Boulder, CO
bd. Columbia Cemetery, Boulder, CO
spouse: George A Clarke
father: Nelson K Smith
mother: Helen Marie Campbell
St Vrain Pioneers Assn Arrival Date: 1860

St Vrain Valley Pioneers

Clawson, Abraham
b. 1832, IN
d. 1899
bd. Fairmount Cemetery, Denver, CO
spouse: Olive Richards Clawson
father: Thomas Clawson
mother: Julia Ives Clawson
St Vrain Pioneers Assn Arrival Date: 1860
1870 US Census, Colorado Territory, Boulder County, Left Hand

Clawson, Albert
b. abt 1862, WI
father: Abraham Clawson
mother: Olive Richards Clawson
1870 US Census, Colorado Territory, Boulder County, Left Hand

Clawson, Earnest
b. abt 1869, MN
father: Abraham Clawson
mother: Olive Richards Clawson
1870 US Census, Colorado Territory, Boulder County, Left Hand

Clawson, Edwin
b. abt 1866, MN
father: Abraham Clawson
mother: Olive Richards Clawson
1870 US Census, Colorado Territory, Boulder County, Left Hand

Clawson, Garrett
b. 6 Feb 1834, IN
d. 31 Dec 1907, Longmont, CO
bd. Mountain View Cemetery, Longmont, Boulder, CO
spouse: Martha Eastwood Clawson
father: Thomas Clawson
mother: Julia Ives Clawson
St Vrain Pioneers Assn Arrival Date: 1860
1870 US Census, Colorado Territory, Boulder County, Left Hand

Clawson, Martha Eastwood
b. May 1838, NY
d. 4 Jan 1922, Longmont, Boulder, CO
spouse: Garrett Clawson
father: John Eastwood
mother: Sarah Ann Lister Eastwood
St Vrain Pioneers Assn Arrival Date: 1860

Clawson, Olive Richards
b. 1842, NY
d. 9 Nov 1899, Ward, Boulder, CO
bd. Fairmount Cemetery, Denver, CO
spouse: Abraham Clawson
1870 US Census, Colorado Territory, Boulder County, Left Hand

Clifton, William
St Vrain Land Club Date: 1861 Mar 5

Clive, Albert
b. abt 1868, Colorado Territory
father: William Clive
mother: Sarah E Clive
1870 US Census, Colorado Territory, Weld County, St Vrain District

Clive, Edwin
b. abt 1865, Colorado Territory
father: William Clive
mother: Sarah E Clive
1870 US Census, Colorado Territory, Weld County, St Vrain District

Clive, Katie
b. abt 1858, IL
father: William Clive
mother: Sarah E
1870 US Census, Colorado Territory, Weld County, St Vrain District

Clive, Mary E
b. abt 1861, Colorado Territory
father: William Clive
mother: Sarah E Clive
1870 US Census, Colorado Territory, Weld County, St Vrain District

Clive, Sarah E
b. abt 1834, PA
spouse: William Clive
1870 US Census, Colorado Territory, Weld County, St Vrain District

Clive, William
b. abt 1828, PA
spouse: Sarah E Clive
1870 US Census, Colorado Territory, Weld County, St Vrain District

St Vrain Valley Pioneers

Clough, Charles E
St Vrain Ditch Owner: Clough & True Private Ditch No. 12, 15 Apr 1862

Clouser, Charles M
b. abt 1825, NY
St Vrain Pioneers Assn Arrival Date: 1858

Clyncke, Mary D
b. 1874
d. 1967
bd. Sacred Heart of Mary Cemetery, Boulder, CO

Cochran, Aurora J
b. abt 1839, MO
spouse: Pearson G Cochran
1870 US Census, Colorado Territory, Boulder County, Left Hand

Cochran, Bedford
St Vrain Pioneers Assn Arrival Date: [not recorded]

Cochran, Edward
b. abt 1840, VA
1870 US Census, Colorado Territory, Weld County, St Vrain District

Cochran, Grace Maria Rannells
b. 29 Sept 1845, Athens, Athens, OH
d. 23 Dec 1933, Longmont, Boulder, CO
bd. Mountain View Cemetery, Longmont, Boulder, CO
spouse: James Allen Cochran
father: Samuel Flemming Rannells
mother: Sarah Bay Rannells
St Vrain Pioneers Assn Arrival Date: 1866
1870 US Census, Colorado Territory, Boulder County, St Vrain District

Cochran, James Allen
b. 1843, MO
d. 24 Mar 1924, San Diego, CA
bd. Mountain View Cemetery, Longmont, Boulder, CO
spouse: Grace M Rannells Cochran
father: Hugh Cochran
mother: Mariah Stockton Cochran
St Vrain Pioneers Assn Arrival Date: 1867
1870 US Census, Colorado Territory, Boulder County, St Vrain District

Cochran, Josephine
b. abt 1869, Colorado Territory
father: Pearson G Cochran
mother: Aurora J Cochran
1870 US Census, Colorado Territory, Boulder County, Left Hand

Cochran, Pearson G
b. abt 1811, NH
spouse: Aurora J Cochran
1870 US Census, Colorado Territory, Boulder County, Left Hand

Cochran, William
b. abt 1866, Colorado Territory
father: Pearson G Cochran
mother: Aurora J Cochran
1870 US Census, Colorado Territory, Boulder County, Left Hand

Cockins, Ezra
b. abt 1840, PA
1870 US Census, Colorado Territory, Weld County, St Vrain District

Code, John
b. abt 1839, NY
1860 US Census, Nebraska Territory, Platte River

Coffin, Emiline M Ainsworth
b. Aug 1842, Warren, PA
d. 19 Nov 1929, Fort Collins, Larimer, CO
spouse: George Wesley Coffin
1870 US Census, Colorado Territory, Weld County, St Vrain District

Coffin, Genevieve
b. 3 Jan 1890, Mead, Weld, CO
d. 16 Mar 1981, Fort Collins, Larimer, CO
bd. Grandview Cemetery, Fort Collins, Larimer, CO
spouse: Vinton Orville Coffin
father: Lawrence Thomas Mulligan
mother: Rachel Frances Trail Mulligan

Coffin, George Emil
b. 4 Dec 1876, Longmont, Boulder, CO
d. 27 Jan 1925, Rochester, Olmsted, MN
bd. Mountain View Cemetery, Longmont, Boulder, CO
spouse: Clara E Specht Coffin

father: George Wesley Coffin
mother: Emiline M Ainsworth Coffin

Coffin, George Wesley
b. abt 1839, NY
spouse: Emiline M Ainsworth Coffin
father: Jacob Coffin
mother: Mary Ann Hull Coffin
St Vrain Pioneers Assn Arrival Date: 1860
Troy District Land Club Claim Date: 1861 Jan 28
St Vrain Ditch Owner: Coffin Meadow Ditch No. 3, 1 May 1860
1870 US Census, Colorado Territory, Weld County, St Vrain District

Coffin, Gertrude
b. 14 Apr 1865, St Vrain, Weld, Colorado Territory
d. 9 May 1945, San Diego, CA
father: George Wesley Coffin
mother: Emiline M Ainsworth Coffin
1870 US Census, Colorado Territory, Weld County, St Vrain District

Coffin, Julia Ann Dunbar
b. 2 Sept 1844, Owego, Tioga, NY
d. 16 Apr 1926, Weld, CO
bd. Mountain Cemetery, Longmont, Boulder, CO
spouse: Morse Houghtaling Coffin
father: Andrew B Dunbar
mother: Dlizabeth Thomas Dunbar
St Vrain Pioneers Assn Arrival Date: 1866

Coffin, Lewis Alfred
b. 19 Feb 1869, St Vrain, Weld, Colorado Territory
d. 1 Nov 1948, Levanworth, Chelan, WA
father: George Wesley Coffin
mother: Emiline M Ainsworth Coffin
1870 US Census, Colorado Territory, Weld County, St Vrain District

Coffin, Mark Ainsworth
b. abt 1867, Afton, DeKalb, IL
d. 15 Jan 1941, Carlsbad, San Diego, CA
father: George Wesley Coffin
mother: Emiline M Ainsworth Coffin
1870 US Census, Colorado Territory, Weld County, St Vrain District

Coffin, Mary Foster
b. 1847, Canada
d. 26 Apr 1921, Flushing, Queens, NY
bd. Arlington National Cemetery, Arlington, VA
spouse: Onsville C Coffin
mother: Betsey S Foster
1870 US Census, Colorado Territory, Boulder County, St Vrain District

Coffin, Merton Dunbar
b. 8 Aug 1868, Afton, DeKalb, IL
d. 22 Oct 1944, Longmont, CO
bd. Mountain View Cemetery, Longmont, Boulder, CO
spouse: Norah Ellen Terry Coffin
father: Morse Houghtaling Coffin
mother: Julia Ann Dunbar Coffin

Coffin, Morse Houghtaling
b. 20 Sept 1836, Roxbury, NY
d. 5 Sept 1913, Longmont, CO
bd. Mountain View Cemetery, Longmont, Boulder, CO
spouse: Julia Ann Dunbar Coffin
father: Jacob Coffin
mother: Mary Ann Hull Coffin
St Vrain Pioneers Assn Arrival Date: 1859
Troy District Land Club Claim Date: 1861 Jan 28
St Vrain Ditch Owner: Coffin-Davis Ditch No. 31, 1 June 1866

Coffin, Onsville C
b. abt 1841, Shapleigh, York, ME
d. 25 Dec 1921, Flushing, Queens, NY
bd. Arlington National Cemetery, Arlington, VA
spouse: Mary Foster Coffin
father: James Coffin
mother: Rachel Garvin Coffin
1870 US Census, Colorado Territory, Boulder County, St Vrain District

Coffin, Reuben Fryer
b. 15 Nov 1842, Rosbury, Delaware, NY
d. 9 Dec 1928, Longmont, Boulder, CO
bd. Mountain View Cemetery, Longmont, Boulder, CO
spouse: Lydia Evangeline Gregg Coffin
father: Jacob Coffin
mother: Mary Ann Hull Coffin
St Vrain Pioneers Assn Arrival Date: 1866
1870 US Census, Colorado Territory, Weld County, St Vrain District

St Vrain Valley Pioneers

Coffin, Vinton Orville
b. 1 Sept 1889, Longmont, Boulder, CO
d. 12 Jan 1977, Fort Collins, Larimer, CO
bd. Grandview Cemetery, Fort Collins, Larimer, CO
spouse: Genevieve Mulligan Coffin
father: Reuben Fryer Coffin
mother: Lydia E Gregg Coffin

Coffman, Arthur W
b. abt 1853, IL
spouse: May Coffman
father: Jacob Coffman
mother: Mary P Stover Coffman
St Vrain Pioneers Assn Arrival Date: 1865
1870 US Census, Colorado Territory, Boulder County, St Vrain District

Coffman, Christe A
b. abt 1835, OH
1870 US Census, Colorado Territory, Boulder County, St Vrain District

Coffman, Daniel Stover
b. 6 July 1832, Enterprise, Preble, OH
d. 8 Feb 1916, Long Beach, CA
bd. Sunnyside Cemetery, Los Angeles, CA
spouse: Sarah P Hall Coffman
father: Jacob Coffman
mother: Mary P Stover Coffman
St Vrain Pioneers Assn Arrival Date: 1865
1870 US Census, Colorado Territory, Boulder County, St Vrain District

Coffman, Elbert Grant
b. abt 1864, Colorado Territory
d. 8 Oct 1922, CA
father: Daniel S Coffman
mother: Sarah Coffman
1870 US Census, Colorado Territory, Boulder County, St Vrain District

Coffman, Electa J
b. abt 1842, OH
spouse: Enoch J Coffman
St Vrain Pioneers Assn Arrival Date: 1861
1870 US Census, Colorado Territory, Boulder County, St Vrain District

Coffman, Enoch J
b. 19 Oct 1837
spouse: Electa McConahay Coffman
father: Jacob Coffman
mother: Mary P Stover Coffman
St Vrain Pioneers Assn Arrival Date: 1861
St Vrain Ditch Owner: Coffman Ditch No. 20, 30 May 1864
1870 US Census, Colorado Territory, Boulder County, St Vrain District

Coffman, George
St Vrain Pioneers Assn Arrival Date: 1865

Coffman, George F
b. abt 1850, IL
spouse: Genevieve S Turrell Coffman
father: Jacob Coffman
mother: Mary P Stover Coffman
1870 US Census, Colorado Territory, Boulder County, St Vrain District

Coffman, Jacob T
b. abt 1802, MD
d. 1 Apr 1876, Longmont, Boulder, CO
bd. Burlington Cemetery?, Longmont, Boulder, CO
spouse: Mary P Stover Coffman
1870 US Census, Colorado Territory, Boulder County, St Vrain District

Coffman, James
St Vrain Pioneers Assn Arrival Date: 1865

Coffman, Jesse D
b. 15 Oct 1839, OH
d. 12 Apr 1921, Denver, CO
bd. Mountain View Cemetery, Longmont, Boulder, CO
father: Jacob Coffman
mother: Mary P Stover Coffman
St Vrain Pioneers Assn Arrival Date: 1865
1870 US Census, Colorado Territory, Boulder County, St Vrain District

Coffman, Lottie
b. abt 1861, IL
father: Daniel Coffman
mother: Sarah Coffman
1870 US Census, Colorado Territory, Boulder County, St Vrain District

Coffman, Maggie
b. abt 1855
d. 8 May 1920, Eaton, CO
spouse: R F Coffman

Coffman, Mary P Stover
b. abt 1810, PA
d. 9 Aug 1877, Longmont, Boulder, CO
bd. Burlington Cemtery?, Longmont, Boulder, CO
spouse: Jacob Coffman
1870 US Census, Colorado Territory, Boulder County, St Vrain District

Coffman, Sarah P Hall
b. 1849, Canada
d. 1922, Long Beach, CA
bd. Sunnyside Cemetery, Los Aneles, CA
spouse: Daniel Stover Coffman
1870 US Census, Colorado Territory, Boulder County, St Vrain District

Coffman, Schuyler
b. abt 1867, Colorado Territory
father: Daniel Coffman
mother: Sarah Coffman
1870 US Census, Colorado Territory, Boulder County, St Vrain District

Coffman, Simon
St Vrain Pioneers Assn Arrival Date: 1865

Cole, Hervey Arthur
b. 1879, Corning, Adams, IA
d. 1968, Longmont, Boulder, CO
bd. Burlington Cemetery, Longmont, Boulder, CO
spouse: Amelia Culver Cole
father: Loren De Loss Cole
mother: Malinda Ward Cole

Collier, David C
b. 13 Oct 1832, NY
St Vrain Land Club (M687) Date: 1860 Feb 21

Coms, Henry
b. abt 1834, Canada
1870 US Census, Colorado Territory, Boulder County, St Vrain District

Conerickly, A P
St Vrain Land Club Date: 1861 May 17

Conley, John
b. abt 1820, Ireland
d. bef 31 Aug 1898, Seattle, WA
1870 US Census, Colorado Territory, Boulder County, St Vrain District

Conlon, Frank
St Vrain Pioneers Assn Arrival Date: [not recorded]

Connelly, Charles
b. abt 1835, NY
1860 US Census, Nebraska Territory, Platte River

Conners, James L
b. abt 1849
d. 11 Dec 1928, Berthoud, Larimer, CO

Connolly, Charles M
St Vrain Land Club (M687) Date: 1859 Sept 15

Cook
St Vrain Land Club (M687) Date: 1859 Oct 6

Cook, Aquilla
b. 7 May 1833
d. abt 20 Apr 1868, St Vrain Canyon, Boulder, CO
bd. Hygiene Cemetery, Hygiene, Boulder, CO
spouse: Esther J Cook
St Vrain Pioneers Assn Arrival Date: 1865

Cook, Caleb
b. abt 1861, IA
father: Aquilla Cook
mother: Ester J Cook Sites
1870 US Census, Colorado Territory, Boulder County, St Vrain District

Cook, Esther J
spouse: Aquila Cook

Cook, Freeman
b. 20 Aug 1863, IA
d. 11 Apr 1889, Balarat, CO
bd. Hygiene Cemetery, Hygiene, Boulder, CO
father: Aquilla Cook
mother: Ester J Cook Sites
1870 US Census, Colorado Territory, Boulder County, St Vrain District

Cooms, James M
St Vrain Pioneers Assn Arrival Date: 1869

St Vrain Valley Pioneers

Corben, John
  b. abt 1844, MA
  1870 US Census, Colorado Territory, Boulder County, St Vrain District

Cornell, Alvin M
  b. abt 1826, NY
  spouse: Sally A Cornell
  St Vrain Pioneers Assn Arrival Date: 1859
  1870 US Census, Colorado Territory, Weld County, St Vrain District

Cornell, Elida
  b. abt 1864, Colorado Territory
  father: Alvin Cornell
  mother: Sally A Cornell
  1870 US Census, Colorado Territory, Weld County, St Vrain District

Cornell, Howard
  b. abt 1852, NY
  father: Alvin Cornell
  mother: Sally A Cornell
  1870 US Census, Colorado Territory, Weld County, St Vrain District

Cornell, Sally A
  b. abt 1831, NY
  d. 26 Dec 1910, Denver, CO
  spouse: Alvin M Cornell
  1870 US Census, Colorado Territory, Weld County, St Vrain District

Corson, William A
  b. Apr 1836, Minion, OH
  d. 15 Jan 1913, El Paso, CO
  bd. Evergreen, El Paso, Colorado Springs
  spouse: Hannah McIntosh Corson

Corwin, Charles A
  b. abt 1846, NY
  1870 US Census, Colorado Territory, Boulder County, St Vrain District

Cosson, Robert
  b. abt 1839, IL
  1870 US Census, Colorado Territory, Boulder County, St Vrain District

Coulson, Clarissa A Rannells
  b. 1 Aug 1837, Guernsey, OH
  d. Sept 1914, Durango, La Plata, CO
  bd. Greenmount Cemetery, La Plata, CO
  spouse: William W Coulson
  father: Samuel Flemming Rannells
  mother: Sarah Bay Rannells
  St Vrain Pioneers Assn Arrival Date: 1864

Coulson, William Wallace
  b. abt 1840, PA
  spouse: Clarissa A Rannells Coulson
  St Vrain Pioneers Assn Arrival Date: 1864

Cowell, S
  b. abt 1839, Canada
  1860 US Census, Nebraska Territory, Platte River

Coyer, John M
  b. abt 1838, OH
  1870 US Census, Colorado Territory, Boulder County, St Vrain District

Craig, John H
  St Vrain Land Club (M687) Date: 1860 Apr 7

Cran, Richard
  b. abt 1842, England
  1870 US Census, Colorado Territory, Boulder County, St Vrain District

Crank, Mrs George
  b. abt 1848
  d. 30 Nov 1923
  spouse: George Crank

Crawford, Arthur
  b. abt 1865, Colorado Territory
  father: Edward Crawford
  mother: Mary J Crawford
  1870 US Census, Colorado Territory, Boulder County, St Vrain District

Crawford, Charles
  b. abt 1864, Colorado Territory
  father: Edward Crawford
  mother: Mary J Crawford
  1870 US Census, Colorado Territory, Boulder County, St Vrain District

Crawford, Edward D
  b. abt 1825
  spouse: Mary D Slaughter Crawford
  St Vrain Pioneers Assn Arrival Date: [not recorded]
  1870 US Census, Colorado Territory, Boulder County, St Vrain District

St Vrain Valley Pioneers

Crawford, John
  b. abt 1847, Canada
  father: Edward Crawford
  mother: Mary J Crawford
  1870 US Census, Colorado Territory, Boulder
    County, St Vrain District

Crawford, Mary D Slaughter
  spouse: Edward D Crawford
  St Vrain Pioneers Assn Arrival Date: [not
    recorded]

Crawford, Mary J
  b. abt 1834, VA
  spouse: Edward Crawford
  1870 US Census, Colorado Territory, Boulder
    County, St Vrain District

Crawford, William
  b. abt 1849, WI
  father: Edward Crawford
  mother: Mary J Crawford
  1870 US Census, Colorado Territory, Boulder
    County, St Vrain District

Cressa
  b. abt 1825, NH
  1870 US Census, Colorado Territory, Boulder
    County, St Vrain District

Crocker, Henry H
  b. 1843
  d. 1898
  bd. Niwot Cemetery, Niwot, Boulder, CO
  spouse: Elizabeth Crocker
  St Vrain Pioneers Assn Arrival Date: 1864
  1870 US Census, Colorado Territory, Boulder
    County, Left Hand

Cronk, David
  b. abt 1839
  d. 6 Jan 1866
  bd. Mountain View Cemetery, Longmont,
    Boulder, CO
  Troy District Land Club Claim Date: 1860 Oct 6

Cronk, Eliza M
  b. abt 1849, OH
  spouse: George Cronk
  1870 US Census, Colorado Territory, Boulder
    County, St Vrain District

Cronk, George
  b. 19 June 1838, NY
  d. 27 Oct 1927, Berthoud, Larimer, CO
  bd. Greenlawn Cemetery, Larimer, CO
  spouse: Eliza M Cronk
  St Vrain Pioneers Assn Arrival Date: 1859
  Troy District Land Club Claim Date: 1861 Feb 19
  1870 US Census, Colorado Territory, Boulder
    County, St Vrain District

Crook, Austin B
  b. abt 1845, NH
  spouse: Lucy Crook
  1870 US Census, Colorado Territory, Boulder
    County, St Vrain District

Crook, Edwin W
  b. abt 1868, WY
  father: Austin B Crook
  mother: Lucy Crook
  1870 US Census, Colorado Territory, Boulder
    County, St Vrain District

Crook, Lucy
  b. abt 1844, NH
  spouse: Austin B Crook
  1870 US Census, Colorado Territory, Boulder
    County, St Vrain District

Crook, R C
  Franklin Township Land Club Claim Date: 1860
    June 24

Crosby, James M
  b. abt 1835, IL
  spouse: Manerva Crosby
  St Vrain Pioneers Assn Arrival Date: 1870

Cross, Louis
  St Vrain Pioneers Assn Arrival Date: [not
    recorded]

Culver, Cary
  b. 24 Feb 1841, Little Valley, Cattaraugus, NY
  d. 8 Aug 1907
  bd. Burlington Cemetery, Longmont, Boulder, CO
  spouse: Elvina E Kennicott Culver
  father: Robert Culver
  mother: Sarah Price Culver
  St Vrain Pioneers Assn Arrival Date: 1866
  St Vrain Land Club Date: 1861 Aug 7

St Vrain Valley Pioneers

1870 US Census, Colorado Territory, Boulder County, St Vrain District

Culver, Elvina E Kennicott
b. 26 Oct 1847, NY
d. 26 Oct 1911, Little Thompson, Larimer, CO
bd. Burlington Cemetery, Longmont, Boulder, CO
spouse: Cary Culver
St Vrain Pioneers Assn Arrival Date: 1865
1870 US Census, Colorado Territory, Boulder County, St Vrain District

Culver, Fred
b. Feb 1870, Colorado Territory
father: Cary Culver
mother: Elvina E Kennicott Culver
1870 US Census, Colorado Territory, Boulder County, St Vrain District

Culver, Mary E
b. 1868, Colorado Territory
d. 11 Jan 1871, Colorado Territory
bd. Burlington Cemetery, Longmont, Boulder, CO
father: Cary Culver
mother: Elvina E Kennicott Culver
1870 US Census, Colorado Territory, Boulder County, St Vrain District

Culver, Robert
b. 6 Mar 1830, Cattaraugas, NY
d. 1 Dec 1906, Baltimore, MD
bd. Columbia Cemetery, Boulder, CO
spouse: Anna Kennicott Culver
father: Lyman Culver
mother: Emeliza Hull Culver
St Vrain Land Club Date: 1861 Aug 27
St Vrain Ditch Owner: Davis & Downing Ditch No. 33, 1 Nov 1866

Culyer, Charles
b. abt 1834, Ireland
1860 US Census, Nebraska Territory, Platte River

Cunningham, Owen
St Vrain Land Club (M687) Date: 1861 May 3

Cushman, Abial Washburn
b. 13 Mar 1839, Lee, Penobscot, ME
d. 9 Aug 1908, Covina, Los Angeles, CA
bd. Mountain View Cemetery, Longmont, Boulder, CO
spouse: Fannie J Skinner Cushman
father: Abial Cushman
mother: Celia Pierce Cushman
St Vrain Pioneers Assn Arrival Date: 1859
St Vrain Ditch Owner: Cushman Ditch No. 8, 20 June 1861
1870 US Census, Colorado Territory, Boulder County, St Vrain District

Cushman, Alfred H
b. 29 Mar 1837, Lee, Penobscot, ME
d. 24 June 1927, Dolores, Montezuma, CO
bd. Cortez Cemetery, Montezuma, CO
spouse: Elisabeth Jane Powell Cushman
father: Abial Cushman
mother: Celia Pierce Cushman
St Vrain Pioneers Assn Arrival Date: 1859
St Vrain Land Club Date: 1861 Apr 19
St Vrain Ditch Owner: South Flat Ditch No. 16, 15 May 1863
1870 US Census, Colorado Territory, Boulder County, St Vrain District

Cushman, Augustus M
b. Oct 1867, Colorado Territory
d. 17 Oct 1912, Delores, Montezuma, CO
spouse: Elizabeth J Closson
father: Alfred Cushman
mother: Elizabeth Jane Powell Cushman
1870 US Census, Colorado Territory, Boulder County, St Vrain District

Cushman, Celia Mary
b. abt 1868, Colorado Territory
d. 1894
father: Abial Washburn Cushman
mother: Fannie J Skinner Cushman
1870 US Census, Colorado Territory, Boulder County, St Vrain District

Cushman, Elizabeth Jane Powell
b. 7 Apr 1840, IN
spouse: Alfred Cushman
father: Aaron Powell
mother: Eliza Priddy Powell
St Vrain Pioneers Assn Arrival Date: 1865
1870 US Census, Colorado Territory, Boulder County, St Vrain District

Cushman, Fannie J Skinner
b. 29 May 1846, OH
d. 31 Mar 1925, Covina City, Los Angeles, CA
bd. Mountain View Cemetery, Longmont, Boulder, CO
spouse: Abiel Washburn Cushman
St Vrain Pioneers Assn Arrival Date: 1859
1870 US Census, Colorado Territory, Boulder County, St Vrain District

Cushman, Madora
b. abt 1868, Colorado Territory
father: Alfred Cushman
mother: Elisabeth Jane Powell Cushman
1870 US Census, Colorado Territory, Boulder County, St Vrain District

Cushman, N
St Vrain Land Club Date: 1861 Apr 24

Cushman, Victor
b. 11 Nov 1869, Colorado Territory
d. 22 Mar 1905, CO
spouse: Linna May Kempton Cushman
father: Abial Washburn Cushman
mother: Fannie J Skinner Cushman
1870 US Census, Colorado Territory, Boulder County, St Vrain District

Cutler, Amanda
b. abt 1852, IA
father: Porter Cutler
mother: Susan Cutler
1870 US Census, Colorado Territory, Weld County, St Vrain District

Cutler, Charles
b. abt 1862, Colorado Territory
father: Porter Cutler
mother: Susan Cutler
1870 US Census, Colorado Territory, Weld County, St Vrain District

Cutler, Cutter
b. abt 1860, IA
father: Porter Cutler
mother: Susan Cutler
1870 US Census, Colorado Territory, Weld County, St Vrain District

Cutler, Mary
b. abt 1856, IA
father: Porter Cutler
mother: Susan Cutler
1870 US Census, Colorado Territory, Weld County, St Vrain District

Cutler, Porter
b. abt 1825, OH
spouse: Susan Cutler
St Vrain Land Club (M687) Date: 1864 Dec 10
1870 US Census, Colorado Territory, Weld County, St Vrain District

Cutler, Sarah
b. abt 1868, Colorado Territory
father: Porter Cutler
mother: Susan Cutler
1870 US Census, Colorado Territory, Weld County, St Vrain District

Cutler, Susan
b. abt 1831, OH
spouse: Porter Cutler
1870 US Census, Colorado Territory, Weld County, St Vrain District

Cutler, Victoria
b. abt 1866, Colorado Territory
father: Porter Cutler
mother: Susan Cutler
1870 US Census, Colorado Territory, Weld County, St Vrain District

Cutler, William
b. abt 1858, IA
father: Porter Cutler
mother: Susan Cutler
1870 US Census, Colorado Territory, Weld County, St Vrain District

St Vrain Valley Pioneers

D

Dagle, Florilla
b. abt 1844, WV
spouse: Joseph Dagle
St Vrain Pioneers Assn Arrival Date: 1863
1870 US Census, Colorado Territory, Boulder County, St Vrain District

Dagle, George S
b. abt 1864, WI
father: Joseph Dagle
mother: Florilla Dagle
1870 US Census, Colorado Territory, Boulder County, St Vrain District

Dagle, Henry
b. abt 1868, WI
father: Joseph Dagle
mother: Florilla Dagle
1870 US Census, Colorado Territory, Boulder County, St Vrain District

Dagle, John L
b. abt 1866, WI
father: Joseph Dagle
mother: Florilla Dagle
1870 US Census, Colorado Territory, Boulder County, St Vrain District

Dagle, Joseph
b. abt 1835, Canada
spouse: Florilla Dagle
St Vrain Pioneers Assn Arrival Date: 1859
1870 US Census, Colorado Territory, Boulder County, St Vrain District

Dailey, Bertha
b. abt 1866, Colorado Territory
father: Dennis Darley
mother: Julia Darley
1870 US Census, Colorado Territory, Weld County, St Vrain District

Dailey, Dempster Harold
b. May 1863, Boulder Creek, Boulder, CO
d. 12 Mar 1931, Boulder, CO
bd. Mountain View Cemetery, Longmont, Boulder, CO
spouse: Laura M Christy Dailey
father: Dennis Dailey
mother: Juliette McDonald Dailey
1870 US Census, Colorado Territory, Weld County, St Vrain District

Dailey, Dempter
b. abt 1862, Colorado Territory
father: Dennis Darley
mother: Julia Darley
1870 US Census, Colorado Territory, Weld County, St Vrain District

Dailey, Dennis
b. 8 Mar 1837, Erie, NY
d. 25 July 1887, Fort Morgan, Weld, CO
bd. Riverside Cemetery, Fort Morgan, Morgan, CO
spouse: Juliette McDonald Green Dailey
father: Peter Dailey
mother: Mary Kenney Dailey
St Vrain Pioneers Assn Arrival Date: 1859
1870 US Census, Colorado Territory, Weld County, St Vrain District

Dailey, Dennis
b. abt 1838, NY
spouse: Julia Darley
1870 US Census, Colorado Territory, Weld County, St Vrain District

Dailey, Harriet
b. abt 1859, WI
father: Dennis Darley
mother: Julia Darley
1870 US Census, Colorado Territory, Weld County, St Vrain District

Dailey, Hawley
b. abt 1864, Colorado Territory
father: Dennis Darley
mother: Julia Darley
1870 US Census, Colorado Territory, Weld County, St Vrain District

Dailey, Imogene
b. abt 1869, Colorado Territory
father: Dennis Darley
mother: Julia Darley
1870 US Census, Colorado Territory, Weld County, St Vrain District

St Vrain Valley Pioneers

Dailey, Juliette McDonald Green
 b. 15 Nov 1840, Rutland, VT
 d. 10 Jan 1914, Fort Morgan, Morgan, CO
 bd. Riverside Cemetery, Fort Morgan, Morgan, CO
 spouse: Dennis Dailey
 father: Nathan Newell Green
 mother: Harriet McDonald Green
 St Vrain Pioneers Assn Arrival Date: 1863
 1870 US Census, Colorado Territory, Weld County, St Vrain District

Dailey, Louisa
 b. abt 1867, Colorado Territory
 father: Dennis Darley
 mother: Julia Darley
 1870 US Census, Colorado Territory, Weld County, St Vrain District

Dakan, Jessie Stanton
 b. 18 Aug 1874
 d. 15 Apr 1968
 bd. Mountain View Cemetery, Longmont, Boulder, CO
 spouse: Albert Dakan
 father: William Stanton
 mother: Mary Ann Blanchard Stanton

Dakan, William Allen
 b. 15 Aug 1840, OH
 d. 14 Aug 1914, Sedalia, Douglas, CO
 spouse: Elizabeth Cahill Dakan
 St Vrain Pioneers Assn Arrival Date: 1862

Daley, Andrew
 St Vrain Pioneers Assn Arrival Date: [not recorded]

Dalton, Patrick
 St Vrain Land Club (M687) Date: 1859 Dec 15

Daniel, Henry
 Troy District Land Club Claim Date: 1861 Jan 28

Daniels, Emmeline Coffin
 b. abt 1845
 d. 20 Oct 1922, Longmont, Boulder, CO
 bd. Mountain View Cemetery, Longmont, Boulder, CO
 spouse: Joseph Warren Daniels
 father: Jacob Coffin
 mother: Mary Ann Hull Coffin

Daniels, W J
 St Vrain Pioneers Assn Arrival Date: 1859

Darclone, Thomas
 St Vrain Land Club Date: 1861 Aug 15

Davidson, Matilda
 b. abt 1820, PA
 spouse: William Davidson
 St Vrain Pioneers Assn Arrival Date: 1859

Davidson, S M
 b. abt 1822, IL
 1860 US Census, Nebraska Territory, Platte River

Davidson, William A
 b. 10 Aug 1817, PA
 d. 20 May 1892
 bd. Columbia Cemetery, Boulder, CO
 spouse: Matilda Davidson
 mother: Elisabeth Davidson
 St Vrain Pioneers Assn Arrival Date: 1859

Davidson, Winifred H
 b. 1895
 d. 17 Feb 1968
 bd. Green Mountain Cemetery, Boulder, CO
 spouse: Frank H Davidson

Davis, Adaline
 b. abt 1856, IA
 father: Joseph Davis
 mother: Alliean Davis
 1870 US Census, Colorado Territory, Boulder County, St Vrain District

Davis, Allisan
 b. abt 1832, OH
 spouse: Joseph Davis
 1870 US Census, Colorado Territory, Boulder County, St Vrain District

Davis, Alvira
 b. abt 1858, IA
 father: Joseph Davis
 mother: Allisan Davis
 1870 US Census, Colorado Territory, Boulder County, St Vrain District

Davis, C M
 b. abt 1839, IL
 1860 US Census, Nebraska Territory, Platte River

St Vrain Valley Pioneers

Davis, Charles
b. abt 1869, Colorado Territory
father: Joseph Davis
mother: Alliean Davis
1870 US Census, Colorado Territory, Boulder County, St Vrain District

Davis, Charles Lorenzo
b. 5 Sept 1850, Waukesha, WI
d. 12 Dec 1915, Boulder, CO
bd. Valmont Cemetery, Boulder, CO
spouse: Della DeBacker Davis
father: John Davis Jr
mother: Lucy S Lyman Davis
1870 US Census, Colorado Territory, Boulder County, St Vrain District

Davis, Charles S
b. abt 1835, MI
spouse: Jane C Davis
1870 US Census, Colorado Territory, Boulder County, St Vrain District

Davis, Frank W
b. 27 May 1855, Hartland, Waukesha, WI
d. 19 May 1918, Boulder, CO
bd. Columbia Cemetery, Boulder, CO
spouse: Elizabeth Jane Hays Davis
father: John Davis Jr
mother: Lucy S Lyman Davis
1870 US Census, Colorado Territory, Boulder County, St Vrain District

Davis, George F
b. abt 1867, Colorado Territory
father: Joseph Davis
mother: Alliean Davis
1870 US Census, Colorado Territory, Boulder County, St Vrain District

Davis, George Martin
b. 16 Oct 1817, NH
d. 18 Nov 1897
bd. Highland Lake Pioneer Cemetery, Weld, CO
spouse: Mary Holden Davis
St Vrain Pioneers Assn Arrival Date: 1864

Davis, James N
b. abt 1862, Colorado Territory
father: Joseph Davis
mother: Alliean Davis
1870 US Census, Colorado Territory, Boulder County, St Vrain District

Davis, Jane C
b. abt 1835, MA
spouse: Charles S Davis
1870 US Census, Colorado Territory, Boulder County, St Vrain District

Davis, John
b. 30 Apr 1817, Franklin, MA
d. 7 Mar 1898, Boulder, CO
bd. Columbia Cemetery, Boulder, CO
spouse: Lucy S Lyman Davis
1870 US Census, Colorado Territory, Boulder County, St Vrain District

Davis, John H
b. abt 1861, IA
father: Joseph Davis
mother: Alliean Davis
1870 US Census, Colorado Territory, Boulder County, St Vrain District

Davis, Joseph
b. abt 1824, OH
spouse: Allisan Davis
St Vrain Pioneers Assn Arrival Date: [not recorded]
1870 US Census, Colorado Territory, Boulder County, St Vrain District

Davis, Lewis
b. abt 1868, MA
father: Charles S Davis
mother: Jane C Davis
1870 US Census, Colorado Territory, Boulder County, St Vrain District

Davis, Lucy S Lyman
b. 1 Mar 1822, Northfield, Franklin, MA
d. 2 Mar 1884, Boulder, CO
bd. Columbia Cemetery, Boulder, CO
spouse: John Davis Jr
father: Henry Lyman
mother: Lucy Field Lyman
1870 US Census, Colorado Territory, Boulder County, St Vrain District

Davis, Mahlon
St Vrain Land Club Date: 1861 Apr 5

St Vrain Valley Pioneers

Davis, Mary Holden
b. 3 Feb 1821, MA
d. 24 Aug 1897
bd. Highland Lake Pioneer Cemetery, Weld, CO
spouse: George Martin Davis
St Vrain Pioneers Assn Arrival Date: 1864

Davis, Sarah Electa
b. 2 Dec 1858, Allamakee, IA
d. 2 Nov 1872, Boulder, Colorado Territory
bd. Columbia Cemetery, Boulder, CO
father: John Davis Jr
mother: Lucy S Lyman Davis
1870 US Census, Colorado Territory, Boulder County, St Vrain District

Davis, William
St Vrain Pioneers Assn Arrival Date: 1863

Davis, William D
b. abt 1867, Colorado Territory
father: Charles S Davis
mother: Jane C Davis
1870 US Census, Colorado Territory, Boulder County, St Vrain District

Davis, William L
b. 31 Jan 1840, IN
d. 13 Mar 1912, Longmont, CO
St Vrain Pioneers Assn Arrival Date: 1862
St Vrain Ditch Owner: Bonus Ditch No. 6, 30 Mar 1861

Dawson, Mrs C E
St Vrain Pioneers Assn Arrival Date: 1863

Day, Edwin W
b. abt 1844, DE/MI
spouse: Mary A Jamison Day
1870 US Census, Colorado Territory, Boulder County, Left Hand

Day, Elizabeth
St Vrain Land Club Date: 1861 Dec 1

Day, John
b. abt 1832, IL
1860 US Census, Nebraska Territory, Platte River

Day, Mary A Jamison
b. abt 1855, MO
spouse: Edwin W Day
father: Joseph H Jamison
mother: Eleanor Jamison
St Vrain Pioneers Assn Arrival Date: 1860
1870 US Census, Colorado Territory, Boulder County, St Vrain District

Deardoff, Cyrus W
b. 22 Feb 1832, Tuscaranas, OH
d. 7 Dec 1915, County Poor Farm, Boulder, CO
bd. Columbia Cemetery, Boulder, CO
spouse: Ellen Perkins Schrader Deardoff
father: Henry Deardoff
mother: Elizabeth Walters Deardoff
1870 US Census, Colorado Territory, Boulder County, St Vrain District

Deaton, Celia L Dean Coleman Burns
b. 1892
d. 1967
bd. Foothills Gardens of Memory, Longmont, Boulder, CO
spouse: William H Coleman, William Burns, Robert Lee Deaton
father: George W Dean
mother: Emma Dean

DeBacker, family of John Franciscus
father: John Franciscus DeBacker
St Vrain Pioneers Assn Arrival Date: 1859

DeBacker, John Franciscus
b. 13 Jan 1827, Moerkerke, West-Vlaanderen, Belgium
d. 26 Feb 1907, Boulder, CO
bd. South Boulder Cemetery, Boulder, CO
spouse: Marie Fouse DeBacker; Marie Dehn DeBacker;. Margery Ellenora Hopkins DeBacker
father: Robert DeBacker
mother: Marie Theresia DeWandel
St Vrain Pioneers Assn Arrival Date: 1859

DeBacker, Marie Dehn
b. 5 June 1836, Prussia
d. 22 Oct 1925, Boulder, CO
bd. South Boulder Cemetery, Boulder, CO
spouse: John DeBacker
St Vrain Pioneers Assn Arrival Date: 1859

St Vrain Valley Pioneers

Dechamp, Joe
  b. abt 1845, Canada
  1870 US Census, Colorado Territory, Boulder County, St Vrain District

Dehn, Alice
  b. 1906
  d. 15 Nov 1967
  bd. Green Mountain Cemetery, Boulder, CO

Delancey, Clara Cassandra Peck Searcy Cranson Butterworth
  b. 7 Nov 1857, Iowa City, Wright, IA
  d. 26 May 1937, Hygiene, Boulder, CO
  spouse: Harden Searcy; John Cranson; John H Butterworth; J Howard Delancey
  father: Thomas Samuel Peck
  mother: Susan Edmund Walthall Peck
  St Vrain Pioneers Assn Arrival Date: 1859
  1870 US Census, Colorado Territory, Boulder County, St Vrain District

Deland, Frank
  b. abt 1839, Canada
  1870 US Census, Colorado Territory, Boulder County, St Vrain District

Delehant, Daniel
  St Vrain Pioneers Assn Arrival Date: 1868

Delehant, Mrs Daniel
  St Vrain Pioneers Assn Arrival Date: 1866

Delongchamp, Mildred Kneale
  b. 2 Dec 1890
  d. 26 Aug 1967, Sussex, NJ
  bd. Green Mountain Cemetery, Boulder, CO
  spouse: James Charles Delongchamp
  mother: Mary Hatfield Kneale

Denio, James Wilbur
  b. 21 Mar 1847, Helena, St Lawrence, NY
  d. 9 Nov 1928, Longmont, Boulder, CO
  bd. Mountain View Cemetery, Longmont, Boulder, CO
  spouse: Hattie Maria Taylor Denio
  father: Hardin Fitzgerald Denio
  mother: Elvira Town Denio
  St Vrain Ditch Owner: Denio & Taylor Ditch No. 28, 15 July 1865

Dennison, Albert
  b. abt 1855, WI
  father: L S Dennison
  mother: Mary Dennison
  1860 US Census, Nebraska Territory, Platte River

Dennison, L S
  b. abt 1830, MO
  spouse: Mary Dennison
  1860 US Census, Nebraska Territory, Platte River

Dennison, Mary
  b. abt 1830, MO
  spouse: L S Dennison
  1860 US Census, Nebraska Territory, Platte River

Dickens, Allen G
  St Vrain Land Club Date: 1861 Mar 5

Dickens, Maria
  b. abt 1846, WI
  1870 US Census, Colorado Territory, Boulder County, St Vrain District

Dickens, William Henry
  b. 26 May 1843, At Sea, Sulawesi Tengah, Indonesia
  d. 30 Nov 1915, Longmont, Boulder, CO
  bd. Mountain View Cemetery, Longmont, Boulder, CO
  spouse: Ida E Kiteley Dickens
  father: John Henry Dickens
  mother: Mary Ann Harris Dickens
  St Vrain Pioneers Assn Arrival Date: 1860
  St Vrain Land Club Date: 1861 Apr 7
  St Vrain Ditch Owner: Dickens Private Ditch No. 12, 15 Apr 1862
  1870 US Census, Colorado Territory, Boulder County, St Vrain District

Dickerson, Daniel
  b. abt 1836, MO
  1860 US Census, Nebraska Territory, Platte River

Dickins, William
  b. abt 1843, WI
  1870 US Census, Colorado Territory, Boulder County, St Vrain District

Dickson, Lewis H
  b. 18 Jan 1834, Franklin, OH
  d. 23 Mar 1911, Longmont, CO

bd. Mountain View Cemetery, Longmont, Boulder, CO
spouse: Emily A Sharp Dickson
father: Hiram Dickson
mother: Elizabeth M Hayward Dickson
St Vrain Pioneers Assn Arrival Date: 1860
Troy District Land Club Claim Date: 1861 Apr 9
St Vrain Ditch Owner: Beckwith Ditch No 5, 8 Mar 1861

Dimick, Frank
b. abt 1838, NY
1870 US Census, Colorado Territory, Boulder County, St Vrain District

Dixon, N
b. abt 1828, Canada
1860 US Census, Nebraska Territory, Platte River

Dixon, Sophia
b. abt 1844, NE Terr
1860 US Census, Nebraska Territory, Platte River

Dodd, Alvah John
b. 29 Jan 1866, Boulder, Boulder, CO
d. 21 Aug 1910, Boulder, CO
bd. Niwot Cemetery, Niwot, Boulder, CO
father: Barnett Dodd
mother: Charlotte Erickson Peterson Dodd
1870 US Census, Colorado Territory, Boulder County, Left Hand

Dodd, Alvah Milford
b. 2 May 1857, Davis, IA
d. 30 June 1936, Niwot, Boulder, CO
bd. Niwot Cemetery, Niwot, Boulder, CO
spouse: Della Lucina Gould Dodd
father: John Dodd
mother: Elizabeth Bell Dodd

Dodd, Barnett
b. 6 Mar 1836, Danville, Hendricks, IN
d. 23 Nov 1920, Niwot, Boulder, CO
bd. Niwot Cemetery, Niwot, Boulder, CO
spouse: Charlotte Erickson Peterson Dodd
father: John Dodd
mother: Elizabeth Bell Dodd
St Vrain Pioneers Assn Arrival Date: 1862
1870 US Census, Colorado Territory, Boulder County, Left Hand

Dodd, Charlotte Erickson Peterson
b. 28 Nov 1838, Sweden
d. 26 Sept 1925, Longmont, Boulder, CO
bd. Niwot Cemetery, Niwot, Boulder, CO
spouse: Barnett Dodd
St Vrain Pioneers Assn Arrival Date: 1861
1870 US Census, Colorado Territory, Boulder County, Left Hand

Dodd, George Washington
b. 6 Oct 1867, Boulder, Colorado Territory
d. 14 June 1960
bd. Mountain View Cemetery, Longmont, Boulder, CO
spouse: Margaret Dawson Dodd
father: Barnett Dodd
mother: Charlotte Erickson Peterson Dodd
1870 US Census, Colorado Territory, Boulder County, Left Hand

Dodd, James Harvey
b. 5 Jan 1870, Niwot, Boulder, Colorado Territory
d. 5 Apr 1959, Boulder, CO
bd. Mountain View Cemetery, Longmont, Boulder, CO
spouse: Mary Elizabeth Dawson Dodd
father: Barnett Dodd
mother: Charlotte Erickson Peterson Dodd
1870 US Census, Colorado Territory, Boulder County, Left Hand

Donnelly, Edward
b. abt 1825, NY
d. 7 July 1887
bd. Valmont Cemetery, Boulder, CO
St Vrain Pioneers Assn Arrival Date: 1859
1860 US Census, Nebraska Territory, Altona

Doolittle, J K
St Vrain Ditch Owner: Bonus Ditch No. 6, 30 Mar 1861

Doran, James
b. abt 1824, Ireland
spouse: Winiford Doran
St Vrain Pioneers Assn Arrival Date: 1862

Doran, Winifred Shanahan
b. abt 1825, Ireland
d. 28 Dec 1903, Boulder, CO
bd. South Boulder Cemetery, Boulder, CO

spouse: James Doran
father: Timothy Shanahan
mother: Winifred Dunn Shanahan
St Vrain Pioneers Assn Arrival Date: 1862

Doughty, Andrew
St Vrain Pioneers Assn Arrival Date: 1860

Douglas, Ormena I Stoddard
b. 1837, NY
d. 9 Jan 1914, Longmont, Boulder, CO
spouse: William Stoddard, Chester W Douglas
St Vrain Pioneers Assn Arrival Date: 1871

Dow, Charlotte Moore
b. abt 1819, VT
spouse: James E Dow
1870 US Census, Colorado Territory, Boulder County, St Vrain District

Dow, James E
b. 6 Nov 1816, NY
d. 3 Apr 1873, Boulder, Colorado Territory
bd. Dow Farm, Boulder, Colorado Territory
spouse: Charlotte Moore Dow
father: Daniel Dow Sr
mother: Susannah Douglas Dow
St Vrain Pioneers Assn Arrival Date: [not recorded]
1870 US Census, Colorado Territory, Boulder County, St Vrain District

Downer, Ada
b. abt 1864, KS
father: Benjamin F Downer
mother: Lydia A Downer
1870 US Census, Colorado Territory, Boulder County, St Vrain District

Downer, Benjamin F
b. abt 1832, IL
spouse: Lydia A Downer
1870 US Census, Colorado Territory, Boulder County, St Vrain District

Downer, Ida
b. abt 1866, Colorado Territory
father: Benjamin F Downer
mother: Lydia A Downer
1870 US Census, Colorado Territory, Boulder County, St Vrain District

Downer, Lewella
b. abt 1868, Colorado Territory
father: Benjamin F Downer
mother: Lydia A Downer
1870 US Census, Colorado Territory, Boulder County, St Vrain District

Downer, Lydia A
b. abt 1837, IL
spouse: Benjamin F Downer
1870 US Census, Colorado Territory, Boulder County, St Vrain District

Downer, Susan
b. abt 1870, Colorado Territory
father: Benjamin F Downer
mother: Lydia A Downer
1870 US Census, Colorado Territory, Boulder County, St Vrain District

Downing, Benjamin A
St Vrain Pioneers Assn Arrival Date: 1860

Druman, Jacob
b. abt 1835 Bavaria
1870 US Census, Colorado Territory, Boulder County, St Vrain District

Dubois, Charles Franklin
b. Oct 1856, IA
d. 5 Jan 1914, Denver, CO
bd. Fairmount Cemetery, Denver, CO
spouse: Mary Winifred Adams DuBois, Catherine McKnight DuBois
father: Ebenezer Collins Dubois
mother: Sarah Ann Cahoon Dubois
St Vrain Pioneers Assn Arrival Date: [not recorded]
1860 US Census, Nebraska Territory, Altona

Dubois, Ebenezer Collins
b. abt 1808, Sutton, Brome, Quebec, Canada
d. 1879, Colorado Territory
spouse: Sarah Ann Cahoon Dubois
father: William Boyce/Henry DuBois
mother: Catherine Collins DuBois
St Vrain Pioneers Assn Arrival Date: [not recorded]
1860 US Census, Nebraska Territory, Altona

DuBois, Ernest Edmund
 b. abt 1862, Colorado Territory
 d. 24 Dec 1898, Boulder, CO
 bd. Columbia Cemetery, Boulder, CO
 spouse: Ida Melcine Richardson DuBois
 father: Ebenezer Collins DuBois
 mother: Sarah Ann Cahoon DuBois
 St Vrain Pioneers Assn Arrival Date: [not recorded]

DuBois, George Samuel
 b. abt 1851, South Bend, St Joseph, IN
 d. 1 Apr 1908, Denver, Adams, CO
 bd. Columbia Cemetery, Boulder, CO
 spouse: Susie E Lasley DuBois
 father: Ebenezer Collins DuBois
 mother: Sarah Ann Cahoon DuBois
 St Vrain Pioneers Assn Arrival Date: [not recorded]
 1860 US Census, Nebraska Territory, Altona

DuBois, James Ebenezer
 b. 16 Nov 1842, OH
 d. 19 May 1899, Fort Collins, Larimer, CO
 bd. Grandview Cemetery, Larimer, CO
 spouse: Hattie LeBeuff DuBois
 father: Ebenezer Collins DuBois
 mother: Sarah Ann Cahoon DuBois
 St Vrain Pioneers Assn Arrival Date: [not recorded]
 1860 US Census, Nebraska Territory, Altona

Dubois, Oren Edward
 b. Sept 1859, Altona, NE Territory
 d. 8 May 1930, Los Angeles, CA
 spouse: Clara Owens
 father: Ebenezer Collins Dubois
 mother: Sarah Ann Cahoon Dubois
 St Vrain Pioneers Assn Arrival Date: [not recorded]
 1860 US Census, Nebraska Territory, Altona

Dubois, Sarah Ann
 b. abt 1848, IN
 d. 1865, Altona?, Colorado Territory
 bd. Altona?, Boulder, Colorado Territory
 father: Ebenezer Collins Dubois
 mother: Sarah Ann Cahoon Dubois
 St Vrain Pioneers Assn Arrival Date: [not recorded]
 1860 US Census, Nebraska Territory, Altona

Dubois, Sarah Ann Cahoon
 b. abt 1817, VA
 d. abt 1869, Colorado Territory
 bd. Altona?. Boulder. Colorado Territory
 spouse: Ebenezer Collins Dubois
 St Vrain Pioneers Assn Arrival Date: [not recorded]
 1860 US Census, Nebraska Territory, Altona

Dubois, William Collins
 b. abt 1839, OH
 d. 23 Feb 1870, Boulder, Colorado Territory
 bd. Faivre Ranch, Boulder, Colorado Territory
 father: Ebenezer Collins Dubois
 mother: Sarah Ann Cahoon Dubois
 St Vrain Pioneers Assn Arrival Date: [not recorded]
 1860 US Census, Nebraska Territory, Altona

Dudley, Ellen
 b. abt 1860, IL
 father: Joseph D Dudley
 mother: Ellen Marcia Howard Dudley
 1870 US Census, Colorado Territory, Weld County, St Vrain District

Dudley, Ellen Marcia Howard
 b. 21 Jan 1839, ME
 d. abt 1900, Longmont, Boulder, CO
 spouse: Joseph B Dudley
 mother: Sarah Howard
 St Vrain Pioneers Assn Arrival Date: 1860
 1870 US Census, Colorado Territory, Weld County, St Vrain District

Dudley, Gerry Elbridge
 b. abt 1862, IL
 father: Joseph D Dudley
 mother: Ellen Marcia Howard Dudley
 1870 US Census, Colorado Territory, Weld County, St Vrain District

Dudley, Joe
 b. abt 1851, MO
 1870 US Census, Colorado Territory, Boulder County, St Vrain District

St Vrain Valley Pioneers

Dudley, Joseph B
b. abt 1858, IL
father: Joseph D Dudley
mother: Ellen Marcia Howard Dudley
1870 US Census, Colorado Territory, Weld County, St Vrain District

Dudley, Joseph B
b. Mar 1834, England
d. 18 Nov 1911, Longmont, Boulder, CO
spouse: Ellen Marcia Howard Dudley
St Vrain Pioneers Assn Arrival Date: 1860
1870 US Census, Colorado Territory, Weld County, St Vrain District

Dulraise, Antonne
b. abt 1856, WY
1870 US Census, Colorado Territory, Boulder County, St Vrain District

Dunbar, Elmer C
b. 30 Mar 1835, Preble, CT
d. 20 Sept 1897, Steamboat Springs, Routt, CO
spouse: Mary Ann Cady Dunbar
1870 US Census, Colorado Territory, Boulder County, St Vrain District

Dunbar, Everet E
b. abt 1845, NY
1870 US Census, Colorado Territory, Boulder County, St Vrain District

Dunbar, Mary Ann Cady
b. 13 Jan 1851, New Hope, Cayuga, NY
d. 17 Oct 1937, Los Angeles, CA
spouse: Elmore C Dunbar
St Vrain Pioneers Assn Arrival Date: 1870

Duncan, Edward Elisha
b. 18 Jan 1863, Golden, Jefferson, Colorado Territory
d. 24 May 1896, Denver, Arapahoe, CO
bd. Mountain View Cemetery, Boulder, CO
spouse: Louisa Elcena Isabel Wright
father: Elisha Duncan
mother: Mary Worthington Myatt Duncan
1870 US Census, Colorado Territory, Weld County, St Vrain District

Duncan, Elisha
b. 13 Sept 1822, Bond, IL
d. 3 July 1893, Boulder, CO
bd. Mountain View Cemetery, Longmont, Boulder, CO
spouse: Mary Worthington Myatt Duncan
father: Robert Duncan
mother: Nancy Bateman Duncan
St Vrain Pioneers Assn Arrival Date: 1860
St Vrain Ditch Owner: Hayseed Ditch No. 1, 1 Jan 1860
1870 US Census, Colorado Territory, Weld County, St Vrain District

Duncan, Guy Dale
b. 5 July 1866, Longmont, Boulder, Colorado Territory
d. 30 Jan 1950, Longmont, Boulder, CO
bd. Mountain View Cemetery, Boulder, CO
spouse: Ida Lillian Crocker Duncan
father: Elisha Duncan
mother: Mary Worthington Myatt Duncan
1870 US Census, Colorado Territory, Weld County, St Vrain District

Duncan, John Thomas
b. 30 Sept 1857, Bond, IL
d. 9 Oct 1950, Custer, Whatcom, WA
bd. Greenacres Memorial Park, Ferndale, Whatcom, WA
spouse: Rolde (Belle Therese) Smith Duncan; May Baldwin Duncan
father: Elisha Duncan
mother: Mary Worthington Myatt Duncan
St Vrain Pioneers Assn Arrival Date: 1861
1870 US Census, Colorado Territory, Weld County, St Vrain District

Duncan, Margaret J
b. 31 July 1853, Bond, IL
d. 11 Dec 1913, Longmont, Boulder, CO
bd. Mountain View Cemetery, Boulder, CO
father: Elisha Duncan
mother: Mary Worthington Myatt Duncan
St Vrain Pioneers Assn Arrival Date: 1861
1870 US Census, Colorado Territory, Weld County, St Vrain District

Duncan, Mary Worthington Myatt
b. 27 Mar 1832, Pocahontas, Bond, IL
d. 21 Feb 1926, Denver, CO
bd. Mountain View Cemetery, Longmont, Boulder, CO

spouse: Elisha Duncan
father: Alexander Myatt
mother: Mary W Chisenhall Myatt
St Vrain Pioneers Assn Arrival Date: 1861
1870 US Census, Colorado Territory, Weld County, St Vrain District

Duncan, Robert Alexander
b. 14 Aug 1855, Bond, IL
d. 16 Jan 1942, Boulder, CO
bd. Mountain View Cemetery, Longmont, Boulder, CO
spouse: Myrtle Mae Wright Duncan
father: Elisha Duncan
mother: Mary Worthington Myatt Duncan
St Vrain Pioneers Assn Arrival Date: 1861
1870 US Census, Colorado Territory, Weld County, St Vrain District

Duncan, Sebastian
b. 1806
d. 25 Jan 1890
bd. Columbia Cemetery, Boulder, CO
St Vrain Ditch Owner: Smead Ditch No. 13, 1 Oct 1862

Dunham, S
Franklin Township Land Club Claim Date: 1860 June 24

Dunham, Wright
Troy District Land Club Claim Date: 1860 Aug 3

Dunkin, John
b. abt 1836, IL
1870 US Census, Colorado Territory, Boulder County, St Vrain District

Dunn, Emma Elizabeth DeBacker
b. 14 Feb 1877, Boulder, CO
d. 13 Jan 1968, Boulder, CO
bd. South Boulder Cemetery, Boulder, CO
spouse: John Edward Dunn
father: John Franciscus DeBacker
mother: Marie Dehn DeBacker

Dunn, Margaret Burke
b. 4 Sept 1835, Tipperary, Ireland
d. 5 Jan 1887, Langford, Boulder, CO
bd. South Boulder Cemetery, Boulder, CO
spouse: Patrick Francis Dunn
St Vrain Pioneers Assn Arrival Date: 1864

Dunn, Patrick Francis
b. 11 Nov 1818, Tipperary, Ireland
d. 16 June 1904, Boulder, CO
bd. South Boulder Cemetery, Boulder, CO
spouse: Margaret Burke Lacey Dunn
St Vrain Pioneers Assn Arrival Date: 1864

Dunn, Thomas
Troy District Land Club Claim Date: 1861 Apr 30

Dunstan, Edwin
St Vrain Land Club Date: 1861 July 31

Dunstan, John H R
Troy District Land Club Claim Date: 1860 July 17
St Vrain Land Club Date: 1861 July 31

Dunstan, Thomas
St Vrain Land Club Date: 1861 July 31

Durham, Edvard/Edward
b. abt 1846, Canada
1870 US Census, Colorado Territory, Boulder County, St Vrain District

Dwight
St Vrain Land Club Date: 1861 Jan 30

E

Eagan, Samuel
b. abt 1843, IA
1870 US Census, Colorado Territory, Boulder County, St Vrain District

Ebi, Daniel/David
St Vrain Land Club Date: 1862 Jan 11

Edwards, James
b. abt 1839, IL
1860 US Census, Nebraska Territory, Platte River

Eisele, Fred W
b. 1 July 1892
d. 7 Feb 1967
bd. Mountain View Cemetery, Longmont, Boulder, CO
spouse: Merl Sanger Eisele
father: David Eisele
mother: Marie Eisele

Eldred, Carrie
b. abt 1865, MI
father: Frederick Hoyt Eldred

St Vrain Valley Pioneers

mother: Sarah A Eldred
1870 US Census, Colorado Territory, Boulder County, St Vrain District

Eldred, Frederick Hoyt
b. 23 Aug 1826, NY
d. 8 Feb 1910
bd. Columbia Cemetery, Boulder, CO
spouse: Sarah A Eldred
1870 US Census, Colorado Territory, Boulder County, St Vrain District

Eldred, Holden Rennington
b. 3 May 1837, York, Medina, OH
d. 24 June 1911, Bonanza, Klamath, OR
bd. Valmont Cemetery, Boulder, CO
spouse: Ophelia Tillie Allen Eldred
father: Holden Eldred
mother: Polly Tryon Eldred

Eldred, Maud
b. abt 1868, Colorado Territory
father: Frederick Hoyt Eldred
mother: Sarah A Eldred
1870 US Census, Colorado Territory, Boulder County, St Vrain District

Eldred, Sarah
b. abt 1844, MI
d. 8 June 1883
bd. Columbia Cemetery, Boulder, CO
spouse: Fred H Eldred
1870 US Census, Colorado Territory, Boulder County, St Vrain District

Ellermeyer, Emma Lee
b. 16 Feb 1870, WV
d. 19 Jan 1949, Cortez, Montezuma, CO
spouse: William H Ellermeyer
father: John Braxton Lee
mother: Margaret Ann Miller Lee
1870 US Census, Colorado Territory, Boulder County, St Vrain District

Elliot, James
St Vrain Land Club Date: 1861 Aug 15

Elliott, Adonis N
b. abt 1855, IL
father: John Elliott
mother: Eliza J Elliott
St Vrain Pioneers Assn Arrival Date: 1859
1870 US Census, Colorado Territory, Weld County, St Vrain District

Elliott, Amy H
b. abt 1869, Colorado Territory
father: Johh Elliott
mother: Eliza J Elliott
1870 US Census, Colorado Territory, Weld County, St Vrain District

Elliott, Andrew J
b. abt 1857, IL
father: John Elliott
mother: Eliza J Elliott
St Vrain Pioneers Assn Arrival Date: 1859
1870 US Census, Colorado Territory, Weld County, St Vrain District

Elliott, Dood N
b. abt 1851, IL
father: John Elliott
mother: Eliza J Elliott
St Vrain Pioneers Assn Arrival Date: 1859
1870 US Census, Colorado Territory, Weld County, St Vrain District

Elliott, Earnest
b. abt 1867, Colorado Territory
father: John Elliott
mother: Eliza J Elliott
1870 US Census, Colorado Territory, Weld County, St Vrain District

Elliott, Eliza J
b. abt 1831, KY
spouse: John Elliott
St Vrain Pioneers Assn Arrival Date: 1859
1870 US Census, Colorado Territory, Weld County, St Vrain District

Elliott, James
b. abt 1860, Colorado Territory
father: John Elliott
mother: Eliza J Elliott
1870 US Census, Colorado Territory, Weld County, St Vrain District

Elliott, John
b. abt 1828, IL
spouse: Eliza J Elliott
St Vrain Pioneers Assn Arrival Date: 1859

1870 US Census, Colorado Territory, Weld County, St Vrain District

Elliott, Minnie
b. abt 1863, Colorado Territory
father: John Elliott
mother: Eliza J Elliott
1870 US Census, Colorado Territory, Weld County, St Vrain District

Elliott, William Anderson
b. 1 Nov 1841, Barren, KY
d. 23 Aug 1922, Boulder, CO
bd. Columbia Cemetery, Boulder, CO
spouse: Sarah J Carpenter Elliott
father: Moses Elliott
mother: Clarissa L Underwood Elliott
St Vrain Pioneers Assn Arrival Date: 1860

Emerich, A J
St Vrain Pioneers Assn Arrival Date: 1864

Emerick, Andrew Jackson
b. 2 Apr 1834, Huntington, IN
d. 25 Apr 1911, Boulder, CO
bd. Columbia Cemetery, Boulder, CO
spouse: Mary Etta White Emerick
father: John Emerick
mother: Nancy Ream Emerick
St Vrain Land Club Date: 1861 May 18

Emmons, Amos Jesse
b. 1838, Chester, NJ
d. 25 Apr 1917, Longmont, CO
bd. Mountain View Cemetery, Longmont, Boulder, CO
spouse: Lovina Robinson Emmons
St Vrain Pioneers Assn Arrival Date: 1866
1870 US Census, Colorado Territory, Weld County, St Vrain District

Emmons, Lovina Robinson
b. 1850
d. 22 June 1923, Niwot, Boulder, CO
bd. Mountain View Cemetery, Longmont, Boulder, CO
spouse: Amos Jesse Emmons

Ereckson, Andrew
bd. Niwot Cemetery, Niwot, Boulder, CO
St Vrain Pioneers Assn Arrival Date: [not recorded]

Ereckson, E Gus
b. 9 Jan 1843
d. 25 Feb 1905
bd. Niwot Cemetery, Niwot, Boulder, CO
spouse: Mary Frances Ereckson
St Vrain Pioneers Assn Arrival Date: 1861

Ereckson, Mary Frances
b. 21 Feb 1851
d. 22 July 1942
bd. Niwot Cemetery, Niwot, Boulder, CO
spouse: E Gus Ereckson
St Vrain Pioneers Assn Arrival Date: 1861

Ereckson, Mrs Andrew
St Vrain Pioneers Assn Arrival Date: [not recorded]

Erickson, E J
St Vrain Pioneers Assn Arrival Date: 1859

Ervine, David W
St Vrain Pioneers Assn Arrival Date: 1869

Eschler, Christian
b. abt 1844, Switzerland
1870 US Census, Colorado Territory, Boulder County, Left Hand

Estes, Anna Elizabeth Calkins
b. 14 Mar 1870, Norwood Park, Cook, IL
d. 7 Dec 1952, Longmont, Boulder, CO
bd. Mountain View Cemetery, Longmont, Boulder, CO
spouse: Edwin Joel Estes
father: Carlton C Calkins
mother: Kate Boyce Calkins

Estes, Carlton
b. 21 Nov 1895
d. 24 May 1982
bd. Mountain View Cemetery, Longmont, Boulder, CO
spouse: Ethelyn Angeline Moore Estes; Gladys Jacobson Estes
father: Edwin J Estes
mother: Anna Calkins Estes

Estes, Ethelyn Angeline Moore
b. 1894
d. 1952
bd. Mountain View Cemetery, Longmont, Boulder, CO

St Vrain Valley Pioneers

spouse: Carlton Chase Estes
father: Ulysses Leonard Moore
mother: Emma Lucretia Miller Moore

Estes, F
b. abt 1835, MS
1860 US Census, Nebraska Territory, Platte River

Estes, Gladys Jacobsen
b. 1914
d. 2002
bd. Mountain View Cemetery, Longmont, Boulder, CO
spouse: Carlton Chase Estes
father: Charles Jacobsen
mother: Barbara Hertha Jacobsen

Estes, J W
b. abt 1815, MS
1860 US Census, Nebraska Territory, Platte River

Estes, Joel
St Vrain Pioneers Assn Arrival Date: 1859

Estes, Mary Louisa Fleming
b. 4 May 1842, Galena, Jo Daviess, IL
d. 15 Aug 1905, Longmont, Boulder, CO
spouse: Milton Estes
father: George Archibald Fleming
mother: Margaret Ellen Gordon Fleming

Estes, Newton Davis
b. 14 Aug 1862, MO
d. 22 Mar 1927, Ogden, Weber, UT
bd. Ogden City Cemetery, Ogden, Weber, UT
spouse: Ida Beenschadler Estes; Rose Estes McDonald Harris
father: Milton Estes
mother: Mary Louise Flemming Estes

Estus, Edna E
St Vrain Pioneers Assn Arrival Date: 1865

Ettinger, Isabella Smith
b. 15 Dec 1857, MN
d. 29 Nov 1916, Czar, Alberta, Canada
spouse: Mahlon D Ettinger
father: James Monroe Smith
mother: Lorinda BurtonSmith
1870 US Census, Colorado Territory, Boulder County, St Vrain District

Evans, Charles
b. abt 1844, MD
spouse: Martha Walthall Evans
1870 US Census, Colorado Territory, Boulder County, St Vrain District

Evans, Colorado A
b. abt 1869, Colorado Territory
father: Charles Evans
mother: Martha Evans
1870 US Census, Colorado Territory, Boulder County, St Vrain District

Evans, Griffith J
b. 1832, Wales
d. 1901
bd. Jamestown Cemetery, Jamestown, Boulder, CO
spouse: Jane A Evans
1870 US Census, Colorado Territory, Boulder County, St Vrain District

Evans, Martha Walthall
b. 24 Mar 1849, North Salem, Hendricks, IN
d. 10 Aug 1923, Sheridan, Sheridan, WY
spouse: Charles Evans
father: Samuel White Walthall
mother: Rebecca Ann Johns Walthall
1870 US Census, Colorado Territory, Boulder County, St Vrain District

Evans, Mattie
b. abt 1851
d. Apr 1924

Evans, Robert
b. abt 1837, Wales
1860 US Census, Nebraska Territory, Platte River

Eves, Gertrude L Wright Campbell
b. Sept 1858, Prairie du Chien, Crawford, WI
d. 4 Mar 1911, Buena Vista, CO
bd. Green Mountain Cemetery, Boulder, CO
spouse: Stephen J Campbell, Geroge Playter Eves
father: Alpheus Stephens Wright
mother: Sarah Jane Hutchinson Wright

F

Farlee, Peter
b. abt 1827, MO
1860 US Census, Nebraska Territory, Platte River

Ferguson, Emily
b. abt 1855, IL
1870 US Census, Colorado Territory, Boulder County, Left Hand

Ferguson, Savannah
b. abt 1858, IL
1870 US Census, Colorado Territory, Boulder County, St Vrain District

Ferrell, Judson
b. abt 1844, PA
spouse: Mary Ferrell
1870 US Census, Colorado Territory, Boulder County, St Vrain District

Ferrell, Mary
b. abt 1850, PA
spouse: Judson Ferrell
1870 US Census, Colorado Territory, Boulder County, St Vrain District

Fickas, John
b. abt 1827, PA
1870 US Census, Colorado Territory, Boulder County, St Vrain District

Fickas, Joseph
b. abt 1849, PA
father: John Fickas
1870 US Census, Colorado Territory, Boulder County, St Vrain District

Fickas, Samuel
b. abt 1852, PA
father: John Fickas
1870 US Census, Colorado Territory, Boulder County, St Vrain District

Fields, A M
St Vrain Pioneers Assn Arrival Date: 1859

Finch, William A
b. abt 1839, IL
1870 US Census, Colorado Territory, Boulder County, St Vrain District

Fink, A
b. abt 1835, OH
1860 US Census, Nebraska Territory, Platte River

Finney, Franklin
St Vrain Land Club (M687) Date: 1861 Mar 15

Fisher, Lullu
b. abt 1864, OH
1870 US Census, Colorado Territory, Boulder County, St Vrain District

Flack, A J
St Vrain Land Club (M687) Date: 1861 Apr 3

Flekeger, John
b. abt 1840, Switzerland
1870 US Census, Colorado Territory, Boulder County, Left Hand

Fleming, George Archibald
b. 12 Oct 1816, Baltimore, MD
d. 20 Feb 1887, Fleming Ranch, Weld, CO
bd. Platteville, Weld, CO
spouse: Margaret Ellen Gordon Fleming
St Vrain Pioneers Assn Arrival Date: 1860
St Vrain Land Club (M687) Date: 1861 July 4
1870 US Census, Colorado Territory, Weld County, St Vrain District

Fleming, John Nelson
b. bef 1860
father: George Archibald Fleming
mother: Margaret Ellen Gordon Fleming

Fleming, Kate
b. abt 1858, IL
father: George Archibald Fleming
mother: Margaret Ellen Gordon Fleming
1870 US Census, Colorado Territory, Weld County, St Vrain District

Fleming, Margaret Ellen Gordon
b. 13 Apr 1817, Chambersburgh, PA
d. 19 Jan 1924, Hardin, CO
bd. Platteville, Weld, CO
spouse: George Archibald Fleming
St Vrain Pioneers Assn Arrival Date: 1861
1870 US Census, Colorado Territory, Weld County, St Vrain District

St Vrain Valley Pioneers

Flemming, John
b. abt 1843
1870 US Census, Colorado Territory, Weld County, St Vrain District

Flemming, Laura May
b. 29 Sept 1860, St Vrain, Colorado Territory
1870 US Census, Colorado Territory, Weld County, St Vrain District

Fletcher, Chandler
Franklin Township Land Club Claim Date: 1860 May 25

Fletcher, John
Franklin Township Land Club Claim Date: 1860 May 25

Fletcher, Lewis
b. abt 1830, KY
1870 US Census, Colorado Territory, Boulder County, Left Hand

Foby, Christopher C
b. abt 1863, IA
1870 US Census, Colorado Territory, Boulder County, St Vrain District

Foby, Elisabeth
b. abt 1859, IA
1870 US Census, Colorado Territory, Boulder County, St Vrain District

Forkner, John
b. abt 1825, FL
1870 US Census, Colorado Territory, Boulder County, St Vrain District

Forsaith, Adele Frances Authur/Austin
b. abt 1846, NY
spouse: Elbridge Forsaith
1870 US Census, Colorado Territory, Boulder County, St Vrain District

Forsaith, Elbridge
b. abt 1839, NY
spouse: Adele F Authur Forsaith
1870 US Census, Colorado Territory, Boulder County, St Vrain District

Forsyth, James Richmond
b. 19 Feb 1847, Nova Scotia, Canada
d. 19 Nov 1926, Longmont, Boulder, CO
bd. Burlington Cemetery, Longmont, Boulder, CO
spouse: Mary Jane Beasley Forsyth
St Vrain Pioneers Assn Arrival Date: 1870

Forsyth, Mary Jane Beasley
b. 2 Apr 1855, MO
d. 23 Nov 1937, Boulder, CO
bd. Burlington Cemetery, Longmont, Boulder, CO
father: William J Beasley
mother: Dulcena Westrope Beasley
St Vrain Pioneers Assn Arrival Date: 1864

Forsythe, James Richmond
d. 19 Nov 1926, Longmont, Boulder, CO

Foster, Betsey Spencer
b. 21 Nov 1802, NY
d. 22 Jan 1881
bd. Valmont Cemetery, Boulder, CO
spouse: Nathan Foster
1870 US Census, Colorado Territory, Boulder County, St Vrain District

Foster, Daniel
b. ab 1828, NY
spouse: Mary Foster
St Vrain Pioneers Assn Arrival Date: [not recorded]
1870 US Census, Colorado Territory, Weld County, St Vrain District

Foster, daughter of Daniel
father: Daniel Foster
St Vrain Pioneers Assn Arrival Date: [not recorded]

Foster, Emma
b. abt 1865, IL
father: Daniel Foster
mother: Mary G Foster
1870 US Census, Colorado Territory, Weld County, St Vrain District

Foster, Frank
b. abt 1867, IL
father: Daniel Foster
mother: Mary Foster
1870 US Census, Colorado Territory, Weld County, St Vrain District

Foster, Mary G
b. abt 1838, Pittsburgh, PA
d. 1 Apr 1893

bd. Burlington Cemetery, Longmont, Boulder, CO
spouse: Daniel Foster
St Vrain Pioneers Assn Arrival Date: 1870
1870 US Census, Colorado Territory, Weld County, St Vrain District

Fowler, Edward
b. abt 1858, IA
mother: Mary E Fowler
1870 US Census, Colorado Territory, Boulder County, St Vrain District

Fowler, Mary E
b. abt 1838, OH
spouse: Henry Fowler
1870 US Census, Colorado Territory, Boulder County, St Vrain District

Fowler, Walter
b. abt 1864, Colorado Territory
mother: Mary E Fowler
1870 US Census, Colorado Territory, Boulder County, St Vrain District

Fox, Charles
b. abt 1844, IA
1870 US Census, Colorado Territory, Weld County, St Vrain District

Francis, James
St Vrain Land Club (M687) Date: 1861 Jan 18

Franklin, Artelesia
b. abt 1859, WI
father: Robert Franklin
mother: Eliza A Franklin
1870 US Census, Colorado Territory, Boulder County, St Vrain District

Franklin, B A
Franklin Township Land Club Claim Date: 1860 Feb 12

Franklin, Benjamin A
d. 22 June 1867, Colorado Territory
bd. Weisner Cemetery, Boulder, CO
St Vrain Pioneers Assn Arrival Date: 1859

Franklin, Eliza A Dickens
b. abt 1840, England
d. 31 Mar 1875
bd. Burlington Cemetery, Longmont, Boulder, CO
spouse: Robert I Franklin
St Vrain Pioneers Assn Arrival Date: 1865
1870 US Census, Colorado Territory, Boulder County, St Vrain District

Franklin, James W
b. abt 1862, ME
father: Robert Franklin
mother: Eliza A Franklin
1870 US Census, Colorado Territory, Boulder County, St Vrain District

Franklin, Robert I
b. abt 1837, NY
spouse: Eliza A Dickens Franklin
St Vrain Pioneers Assn Arrival Date: 1865
1870 US Census, Colorado Territory, Boulder County, St Vrain District

Franklin, Will
father: Robert I Franklin
mother: Eliza Dickens Franklin
St Vrain Pioneers Assn Arrival Date: 1865

Frederick, Albert
b. abt 1844, IN
father: Daniel Frederick
mother: Iva Frederick
1870 US Census, Colorado Territory, Boulder County, Left Hand

Frederick, Daniel
b. abt 1797, IN
spouse: Iva Frederick
St Vrain Pioneers Assn Arrival Date: [not recorded]
1870 US Census, Colorado Territory, Boulder County, Left Hand

Frederick, Iva
b. abt 1806, IN
spouse: Daniel Frederick
St Vrain Pioneers Assn Arrival Date: [not recorded]
1870 US Census, Colorado Territory, Boulder County, Left Hand

Frederick, Marcellus
b. abt 1846, IN
father: Daniel Frederick
mother: Iva Frederick
1870 US Census, Colorado Territory, Boulder County, Left Hand

St Vrain Valley Pioneers

Friday, Frank
b. abt 1845, MI
1870 US Census, Colorado Territory, Boulder County, St Vrain District

Friday, James
b. abt 1836, IN
1870 US Census, Colorado Territory, Boulder County, St Vrain District

Fullen, Hiram
b. 29 Apr 1839, VA
d. 5 Apr 1900, Boulder, Boulder, CO
bd. Columbia Cemetery, Boulder, CO
St Vrain Pioneers Assn Arrival Date: [not recorded]
1870 US Census, Colorado Territory, Boulder County, St Vrain District

Fulton, Walter
b. 1 Sept 1882
d. 17 Oct 1966
bd. Mountain View Cemetery, Longmont, Boulder, CO
spouse: Ida Ethel Shippee Fulton

G

Gaines, Richard
Franklin Township Land Club Claim Date: 1860 Feb 15

Gallagher
b. abt 1870, Colorado Territory
father: Francis Gallagher
mother: Sophronia Gallagher
1870 US Census, Colorado Territory, Boulder County, St Vrain District

Gallagher, Charles P
b. abt 1867, Colorado Territory
father: Francis Gallagher
mother: Sophronia Gallagher
1870 US Census, Colorado Territory, Boulder County, St Vrain District

Gallagher, Delois A
b. abt 1868, Colorado Territory
father: Francis Gallagher
mother: Sophronia Gallagher
1870 US Census, Colorado Territory, Boulder County, St Vrain District

Gallagher, Francis
b. abt 1841, KY
spouse: Sophronia Gallagher
1870 US Census, Colorado Territory, Boulder County, St Vrain District

Gallagher, Sophronia A White
b. abt 1848, Gallia, OH
d. 30 Dec 1887, Boulder, CO
bd. Columbia Cemetery, Boulder, CO
spouse: Francis M Gallagher
father: Perry White
mother: Rachel Barlow Irvine White
1870 US Census, Colorado Territory, Boulder County, St Vrain District

Gammon, Orson
b. abt 1840, MO
1870 US Census, Colorado Territory, Boulder County, St Vrain District

Gane, Benjamin
b. abt 1849, WI
1870 US Census, Colorado Territory, Boulder County, St Vrain District

Gardner, Charles H
b. 20 Apr 1831, Schaghticoke, Rensselaer, NY
d. 7 Nov 1905, Longmont, CO
bd. Mountain View Cemetery, Longmont, Boulder, CO
spouse: Sarah H Smith Gardner
father: Alphaeus Nelson Gardner
mother: Roxa Lana Townsend Gardner
St Vrain Pioneers Assn Arrival Date: 1859
Troy District Land Club Claim Date: 1861 Jan 26

Gardner, Isaac Newton
b. 1829, Pittstown, Rensselaer, NY
d. 7 May 1909, Berthoud, Larimer, CO
bd. Greenlawn Cemetery, Larimer, CO
spouse: Emily L Gardner
father: Alphaeus Nelson Gardner
mother: Roxa Lana Townsend Gardner
St Vrain Pioneers Assn Arrival Date: 1861

Gardner, John
St Vrain Land Club (M687) Date: 1861 May 21

St Vrain Valley Pioneers

Gardner, Sarah H Smith
b. abt 1847, NY
d. abt 1879, Longmont, Boulder, CO
spouse: Charles H Gardner
St Vrain Pioneers Assn Arrival Date: 1859

Gardner, William
St Vrain Land Club Date: 1861 Aug 29

Gates, Mary H Shepherd
b. abt 1858, IA
spouse: Henry S Gates
father: David S Shepherd
mother: Mary S Shepherd
St Vrain Pioneers Assn Arrival Date: 1861

Geer, Charles O
b. abt 1850, IL
spouse: Allie Kilgore O'Dell Geer
father: Solomon Geer
mother: Nancy Phenix Geer
St Vrain Pioneers Assn Arrival Date: 1866
1870 US Census, Colorado Territory, Boulder County, St Vrain District

Geer, Elmer Harmon
b. 1866, Colorado Territory
d. Mar 1935, Longmont, CO
spouse: Nida Smith Geer
father: Solomon Geer
mother: Nancy Phenix Geer
St Vrain Pioneers Assn Arrival Date: 1866
1870 US Census, Colorado Territory, Boulder County, St Vrain District

Geer, Mary E
b. abt 1855, IL
father: Solomon Geer
mother: Nancy Phenix Geer
St Vrain Pioneers Assn Arrival Date: 1866
1870 US Census, Colorado Territory, Boulder County, St Vrain District

Geer, Nancy Phenix
b. abt 1825, Pennsylvania Township, IL
d. 15 Jan 1899, Altona, Boulder, CO
bd. Niwot Cemetery, Niwot, Boulder, CO
spouse: Solomon Geer
St Vrain Pioneers Assn Arrival Date: 1866
1870 US Census, Colorado Territory, Boulder County, St Vrain District

Geer, Solomon
b. 23 Oct/24 Nov 1819, CT
d. 18 July 1892, Altona, Boulder, CO
bd. Niwot Cemetery, Niwot, Boulder, CO
spouse: Nancy Phenix Geer
St Vrain Pioneers Assn Arrival Date: 1859
1870 US Census, Colorado Territory, Boulder County, St Vrain District

Gentry, Joseph
b. abt 1823, NY
1860 US Census, Nebraska Territory, Platte River

Gibb, William
b. abt 1838, NY
1860 US Census, Nebraska Territory, Platte River

Gifford, Abram D
b. abt 1832, OH
spouse: Sarah Gifford
St Vrain Pioneers Assn Arrival Date: 1862
1870 US Census, Colorado Territory, Boulder County, St Vrain District

Gifford, Abram Delas
b. 3 July 1833, Delaware, OH
d. 21 Sept 1905, Larimer, CO
bd. Lakeside Cemetery, Loveland, Larimer, CO
spouse: Sarah Bond Gifford
father: Humphrey Gifford
mother: Jane Caroline Jenney Gifford
St Vrain Land Club Date: 1861 Aug 11

Gifford, Ada J
b. abt 1866, IA
father: William H Gifford
mother: Clementine Gifford
St Vrain Pioneers Assn Arrival Date: 1866
1870 US Census, Colorado Territory, Boulder County, St Vrain District

Gifford, Clementine
b. abt 1842, NY
spouse: William H Gifford
St Vrain Pioneers Assn Arrival Date: 1866
1870 US Census, Colorado Territory, Boulder County, St Vrain District

Gifford, George
b. abt 1867, Colorado Territory
father: Abram D Gifford
mother: Sarah Gifford

St Vrain Valley Pioneers

1870 US Census, Colorado Territory, Boulder County, St Vrain District

Gifford, Lida M
b. abt 1869, Colorado Territory
father: Abram D Gifford
mother: Sarah Gifford
1870 US Census, Colorado Territory, Boulder County, St Vrain District

Gifford, Mary
b. abt 1865, Colorado Territory
father: Abram D Gifford
mother: Sarah Gifford
1870 US Census, Colorado Territory, Boulder County, St Vrain District

Gifford, Sarah Bond
b. 6 Sept 1836, Wheeling, Ohio, VA
d. 13 Feb 1898, Loveland, Larimer, CO
bd. Lakeside Cemetery, Loveland, Larimer, CO
spouse: Abram D Gifford
father: George Bond
mother: Mary Furbee Bond
1870 US Census, Colorado Territory, Boulder County, St Vrain District

Gifford, Sarah F
b. 5 Jan 1868, Colorado Territory
father: William H Gifford
mother: Clementine Gifford
1870 US Census, Colorado Territory, Boulder County, St Vrain District

Gifford, William H
b. abt 1841, OH
spouse: Clementine Gifford
St Vrain Pioneers Assn Arrival Date: 1862
1870 US Census, Colorado Territory, Boulder County, St Vrain District

Gifford, William H
b. abt 1864, Colorado Territory
father: Abram D Gifford
mother: Sarah Gifford
1870 US Census, Colorado Territory, Boulder County, St Vrain District

Giggey, Arthur Weir
b. 9 Apr 1896, CO
d. 15 Feb 1968, Boulder, CO
bd. Mountain View Memorial Park, Boulder, CO
spouse: Mary Phillips Williams Giggey
father: Adelbert Alonzo Giggey
mother: Anna Lefforts Berkley Giggey

Gill, Edward J
b. abt 1843, ME
1870 US Census, Colorado Territory, Boulder County, St Vrain District

Gillaspie, Henry B
St Vrain Pioneers Assn Arrival Date: [not recorded]

Gillespie, John
St Vrain Pioneers Assn Arrival Date: 1859

Gillispie, Armeda
b. abt 1869, Colorado Territory
father: William Gillispie
mother: Sarah Gillispie
1870 US Census, Colorado Territory, Boulder County, Left Hand

Gillispie, Harvey
b. abt 1853, MO
father: William Gillispie
mother: Sarah Gillispie
1870 US Census, Colorado Territory, Boulder County, Left Hand

Gillispie, John
b. abt 1855, MO
father: William Gillispie
mother: Sarah Gillispie
1870 US Census, Colorado Territory, Boulder County, Left Hand

Gillispie, Sarah
b. abt 1833, MO
spouse: William Gillispie
1870 US Census, Colorado Territory, Boulder County, Left Hand

Gillispie, Thomas
b. abt 1867, Colorado Territory
father: William Gillispie
mother: Sarah Gillispie
1870 US Census, Colorado Territory, Boulder County, Left Hand

Gillispie, William
b. abt 1830, KY
1870 US Census, Colorado Territory, Boulder County, Left Hand

St Vrain Valley Pioneers

Gilman, Alice
b. abt 1858
d. 16 Sept 1924

Gilman, John A
St Vrain Pioneers Assn Arrival Date: 1869

Gilman, Mrs John A
St Vrain Pioneers Assn Arrival Date: 1869

Girioux, Louis
b. abt 1829, Canada
1860 US Census, Nebraska Territory, Platte River

Girioux, Mary
b. abt 1843, NE Terr
1860 US Census, Nebraska Territory, Platte River

Gist, William
b. abt 1840, OH
1860 US Census, Nebraska Territory, Platte River

Godding, Evan
b. abt 1854, WI
father: Talmai F Godding
mother: Mary Godding
1870 US Census, Colorado Territory, Weld County, St Vrain District

Godding, Mary
b. abt 1831, WI
spouse: Talmai F Godding
St Vrain Pioneers Assn Arrival Date: 1863
1870 US Census, Colorado Territory, Weld County, St Vrain District

Godding, T F
b. abt 1865, Colorado Territory
father: Talmai F Godding
mother: Mary Godding
1870 US Census, Colorado Territory, Weld County, St Vrain District

Godding, Talmai F
b. abt 1826, NY
spouse: Mary Godding
St Vrain Pioneers Assn Arrival Date: 1859
1870 US Census, Colorado Territory, Weld County, St Vrain District

Godding, William
b. abt 1849, WI
father: Talmai F Godding
mother: Mary Godding
1870 US Census, Colorado Territory, Weld County, St Vrain District

Golden, Florence Cushman
b. 18 Mar 1866, Colorado Territory
d. 28 Dec 1940, Longmont, Boulder, CO
spouse: James H Golden
father: Abiel Washburn Cushman
mother: Fannie J Skinner Cushman
1870 US Census, Colorado Territory, Boulder County, St Vrain District

Goodhue, Abner Cushman
b. 1833, Canada
d. 1912
bd. Green Mountain Cemetery, Boulder, CO
St Vrain Pioneers Assn Arrival Date: 1865

Goodman, W F
b. abt 1832, KY
1860 US Census, Nebraska Territory, Platte River

Goodwin, Alice White
b. abt 1855, IA
spouse: Frank C Goodwin
father: Perry White
mother: Rachel Barlow Irvine White
1870 US Census, Colorado Territory, Boulder County, St Vrain District

Goodwin, Frank C
b. abt 1855, IN
spouse: Alice White Goodwin
father: Harrison O Goodwin
mother: Lizzie Goodwin
St Vrain Pioneers Assn Arrival Date: 1859
1870 US Census, Colorado Territory, Boulder County, St Vrain District

Goodwin, Harrison O
b. abt 1826, IN
d. 10 June 1885
bd. Mountain View Cemetery, Longmont, Boulder, CO
spouse: Lizzie Goodwin
St Vrain Pioneers Assn Arrival Date: 1859
Franklin Township Land Club Claim Date: 1860 June 24
St Vrain Land Club Date: 1861 Apr 18
1870 US Census, Colorado Territory, Boulder County, St Vrain District

St Vrain Valley Pioneers

Goodwin, Lizzie K
b. 1834, IN
d. 11 Apr 1929, Loveland, Larimer, CO
spouse: Harrison O Goodwin
St Vrain Pioneers Assn Arrival Date: 1859
1870 US Census, Colorado Territory, Boulder County, St Vrain District

Gordon, David
St Vrain Pioneers Assn Arrival Date: 1858

Gordon, E E
b. abt 1838, KY
1860 US Census, Nebraska Territory, Platte River

Gordon, W F
b. abt 1830, England
1860 US Census, Nebraska Territory, Platte River

Goss, Carver Johnathan
b. 21 Mar 1821, Brandon, Rutland, VT
d. 30 Nov 1882, Denver, Arapahoe, CO
bd. Riverside, Denver, CO
spouse: Betsey Green Shepard
father: Carver Goss
mother: Levina Hulett
St Vrain Pioneers Assn Arrival Date: 1859

Goss, Elizabeth Lettice Manners Blore
b. 4 Feb 1848, Crawfordsville, Montgomery, IN
d. 12 July 1917, CO
spouse: William Richard Blore; Percy Darius Goss
father: Harvey Manners
mother: Sarah Oppy Manners
St Vrain Pioneers Assn Arrival Date: 1868

Goss, Ellen Augusta Olcott
b. 24 Apr 1845, Granby, Oswego, NY
d. 19 Dec 1941, Longmont, Boulder, CO
spouse: John Wesley Goss
father: Philander Wilcox Olcott
mother: Elizabeth Hannah Stevens
St Vrain Pioneers Assn Arrival Date: 1868
1870 US Census, Colorado Territory, Boulder County, St Vrain District

Goss, John Wesley
b. 11 May 1840, Morristown, St Lawrence, NY
d. 4 Sept 1927, Longmont, CO
bd. Mountain View Cemetery, Longmont, Boulder, CO
spouse: Ellen Augusta Olcott Goss, Mary Hummell Goss
father: Darius Goss
mother: Sophia Blackstone Goss
St Vrain Pioneers Assn Arrival Date: 1864
St Vrain Ditch Owner: Goss Private Ditch 1, No. 25, 30 June 1865
1870 US Census, Colorado Territory, Boulder County, St Vrain District

Goss, Mayme Eddings
d. abt 1966
spouse: James Olcott Goss

Goss, Percy A
b. 15 June 1875, Hygiene, Boulder, Colorado Territory
d. 14 Feb 1967, Longmont, Boulder, CO
bd. Hygiene Cemetery, Hygiene, Boulder, CO
spouse: Jennie Maud Lee Goss
father: John Wesley Goss
mother: Ellen Augusta Olcott Goss

Goss, Peter
b. abt 1845, NY
1870 US Census, Colorado Territory, Boulder County, St Vrain District

Goss, Wilder Darius
b. 3 June 1870, Goss Homestead, Boulder, CO
d. 27 June 1922, Parma, Cannon, ID
spouse: Sarah Barshaw Goss
father: John Wesley Goss
mother: Ellen Augusta Olcott Goss
1870 US Census, Colorado Territory, Boulder County, St Vrain District

Goudy, Isaac
b. abt 1832, OH
1870 US Census, Colorado Territory, Boulder County, St Vrain District

Gould, Amy Foster
b. 1838, OH
d. 21 Apr 1883
bd. Niwot Cemetery, Niwot, Boulder, CO
spouse: Jerome Fuller Gould
St Vrain Pioneers Assn Arrival Date: 1861
1870 US Census, Colorado Territory, Boulder County, St Vrain District

Gould, Ernest W
b. 1868, Colorado Territory
d. 6 Aug 1881
bd. Niwot Cemetery, Niwot, Boulder, CO
father: Jerome Fuller Gould
mother: Amy Foster Gould
1870 US Census, Colorado Territory, Boulder County, St Vrain District

Gould, Euphemia
b. 5 Apr 1898
d. 30 Dec 1980
bd. Mountain View Memorial Park, Boulder, CO
spouse: Lee G Gould

Gould, Jerome Fuller
b. 21 Apr 1834, Naples, Ontario, NY
d. 22 June 1924, Niwot, Boulder, CO
bd. Niwot Cemetery, Niwot, Boulder, CO
spouse: Amy Foster Gould
father: Jothan S Gould
mother: Marinda Patterson Gould
St Vrain Pioneers Assn Arrival Date: 1861
1870 US Census, Colorado Territory, Boulder County, St Vrain District

Gould, Lacinda P
b. abt 1865, Colorado Territory
father: Jerome Fuller Gould
mother: Amy Foster Gould
1870 US Census, Colorado Territory, Boulder County, St Vrain District

Gould, Lee G
b. 1 Nov 1892
d. 14 Feb 1963
bd. Mountain View Memorial Park, Boulder, CO
spouse: Euphemia Gould
father: LeGrand Patterson Gould
mother: Emma Jane Doud Gould

Gould, Mary
b. abt 1867, Colorado Territory
father: Jerome Fuller Gould
mother: Amy Foster Gould
1870 US Census, Colorado Territory, Boulder County, St Vrain District

Goyn, Richard
b. abt 1823, England
spouse: Catherine Goyn
St Vrain Pioneers Assn Arrival Date: [not recorded]
St Vrain Ditch Owner: Titus & Goyn Ditch No. 72, 1 Apr 1878

Grafflin, William H
St Vrain Land Club (M687) Date: 1865 Feb 9

Graham, Ellen D
St Vrain Land Club (M687) Date: 1860 Jan 7

Graham, Samuel D
b. abt 1815, PA
spouse: Rebecca S Knopple Graham
St Vrain Pioneers Assn Arrival Date: 1868

Graham, Thomas Jefferson
b. 25 Nov 1830, PA
d. 15 Aug 1892, Boulder, BO
bd. Green Mountain Cemetery, Boulder, CO
father: George M Graham
mother: Eliza Alter Graham
St Vrain Pioneers Assn Arrival Date: 1860
St Vrain Land Club Date: 1861 Aug 18

Grant, Edward
Franklin Township Land Club Claim Date: 1860 Feb 16
St Vrain Land Club Date: 1860 Feb 1

Grayham, James
b. abt 1849, England
1870 US Census, Colorado Territory, Weld County, St Vrain District

Greenly, Allen
b. abt 1856, IL
father: Jesse Greenly
mother: Malissa Greenly
1870 US Census, Colorado Territory, Boulder County, St Vrain District

Greenly, Arthur Chase
b. 25 Jan 1865, Burlington, Boulder, Colorado Territory
d. 17 Mar 1922, WY
spouse: Francis Arvilla Shafer Greenly
father: Jesse Hamilton Greenly
mother: Melissa Sophia Corwin Greenly
1870 US Census, Colorado Territory, Boulder County, St Vrain District

St Vrain Valley Pioneers

Greenly, Edith
b. 27 Feb 1867, Burlington, Boulder, Colorado Territory
d. 27 Feb 1937, Compton, Los Angeles, CA
father: Jesse Hamilton Greenly
mother: Melissa Sophia Corwin Greenly
1870 US Census, Colorado Territory, Boulder County, St Vrain District

Greenly, Ernest Charles
b. 1869, Colorado Territory
d. 29 Mar 1930, Salina, Gloucester, NJ
bd. Burlington Cemetery, Longmont, Boulder, CO
father: Jesse Hamilton Greenly
mother: Melissa Sophia Corwin Greenly
1870 US Census, Colorado Territory, Boulder County, St Vrain District

Greenly, Jesse Hamilton
b. 13 Oct 1826, OH
d. 28 Sept 1903, Blackfoot, Bingham, ID
bd. State Hospital South Cemetery, Bingham, ID
spouse: Melissa Sophia Corwin Greenly Belcher; Margarette Alice Rose Greenly
St Vrain Pioneers Assn Arrival Date: 1859
1870 US Census, Colorado Territory, Boulder County, St Vrain District

Greub, Elizabeth Affolter
b. 7 Oct 1821, Switzerland
d. 26 Aug 1885, Boulder, CO
bd. Burlington Cemetery, Longmont, Boulder, CO
spouse: Rudolph Greub
father: Jacob Affolter
mother: Elizabeth Baumberger Affolter
St Vrain Pioneers Assn Arrival Date: 1864
1870 US Census, Colorado Territory, Boulder County, Left Hand

Greub, Fred Rupert
b. 4 Oct 1857, Easton, Buchanan, MO
d. 8 Mar 1943, Boulder, CO
bd. Fairmount Cemetery, Denver, CO
father: Rudolph Greub
mother: Elizabeth Affolter Greub
St Vrain Pioneers Assn Arrival Date: 1864
1870 US Census, Colorado Territory, Boulder County, Left Hand

Greub, Jacob Ernest
b. 12 July 1861, St Joseph, Andrew, MO
d. 3 Feb 1913, Greub Ranch, Kearney, WY
father: Rudolph Greub
mother: Elizabeth Affolter Greub
St Vrain Pioneers Assn Arrival Date: 1864
1870 US Census, Colorado Territory, Boulder County, Left Hand

Greub, John N
b. 12 Mar 1859, St Joseph, Andrew, MO
d. 29 Apr 1943, Buffalo, Johnson, WY
father: Rudolph Greub
mother: Elizabeth Affolter Greub
St Vrain Pioneers Assn Arrival Date: 1864
1870 US Census, Colorado Territory, Boulder County, Left Hand

Greub, Rudolph
b. abt 1823
d. 2 Mar 1883, Longmont, Boulder, CO
bd. Burlington Cemetery, Longmont, Boulder, CO
spouse: Elizabeth Affolter Greub
father: Johannes Greub
mother: Suzanne Pfister Greub
St Vrain Pioneers Assn Arrival Date: 1864
1870 US Census, Colorado Territory, Boulder County, Left Hand

Griffin, Josephine Virden
b. abt 1856, Nebraska Territory
spouse: Thomas J Griffin
father: John Virden
mother: Jane Hunt Virden
1870 US Census, Colorado Territory, Boulder County, St Vrain District

Griffith, Edward W
Franklin Township Land Club Claim Date: 1860 Feb 15
St Vrain Land Club Date: 1860 Feb 15

Groseclose, Albert
b. 10 May 1868, Colorado Territory
d. 21 Apr 1887, Boulder, CO
father: Peter Groseclose
mother: Helena Sophia Anderson Groseclose
1870 US Census, Colorado Territory, Weld County, St Vrain District

St Vrain Valley Pioneers

Groseclose, Andrew
b. abt 1801, VA
1870 US Census, Colorado Territory, Weld County, St Vrain District

Groseclose, Austin T
b. abt 1858, IA
father: Jacob Groseclose
mother: Elisobett Groseclose
1870 US Census, Colorado Territory, Weld County, St Vrain District

Groseclose, Charles
b. abt 1862, IA
father: Peter Groseclose
mother: Helena Sophia Anderson Groseclose
1870 US Census, Colorado Territory, Weld County, St Vrain District

Groseclose, Charlotte
b. abt 1866, IA
father: Jacob Groseclose
mother: Elisobett Groseclose
1870 US Census, Colorado Territory, Weld County, St Vrain District

Groseclose, Elisobett
b. abt 1827, VA
spouse: Jacob Groseclose
1870 US Census, Colorado Territory, Weld County, St Vrain District

Groseclose, Fannie
b. abt 1803, VA
d. bef 1885?
spouse: Andrew Groseclose
1870 US Census, Colorado Territory, Weld County, St Vrain District

Groseclose, Frances M
b. abt 1864, Colorado Territory
father: Peter Groseclose
mother: Helena Sophia Anderson Groseclose
1870 US Census, Colorado Territory, Weld County, St Vrain District

Groseclose, George
St Vrain Pioneers Assn Arrival Date: 1860

Groseclose, Helena Sophia Anderson
b. 5 Feb 1830, Vastra Eneby, Ostergotlands Ian, Sweden
d. 2 Dec 1913, Weld, CO
bd. Mountain View Cemetery, Longmont, Boulder, CO
spouse: Peter Groseclose
father: Magnus Anderson
mother: Elizabeth Bengtsson Anderson
St Vrain Pioneers Assn Arrival Date: 1859
1870 US Census, Colorado Territory, Weld County, St Vrain District

Groseclose, Isaac
b. abt 1861, MO
father: Jacob Groseclose
mother: Elisobett Groseclose
1870 US Census, Colorado Territory, Weld County, St Vrain District

Groseclose, Jacob
b. abt 1824, IN
d. 1876?
spouse: Elisobett Groseclose
1870 US Census, Colorado Territory, Weld County, St Vrain District

Groseclose, Jacob
b. abt 1855, IN
father: Jacob Groseclose
mother: Elisobett Groseclose
1870 US Census, Colorado Territory, Weld County, St Vrain District

Groseclose, John
b. abt 1855, IA
father: Peter Groseclose
mother: Helena Sophia Anderson Groseclose
1870 US Census, Colorado Territory, Weld County, St Vrain District

Groseclose, John
b. abt 1855, IA
1870 US Census, Colorado Territory, Weld County, St Vrain District

Groseclose, Mary Sophia
b. 27 Sept 1865, Weld, Colorado Territory
d. 28 Sept 1886, Boulder, CO
bd. Mountain View Cemetery, Longmont, Boulder, CO
father: Peter Groseclose
mother: Helena Sophia Anderson Groseclose
1870 US Census, Colorado Territory, Weld County, St Vrain District

St Vrain Valley Pioneers

Groseclose, Mrs George
spouse: George Groseclose
St Vrain Pioneers Assn Arrival Date: 1860

Groseclose, Peter
b. 13 Nov 1826, Johnson, IN
d. 30 Oct 1903, Boulder, CO
bd. Mountain View Cemetery, Longmont, Boulder, CO
spouse: Helena Sophia Anderson Groseclose
father: Andrew Groseclose
mother: Fannie Groseclose
St Vrain Pioneers Assn Arrival Date: 1859

Groseclose, Rosana
b. abt 1867, Colorado Territory
father: Jacob Groseclose
mother: Elisobett Groseclose
1870 US Census, Colorado Territory, Weld County, St Vrain District

Groseclose, Sarah F
b. abt 1863, IA
father: Jacob Groseclose
mother: Elisobett Groseclose
1870 US Census, Colorado Territory, Weld County, St Vrain District

Groves, Joseph
b. abt 1841, Baden, Germany
1870 US Census, Colorado Territory, Boulder County, St Vrain District

Grubb, Burr
St Vrain Pioneers Assn Arrival Date: 1867

Gubins, G E
St Vrain Land Club Date: 1861 Jan 30

Guin, G C
St Vrain Land Club Date: 1860 Oct 29

Guin, Richard
St Vrain Land Club Date: 1860 Oct 29

Guinn, T
Franklin Township Land Club Claim Date: 1860 Feb 11

Gulick, William
b. abt 1846, IN
1870 US Census, Colorado Territory, Boulder County, St Vrain District

Gumeson, Amanda C Nelson
b. 1882
d. 1966
bd. Mountain View Cemetery, Longmont, Boulder, CO
spouse: Albert P Gumeson
father: John L Nelson
mother: Ingeborg Mossberg Nelson

Gummeson, Samuel
b. 29 Mar 1839
d. 29 Oct 1921
bd. Ryssby Cemetery, Boulder, CO
spouse: Eva Marie Gummeson
St Vrain Pioneers Assn Arrival Date: 1869

H

Hadson, John
b. abt 1840, England
spouse: Samantha Hadson
1870 US Census, Colorado Territory, Boulder County, Left Hand

Hadson, Samantha
b. abt 1855, IA
spouse: John Hadson
1870 US Census, Colorado Territory, Boulder County, Left Hand

Hafford, George
b. abt 1830, Germany
1860 US Census, Nebraska Territory, Platte River

Hager, John Henry
b. 21 Mar 1826, Wurtemberg, Germany
d. 23 Nov 1891
bd. Hygiene Cemetery, Hygiene, Boulder, CO
spouse: Mary M Hager, Catherine M Hager
St Vrain Pioneers Assn Arrival Date: 1859
St Vrain Ditch Owner: Hager's Meadow Ditch No. 18, 1 Jan 1864
1870 US Census, Colorado Territory, Boulder County, St Vrain District

Hager, Mary M
b. abt 1828, KY
d. 16 Dec 1878
bd. Burlington Cemetery, Longmont, Boulder, CO
spouse: John H Hager

1870 US Census, Colorado Territory, Boulder County, St Vrain District

Haight, Charles
b. abt 1839, OH
spouse: Lucy Haight
1870 US Census, Colorado Territory, Boulder County, St Vrain District

Haight, Lucy
b. abt 1840, OH
spouse: Charles Haight
1870 US Census, Colorado Territory, Boulder County, St Vrain District

Haines, Martin S
b. 1838, IN
d. 1911
bd. Lafayette Cemetery, Lafayette, Boulder, CO
spouse: Rachel Haines
1870 US Census, Colorado Territory, Weld County, St Vrain District

Hake, Mary Elizabeth Riddle Stotts
b. 22 July 1845, Marion Cty, IA
d. 7 Nov 1927, Boulder, CO
bd. Columbia Cemetery, Boulder, CO
spouse: Lewis Stotts; Levi Hake
father: John G Riddle
mother: Frances May
St Vrain Pioneers Assn Arrival Date: 1859

Hall, George H
b. 21 Sept 1842, Canada
d. 4 Sept 1917, Longmont, Boulder, CO
bd. Mountain View Cemetery, Longmont, Boulder, CO
spouse: Nellie Mumford Hall
father: David Hall
St Vrain Pioneers Assn Arrival Date: 1865

Hall, Henry B
b. abt 1840, KY
spouse: Mandy Hall
1870 US Census, Colorado Territory, Boulder County, St Vrain District

Hall, Mandy
b. abt 1846, IL
spouse: Henry B Hall
1870 US Census, Colorado Territory, Boulder County, St Vrain District

Hamblin, Charles D
b. abt 1861, Colorado Territory
d. 21 Feb 1923, WY
bd. Willow Grove Cemetery, Buffalo, Johnson, WY
father: Charles P Hamblin
mother: Hellen Munger Hamblin
1870 US Census, Colorado Territory, Boulder County, St Vrain District

Hamblin, Charles Phineas
b. 1 Feb 1829, VT
d. 16 Sept 1871, Boulder, CO
bd. Columbia Cemetery, Boulder, CO
spouse: Hellen Munger Hamblin
father: William B Hamblin
mother: Sally Kitchell Hamblin
1870 US Census, Colorado Territory, Boulder County, St Vrain District

Hamblin, Fannie
b. abt 1858, IL
father: Charles P Hamblin
mother: Hellen Munger Hamblin
1870 US Census, Colorado Territory, Boulder County, St Vrain District

Hamblin, Hellen Munger
b. abt 1828, VT
spouse: Charles P Hamblin
1870 US Census, Colorado Territory, Boulder County, St Vrain District

Hamblin, Hellen M
b. abt 1865, Colorado Territory
father: Charles P Hamblin
mother: Hellen Munger Hamblin
1870 US Census, Colorado Territory, Boulder County, St Vrain District

Hamby, James
St Vrain Pioneers Assn Arrival Date: [not recorded]

Hamlin, Charles
St Vrain Pioneers Assn Arrival Date: 1861

Hamlin, Frank M
b. abt 1861, Colorado Territory
father: Oliver T Hamlin
mother: Lucinda Hamlin

St Vrain Valley Pioneers

1870 US Census, Colorado Territory, Boulder County, St Vrain District

Hamlin, Georgie A
b. abt 1859, IA
father: Oliver T Hamlin
mother: Lucinda Hamlin
1870 US Census, Colorado Territory, Boulder County, St Vrain District

Hamlin, Lucinda
b. abt 1833, OH
spouse: Oliver T Hamlin
St Vrain Pioneers Assn Arrival Date: 1859
1870 US Census, Colorado Territory, Boulder County, St Vrain District

Hamlin, Oliver T
b. abt 1831, PA
d. 24 Jan 1912, Loveland, CO
spouse: Lucinda Hamlin
St Vrain Pioneers Assn Arrival Date: 1859
1870 US Census, Colorado Territory, Boulder County, St Vrain District

Hammett, Mary
b. abt 1840, IA
spouse: T W Hammett
1860 US Census, Nebraska Territory, Platte River

Hammett, T W
b. abt 1834, IA
spouse: Mary Hammett
1860 US Census, Nebraska Territory, Platte River

Hammond, John
b. abt 1816, England
1870 US Census, Colorado Territory, Boulder County, St Vrain District

Hanby, James
b. abt 1848, OH
spouse: Laura Hanby
1870 US Census, Colorado Territory, Boulder County, Left Hand

Haney, Lawrence
b. abt 1851, OH
father: John S Haney
1870 US Census, Colorado Territory, Boulder County, St Vrain District

Hank, Austin
b. abt 1840, Sachsen, Germany
spouse: Robert Hank
1870 US Census, Colorado Territory, Weld County, St Vrain District

Hank, Edward
b. abt 1869, Colorado Territory
father: Robert Hank
mother: Austin Hank
1870 US Census, Colorado Territory, Weld County, St Vrain District

Hank, Robert
b. abt 1830, Prussia
spouse: Austin Hank
1870 US Census, Colorado Territory, Weld County, St Vrain District

Hanna, George
b. abt 1846, England
1870 US Census, Colorado Territory, Weld County, St Vrain District

Hansen, Charles C
b. 1 Oct 1889
d. 26 Oct 1981
bd. Lafayette Cemetery, Lafayette, Boulder, CO
spouse: Mary Alice Prince Knutson

Hansen, William
b. 1895
d. 1981
bd. Foothills Garden of Memory, Longmont, Boulder, CO
spouse: Delia C Hansen

Hanson, Andrew J
St Vrain Pioneers Assn Arrival Date: 1867

Hanson, Mrs Andrew J
St Vrain Pioneers Assn Arrival Date: 1867

Hardenberg, Norma Bell
b. 27 June 1896
d. 2 Jan 1968
bd. Mountain View Cemetery, Longmont, Boulder, CO
father: Guy Hardenberg
mother: Gretta E Jackman Hardenberg

Harley, Chriss
b. abt 1840, England
spouse: Elisabeth Harley
1870 US Census, Colorado Territory, Boulder County, St Vrain District

Harley, Elisabeth
b. abt 1843, England
spouse: Chriss Harley
1870 US Census, Colorado Territory, Boulder County, St Vrain District

Harley, Louisa
b. abt 1869, Colorado Territory
father: Chriss Harley
mother: Elisabeth Harley
1870 US Census, Colorado Territory, Boulder County, St Vrain District

Harmon, Manning S
b. abt 1831
d. 10 Dec 1905
bd. Louisville Cemetery, Louisville, Boulder, CO
St Vrain Pioneers Assn Arrival Date: 1861

Harmon, Mrs Manning S
St Vrain Pioneers Assn Arrival Date: 1861

Harrigan, Edward
b. abt 1843, Ireland
1870 US Census, Colorado Territory, Boulder County, St Vrain District

Harris, Addison W
b. abt 1836, IN
d. , Silver City, NM?
St Vrain Pioneers Assn Arrival Date: 1859

Harris, Charles
b. abt 1849, MA
1870 US Census, Colorado Territory, Boulder County, St Vrain District

Harris, family of Addison
St Vrain Pioneers Assn Arrival Date: 1859

Hart, Orton Burton
b. 7 Sept 1908
d. 25 Sept 1929, Pendleton, OR
bd. Burlington Cemetery, Longmont, Boulder, CO
father: Burton O Hart
mother: Eliza Margaret Forsyth Hart

Hart, Sarah
b. abt 1844, OH
1870 US Census, Colorado Territory, Weld County, St Vrain District

Hartgrove, Nelson
St Vrain Land Club Date: 1861 Apr 5

Hartgrove, William
St Vrain Land Club Date: 1861 Apr 8

Hartsook, Minnie
b. abt 1887
d. 20 Feb 1923
mother: Mrs H H Hornbaker

Hauck, Ernestine Lange
b. abt 1842, Prussia
St Vrain Pioneers Assn Arrival Date: 1863

Hauck, Robert August
b. abt 1828, Prussia
spouse: Ernestine Lange Hauck
St Vrain Pioneers Assn Arrival Date: 1859

Hause, Harriet
b. abt 1855, IA
spouse: Lewis F Hause
1870 US Census, Colorado Territory, Boulder County, St Vrain District

Hause, Lewis F
b. abt 1843, KY
spouse: Harriet Hause
1870 US Census, Colorado Territory, Boulder County, St Vrain District

Hawkins, Hiram
St Vrain Land Club (M687) Date: 1860 Oct 23

Hayden, Samuel
b. 1831
d. 21 July 1906
bd. Green Mountain Cemetery, Boulder, CO
spouse: Matilda J Hayden
St Vrain Pioneers Assn Arrival Date: 1864

Henderson, Joseph
b. abt 1808, NY
St Vrain Pioneers Assn Arrival Date: [not recorded]
Franklin Township Land Club Claim Date: 1860 June 24

St Vrain Valley Pioneers

Henderson, William S
b. 4 Aug 1828, DuBoise, IN
d. 18 Oct 1911
bd. Hygiene Cemetery, Hygiene, Boulder, CO
spouse: Lucy E Henderson, Eveline McEwan Henderson
St Vrain Pioneers Assn Arrival Date: 1865

Hendren, Harriet A Caywood
b. 10 Jan 1857, Wapello, IA
d. 31 Aug 1936, Boulder, CO
bd. Green Mountain Cemetery, Boulder, CO
father: William Wesley Caywood
mother: Katharine Donovan Newman Caywood
St Vrain Pioneers Assn Arrival Date: 1864
1870 US Census, Colorado Territory, Boulder County, Left Hand

Henney, family of Lawrence
St Vrain Pioneers Assn Arrival Date: 1862

Henney, Lawrence
St Vrain Pioneers Assn Arrival Date: 1862

Henney, Mrs Lawrence
St Vrain Pioneers Assn Arrival Date: 1862

Henry, Charles W
b. abt 1869, Colorado Territory
father: Orin H Henry
mother: Katie Henry
1870 US Census, Colorado Territory, Boulder County, St Vrain District

Henry, Katie
b. abt 1843, France
spouse: Orin H Henry
1870 US Census, Colorado Territory, Boulder County, St Vrain District

Henry, Nimrod Milton
b. 29 Aug 1847, Parke, Greene, IN
d. 19 Jan 1940, Boulder, Boulder, CO
bd. Green Mountain Cemetery, Boulder, CO
spouse: Melissa Ann Linson Henry
father: Thomas Shrpe Henry
mother: Phoebe Philson Brown Henry
St Vrain Pioneers Assn Arrival Date: 1865
1870 US Census, Colorado Territory, Boulder County, Left Hand

Henry, Oren G
b. abt 1867, Colorado Territory
father: Oren H Henry
mother: Katie Henry
1870 US Census, Colorado Territory, Boulder County, St Vrain District

Henry, Oren H
b. abt 1843, VT
spouse: Katie Henry
1870 US Census, Colorado Territory, Boulder County, St Vrain District

Henry, Ormal E
b. abt 1838, VT
spouse: Mary J Entwistle Henry
1870 US Census, Colorado Territory, Boulder County, St Vrain District

Herdrick, William
b. abt 1837, KY
1860 US Census, Nebraska Territory, Platte River

Heriman, A
St Vrain Land Club Date: 1861 Apr 11

Herington, C G
St Vrain Land Club Date: 1861 Feb 18

Herring, Leonidas Marquette
b. 17 Nov 1846, IL
d. 27 May 1918, Longmont, CO
bd. Mountain View Cemetery, Longmont, Boulder, CO
spouse: Amanda S Raymond Herring
St Vrain Pioneers Assn Arrival Date: 1866
1870 US Census, Colorado Territory, Weld County, St Vrain District

Hershey, Nellie Carr
b. abt 1860, NE Terr
d. 9 Feb 1889, Longmont, CO
spouse: Benjamin F Hershey
father: Stephen H Carr
mother: Lizzie Oliphant Carr
1870 US Census, Colorado Territory, Weld County, St Vrain District

Hertha, Henry
St Vrain Pioneers Assn Arrival Date: [not recorded]

Hertha, John Nicholaus
b. 10 Oct 1836, Saxony, Germany
d. 20 Aug 1901, Longmont, CO
bd. Mountain View Cemetery, Longmont, Boulder, CO
spouse: Mary Augusta Meinhardt Hertha
mother: Margaret Hertha
St Vrain Pioneers Assn Arrival Date: 1868

Hertha, William
St Vrain Pioneers Assn Arrival Date: [not recorded]

Hess, Mr
St Vrain Pioneers Assn Arrival Date: [not recorded]

Hess, Mrs
St Vrain Pioneers Assn Arrival Date: [not recorded]

Hess, William
b. abt 1832, OH
1870 US Census, Colorado Territory, Boulder County, St Vrain District

Higginbotham, Elijah
b. abt 1824, FL
1870 US Census, Colorado Territory, Boulder County, St Vrain District

Hildreth, Isaac Howell
b. 13 Oct 1839, Canada
d. 12 Dec 1918, Longmont, Boulder, CO
bd. Mountain View Cemetery, Longmont, Boulder, CO
spouse: Emma Vennum Hildreth
St Vrain Pioneers Assn Arrival Date: 1859

Hildreth, Emma Vennum
b. 3 Mar 1846, Union Grove, Whiteside, IL
d. 12 Aug 1914, Caldwell, Canyon, ID
bd. Grove Hill Cemetery, Morrison, Whiteside, IL
spouse: Isaac Howell Hildreth
St Vrain Pioneers Assn Arrival Date: 1859

Hill, Caroline E Brown
b. abt 1836, NY
spouse: Nathan Brown, Thomas J Hill
1870 US Census, Colorado Territory, Boulder County, St Vrain District

Hill, Miles
St Vrain Land Club Date: 1861 Apr 1

Hill, Sylvester L
b. abt 1815, NY
d. 1 Feb 1889
bd. Columbia Cemetery, Boulder, CO
spouse: Harriet N Hill
St Vrain Land Club Date: 1861 Aug 19

Hill, Thomas J
b. 25 Dec 1841
d. 25 May 1873
bd. Columbia Cemetery, Boulder, CO
spouse: Caroline E Brown Hill
1870 US Census, Colorado Territory, Boulder County, St Vrain District

Hinman, Frank Alfred
b. 26 Jan 1857, Sailorville, IA
d. 16 June 1900, Colorado City, Pueblo, CO
father: Porter Timothy Hinman
mother: Mary A Smith Hinman
1870 US Census, Colorado Territory, Boulder County, Left Hand

Hinman, Ida Dale
b. abt 1843
d. 20 Mar 1874, Left Hand, Boulder, CO
bd. Columbia Cemetery, Boulder, CO
spouse: Porter Mortimer Hinman
mother: Prudence Dale
St Vrain Pioneers Assn Arrival Date: 1863

Hinman, Mary A Smith
b. 1819, CT
d. 28 Feb 1903, Canfield, Boulder, CO
bd. Columbia Cemetery, Boulder, CO
spouse: Porter Timothy Hinman
father: Stephen Smith
mother: Polly Betts Smith
1870 US Census, Colorado Territory, Boulder County, Left Hand

Hinman, Merritt L
b. 14 Mar 1853, IL
d. 1895, Leadville, Lake, CO
spouse: Sarah Elizabeth Cavey Hinman
father: Porter Timothy Hinman
mother: Mary A Smith Hinman

St Vrain Valley Pioneers

1870 US Census, Colorado Territory, Boulder County, Left Hand

Hinman, Otto Thomas
b. 3 June 1883, Boulder, CO
d. 8 Dec 1921, Kremmling, Grand, CO
bd. Mountain View Cemetery, Longmont, Boulder, CO
spouse: Ethel Irene Richards Hinman
father: Merritt L Hinman
mother: Sarah E Cavey Hinman

Hinman, Platte A
b. Apr 1846, IN
d. 28 Dec 1925, Los Angeles, CA
bd. Los Angeles National Cemetery, Los Angeles, CA
spouse: Nannie L Hinman
father: Porter Timothy Hinman
mother: Mary A Smith Hinman
1870 US Census, Colorado Territory, Boulder County, Left Hand

Hinman, Porter Mortimer
b. 9 Aug 1844, Millersburg, Holmes, OH
d. 21 Jan 1884, St James Hotel, Denver, CO
bd. Columbia Cemetery, Boulder, CO
spouse: Ida Dale Hinman; Estelle Turrell Hinman
father: Porter Timothy Hinman
mother: Mary A Smith Hinman
St Vrain Pioneers Assn Arrival Date: 1860
1870 US Census, Colorado Territory, Boulder County, Left Hand

Hinman, Porter Timothy
b. 6 July 1816, Allegheny, NY
d. bef 14 June 1894, Snake River, WY
spouse: Mary A Smith Hinman
father: Timothy Judge Hinman
mother: Phoebe Stoddard Hinman
1870 US Census, Colorado Territory, Boulder County, Left Hand

Hite, Gabriel J
b. abt 1838, WV
1870 US Census, Colorado Territory, Boulder County, St Vrain District

Hitt, John G
b. abt 1808, PA
1860 US Census, Nebraska Territory, Platte River

Hitt, Sarah
b. abt 1856, NE Terr
1860 US Census, Nebraska Territory, Platte River

Hobbs, Robert
b. abt 1846, IN
1870 US Census, Colorado Territory, Weld County, St Vrain District

Hockaday, Charles
b. 16 Mar 1869, Colorado Territory
d. 16 Apr 1960
bd. Littleton Cemetery, Littleton, Arapahoe, CO
spouse: Retta Lehman Hockaday
father: Charles Newton Hockaday
mother: Hannah Hockaday
1870 US Census, Colorado Territory, Boulder County, St Vrain District

Hockaday, Charles Newton
b. 24 May 1834, KY
d. 6 Oct 1910, Boulder, CO
bd. Kossler Ranch, Boulder, CO
spouse: Hannah Hockaday
1870 US Census, Colorado Territory, Boulder County, St Vrain District

Hockaday, Edward
b. abt 1867, Colorado Territory
father: Charles Hockaday
mother: Hannah Hockaday
1870 US Census, Colorado Territory, Boulder County, St Vrain District

Hockaday, Hannah Sheppard Kelsay
b. Nov 1842
d. 6 Dec 1898
bd. Kossler Ranch, Boulder, CO
spouse: Charles Newton Hockaday
father: James Sheppard Kelsay
mother: Harriet Westcott Sheppard Kelsay
1870 US Census, Colorado Territory, Boulder County, St Vrain District

Hodgson, Christine
b. abt 1834
d. 18 Oct 1911, Platteville, Weld, CO
spouse: David Hodgson
St Vrain Pioneers Assn Arrival Date: 1863

Hodgson, David
spouse: Christine Hodgson
St Vrain Pioneers Assn Arrival Date: 1863

Hodgson, Frank
St Vrain Pioneers Assn Arrival Date: 1863

Hodgson, George
St Vrain Pioneers Assn Arrival Date: 1863

Holck, Chris
b. abt 1830, Denmark
1870 US Census, Colorado Territory, Boulder County, St Vrain District

Hollenbeck, Hattie Levey
spouse: Michael Hollenbeck
father: William Levey
mother: Roxanna Beach Levey
St Vrain Pioneers Assn Arrival Date: 1869

Hollenbeck, Michael
spouse: Hattie Levey Hollenbeck
St Vrain Pioneers Assn Arrival Date: 1860

Hollingshead, Thomas
St Vrain Land Club (M687) Date: 1861 Apr 15

Hollman, J W
b. abt 1839, WI
1860 US Census, Nebraska Territory, Platte River

Hollowell, J W
St Vrain Pioneers Assn Arrival Date: 1860
St Vrain Land Club Date: 1861 Nov 28

Holmes, J W
St Vrain Pioneers Assn Arrival Date: 1859

Holmes, John H
b. abt 1838, NY
d. 8 Nov 1910, Denver, CO
spouse: Marion A Holmes

Holmes, Mrs J W
St Vrain Pioneers Assn Arrival Date: 1859

Homer, Joseph
b. abt 1844, Bohemia
St Vrain Pioneers Assn Arrival Date: [not recorded]
1870 US Census, Colorado Territory, Boulder County, Left Hand

Hood, Walter John
b. 15 May 1907, Lafayette, Boulder, CO
d. 28 Oct 1966, Boulder, CO
bd. Green Mountain Cemetery, Boulder, CO

Hooper, J B
b. abt 1825, VA
1860 US Census, Nebraska Territory, Platte River

Hoover, D C
Franklin Township Land Club Claim Date: 1860 June 25

Hoover, R C
Franklin Township Land Club Claim Date: 1860 June 25

Hopkins, D J
St Vrain Land Club (M687) Date: 1861 Feb 4

Hopkins, William LeSeur
b. 13 Feb 1833, Shelby, Richland, OH
d. 20 Feb 1889, Denver, Arapahoe, CO
bd. Monument Cemetery, Monument, El Paso, CO
spouse: Emily J Hopkins
father: Isaac Daniel Hopkins
mother: Sarah Henry Hopkins
St Vrain Land Club (M687) Date: 1859 Oct 22
Troy District Land Club Claim Date: 1860 Dec 25

Hornbaker, Arabell
b. abt 1867, Colorado Territory
father: Henry Harrison Hornbaker
mother: Sarah Isabelle Way Hornbaker
1870 US Census, Colorado Territory, Boulder County, Left Hand

Hornbaker, Arminta A Richardson McLaren
b. 21 Apr 1858, Des Moines, IA
d. 4 Jan 1926, Niwot, Boulder, CO
bd. Green Mountain Cemetery, Boulder, CO
spouse: John Lapsley McLaren, Franklin L Hornbaker; John Lapsley McLaren

Hornbaker, Franklin Leroy
b. 6 Aug 1865, Colorado Territory
d. 26 Sept 1948
bd. Columbia Cemetery, Boulder, CO
spouse: Cora A Wellman Hornbaker
father: Henry Harrison Hornbaker
mother: Sarah Isabelle Way Hornbaker

St Vrain Valley Pioneers

1870 US Census, Colorado Territory, Boulder County, Left Hand

Hornbaker, Henry Harrison
b. 22 Oct 1839, Munce, IN
d. 6 Jan 1924, Longmont, Boulder, CO
bd. Burlington Cemetery, Longmont, Boulder, CO
spouse: Sarah Isabelle Way Hornbaker
St Vrain Pioneers Assn Arrival Date: 1864
1870 US Census, Colorado Territory, Boulder County, Left Hand

Hornbaker, Jesse B
b. 23 Mar 1893, Ward, Boulder, CO
d. 1980
bd. Mountain View Memorial Park, Boulder, CO
spouse: Gertrude Simonton Hornbaker
father: Franklin LeRoy Hornbaker
mother: Cora Ann Wellman Hornbaker

Hornbaker, Pansy B Manke
b. 19 Jan 1904
d. 28 Jan 1967
bd. Mountain View Cemetery, Longmont, Boulder, CO
spouse: James Harrison Hornbaker
father: William Manke
mother: Eliza K Manke

Hornbaker, Sarah Isabelle Way
b. 11 Jan 1842, Wapello, IA
d. 18 Apr 1898, Boulder, CO
bd. Burlington Cemetery, Longmont, Boulder, CO
spouse: Henry Harrison Hornbaker
father: Enoch Way
mother: Paulina Burlington Way
St Vrain Pioneers Assn Arrival Date: 1864
1870 US Census, Colorado Territory, Boulder County, Left Hand

Hornbaker, William Goldwin Dimineous
b. 22 June 1863, Wapello, IA
d. 11 Mar 1958, Longmont, CO
bd. Burlington Cemetery, Longmont, Boulder, CO
spouse: S Ella Hornbaker
father: Henry Harrison Hornbaker
mother: Sarah Isabelle Way Hornbaker
St Vrain Pioneers Assn Arrival Date: 1864
1870 US Census, Colorado Territory, Boulder County, Left Hand

Horsfal, David
St Vrain Pioneers Assn Arrival Date: 1859

House, Lewis L
spouse: Harriet Hutchinson House
St Vrain Pioneers Assn Arrival Date: [not recorded]

Housel, Louisa Payson Bixby Wolcott
b. 6 Sept 1835, ME
d. 2 May 1917, Boulder, CO
bd. Green Mountain Cemetery, Boulder, CO
spouse: Horace Alanson Wolcott; Peter Mandeville Housel
1870 US Census, Colorado Territory, Boulder County, St Vrain District

Houston, Ageal
b. abt 1839, MO
1860 US Census, Nebraska Territory, Platte River

Houston, Albert
b. abt 1849, MO
1860 US Census, Nebraska Territory, Platte River

Houston, John
b. abt 1833, MO
spouse: Ageal Houston
1860 US Census, Nebraska Territory, Platte River

Houston, Mary
b. abt 1859
father: John Houston
mother: Ageal Houston
1860 US Census, Nebraska Territory, Platte River

How, Joseph
St Vrain Land Club (M687) Date: 1859 Oct 12

Howard, Charles
d. 6 May 1921, Long Beach, CA
father: Charles Pierpont Howard

Howard, Charles Pierpont
b. 9 Feb 1844, Warren Jo Davies, IL
d. 18 Apr 1911, Longmont, CO
bd. Mountain View Cemetery, Longmont, Boulder, CO
spouse: Lizzie Howard
father: E G Howard
mother: Sarah Howard
St Vrain Pioneers Assn Arrival Date: 1866

St Vrain Valley Pioneers

Howard, family of Ross
St Vrain Pioneers Assn Arrival Date: 1862

Howard, Mrs Ross
spouse: Ross Howard
St Vrain Pioneers Assn Arrival Date: 1862

Howard, Ross
St Vrain Pioneers Assn Arrival Date: 1862

Howard, Sarah
b. abt 1820, ME
1870 US Census, Colorado Territory, Weld County, St Vrain District

Howell, Cornelia Ann Sheldon
b. 24 July 1841, New Haven, Oswego, NY
d. 9 Aug 1922, Los Angeles, CA
bd. Inglewood Park Cemetery, Inglewood, Los Angeles, CA
spouse: William Rice Howell
St Vrain Pioneers Assn Arrival Date: 1861

Howell, James J
b. abt 1848, VA
1870 US Census, Colorado Territory, Boulder County, St Vrain District

Howell, William Rice
b. 17 Aug 1834, St Thomas, Canada
d. 19 Dec 1889, Needles, San Bernardino, CA
bd. Mountain View Cemetery, Longmont, Boulder, CO
spouse: Cornelia Ann Sheldon Howell
father: Hugh Howell
mother: Lucretia C Morton Howell
St Vrain Pioneers Assn Arrival Date: 1861

Hubbard, James Edwin
b. 22 Sept 1851, Sanford, York, ME
d. 27 Feb 1927, Boulder, CO
bd. Columbia Cemetery, Boulder, CO
spouse: Rhoda Maud Duke Hubbard
father: James Deacon Hubbard
mother: Hannah H Adams Hubbard
St Vrain Pioneers Assn Arrival Date: 1862

Huey, William
St Vrain Pioneers Assn Arrival Date: 1859

Hughes, Edward C
St Vrain Pioneers Assn Arrival Date: 1869

Hughes, Thomas
d. 11 Oct 1873
bd. Valmont Cemetery?, Boulder, CO
St Vrain Pioneers Assn Arrival Date: 1867

Hulversen, Chris
b. abt 1825, Norway
1870 US Census, Colorado Territory, Boulder County, St Vrain District

Hunter, Gilbert D
b. abt 1834, Scotland
spouse: Mary Hunter
1870 US Census, Colorado Territory, Boulder County, Left Hand

Hunter, Mary
b. abt 1834, OH
spouse: Gilbert Hunter
1870 US Census, Colorado Territory, Boulder County, Left Hand

Hunter, Samuel F/T
b. abt 1839
St Vrain Pioneers Assn Arrival Date: [not recorded]

Huppe, Walter
b. 21 June 1879, Berthoud, Larimer, CO
d. 6 Feb 1968, Longmont, Boulder, CO
bd. Greenlawn Cemetery, Berthoud, Larimer, CO
spouse: Florence Waite Huppe, Minnie A Huppe
father: Henry Albert Huppe
mother: Frieda H Huppe

Hutchinson, Daniel W
b. abt 1856, IA
father: Joseph Hutchinson
mother: Rhoda E Hutchinson
1870 US Census, Colorado Territory, Boulder County, St Vrain District

Hutchinson, Joseph
b. abt 1820, OH
d. 3 Sept 1889
bd. Burlington Cemetery, Longmont, Boulder, CO
spouse: Rhoda E Hutchinson
1870 US Census, Colorado Territory, Boulder County, St Vrain District

Hutchinson, Joseph
b. abt 1858, IA
father: Joseph Hutchinson
mother: Rhoda E Hutchinson
1870 US Census, Colorado Territory, Boulder County, St Vrain District

Hutchinson, Josephine
b. abt 1866 Canada
father: Joseph Hutchinson
mother: Rhoda E Hutchinson
1870 US Census, Colorado Territory, Boulder County, St Vrain District

Hutchinson, Rhoda E
b. abt 1827, OH
spouse: Joseph Hutchinson
1870 US Census, Colorado Territory, Boulder County, St Vrain District

I

Idler, Jane
b. abt 1842, Wurtemburg, Germany
1870 US Census, Colorado Territory, Boulder County, St Vrain District

Inglefield, Samuel J
b. abt 1848, OH
1870 US Census, Colorado Territory, Boulder County, St Vrain District

Irish Johnny
St Vrain Land Club (M687) Date: 1861 July 4

Iron, John
b. abt 1841
spouse: Kate Iron
1870 US Census, Colorado Territory, Weld County, St Vrain District

Iron, Kate
b. abt 1841, Wales
spouse: John Iron
1870 US Census, Colorado Territory, Weld County, St Vrain District

Irvin, David
b. abt 1840, PA
spouse: Elisobeth Irvin
1870 US Census, Colorado Territory, Weld County, St Vrain District

Irvin, Elisobeth
b. abt 1846, Canada
spouse: David Irvin
1870 US Census, Colorado Territory, Weld County, St Vrain District

Irvin, Mary E
b. abt 1865, Colorado Territory
father: David Irvin
mother: Elisobeth Irvin
1870 US Census, Colorado Territory, Weld County, St Vrain District

Irvin, Sarah
b. abt 1870, Colorado Territory
father: David Irvin
mother: Elisobeth Irvin
1870 US Census, Colorado Territory, Weld County, St Vrain District

J

Jackson, Daniel
b. abt 1844, IL
spouse: Phebe Jackson
1870 US Census, Colorado Territory, Boulder County, Left Hand

Jackson, George
b. abt 1847, VA
1870 US Census, Colorado Territory, Boulder County, St Vrain District

Jackson, Rhebe
b. abt 1851, MO
spouse: Daniel Jackson
1870 US Census, Colorado Territory, Boulder County, Left Hand

Jain, Jules Francois Emil
b. 31 Dec 1839, Ecublens, Vaud, Switzerland
d. 21 Nov 1910, Boulder, CO
bd. Green Mountain Cemetery, Boulder, CO
spouse: Mary Jane Case Jain
father: William Benjamin Jain
mother: Anna Rose Suzanne Mennett Jain
St Vrain Pioneers Assn Arrival Date: 1860

Jain, Mary Jane Case
b. 29 Jan 1852, Libertyville, Jefferson, IA
d. 7 June 1943, Boulder, CO

spouse: Jules Francois Emil Jain
father: Milton Bell Case
mother: Catherine Wolphe Case
St Vrain Pioneers Assn Arrival Date: 1862

James, Gilbert
St Vrain Land Club Date: 1861 June 23

James, Michael Sylvestor
b. 28 Apr 1893, Louisville, Boulder, CO
d. 9 Mar 1968, Longmont, Boulder, CO
bd. Mountain View Cemetery, Longmont, Boulder, CO
spouse: Angelina Lucille DiGiacomo James
father: Peter James
mother: Mary Ricci James

Jamison, Aaron Parker
b. abt 1861, Colorado Territory
father: Joseph H Jamison
mother: Eleanor Jamison
1870 US Census, Colorado Territory, Boulder County, St Vrain District

Jamison, Eleanor
b. abt 1824, KY
spouse: Joseph H Jamison
1870 US Census, Colorado Territory, Boulder County, St Vrain District

Jamison, Francis Van Doren
b. 24 Oct 1857, MO
d. 26 Mar 1915
bd. Lyons Cemetery, Lyons, Boulder, CO
father: Joseph H Jamison
mother: Eleanor Jamison
1870 US Census, Colorado Territory, Boulder County, St Vrain District

Jamison, Harriet Lorinda
b. abt 1863, Colorado Territory
father: Joseph H Jamison
mother: Eleanor Jamison
1870 US Census, Colorado Territory, Boulder County, St Vrain District

Jamison, James L
b. abt 1850, MO
spouse: Amanda B Keller Jamison
father: Joseph H Jamison
mother: Eleanor Jamison
1870 US Census, Colorado Territory, Boulder County, St Vrain District

Jamison, John Milborn
b. abt 1865, Colorado Territory
d. 26 Oct 1876
bd. Columbia Cemetery, Boulder, CO
father: Joseph H Jamison
mother: Eleanor Jamison
1870 US Census, Colorado Territory, Boulder County, St Vrain District

Jamison, Joseph H
b. abt 1823, KY
spouse: Eleanor Jamison
St Vrain Pioneers Assn Arrival Date: [not recorded]
1870 US Census, Colorado Territory, Boulder County, St Vrain District

Jamison, Rufus C
b. abt 1858, MO
father: Joseph H Jamison
mother: Eleanor Jamison
1870 US Census, Colorado Territory, Boulder County, St Vrain District

Jemes, Elisabeth
b. abt 1832, MO
father: Henry H Jemes
mother: Manerva Jemes
1870 US Census, Colorado Territory, Boulder County, Left Hand

Jemes, Henry H
b. abt 1832, MO
spouse: Manerva Jemes
1870 US Census, Colorado Territory, Boulder County, Left Hand

Jemes, Manerva
b. abt 1836, NC
spouse: Henry H Jemes
1870 US Census, Colorado Territory, Boulder County, Left Hand

Jemes, Martha E
b. abt 1865, MO
father: Henry H Jemes
mother: Manerva Jemes
1870 US Census, Colorado Territory, Boulder County, Left Hand

St Vrain Valley Pioneers

Jemes, Montgomery
b. abt 1858, MO
father: Henry H Jemes
mother: Manerva Jemes
1870 US Census, Colorado Territory, Boulder County, Left Hand

Jensen, Gertrude Isabella Peck
b. abt 1870, Colorado Territory
spouse: Robert Jensen
father: Thomas Samuel Peck
mother: Susan Edmund Walthall Peck
1870 US Census, Colorado Territory, Boulder County, St Vrain District

Jinks, Julius
b. abt 1819, NY
1870 US Census, Colorado Territory, Boulder County, St Vrain District

Johnson, A W
St Vrain Pioneers Assn Arrival Date: 1869

Johnson, Amanda
b. abt 1868, IL
father: Carl August Johnson
mother: Anna Sophia Jonsdotter Johnson
St Vrain Pioneers Assn Arrival Date: 1869
1870 US Census, Colorado Territory, Boulder County, Left Hand

Johnson, Amelia
b. abt 1843, OH
spouse: David Johnson
1870 US Census, Colorado Territory, Boulder County, Left Hand

Johnson, Andrew William
b. 14 Sept 1843
d. 8 Sept 1922, Longmont, Boulder, CO
bd. Mountain View Cemetery, Longmont, Boulder, CO
spouse: Christina Larson Johnson

Johnson, Anna Sophia Jonsdotter
b. 15 Oct 1835, Sweden
d. 7 May 1905, Longmont, Boulder, CO
bd. Mountain View Cemetery, Longmont, Boulder, CO
spouse: Carl August Johnson
father: Jonas Nilsson
mother: Stina Svensdotter
St Vrain Pioneers Assn Arrival Date: 1869
1870 US Census, Colorado Territory, Boulder County, Left Hand

Johnson, August
St Vrain Pioneers Assn Arrival Date: 1869

Johnson, Bengt Mason
b. 28 Jan 1842
d. 26 Apr 1908, Ryssby, Boulder, CO
bd. Ryssby Cemetery, Boulder, CO
spouse: Eva Charlotta Erickson Johnson

Johnson, Bertha May Goss
b. 12 May 1869, Goss Homestead, Boulder, CO
d. 24 Apr 1964, Parma, Cannon, Idaho
spouse: Francis Lee Berry Johnson
father: John Wesley Goss
mother: Ellen Olcott Goss
1870 US Census, Colorado Territory, Boulder County, St Vrain District

Johnson, Capitola Lazella
b. abt 1869, Colorado Territory
father: Harvey Johnson
mother: Elisabeth Johnson
1870 US Census, Colorado Territory, Boulder County, St Vrain District

Johnson, Carl August
b. 21 Oct 1832, Parish of Saby, Smaland, Sweden
d. 4 Aug 1898, Pueblo, CO
bd. Roselawn Cemetery, Pueblo, CO
spouse: Anna Sophia Jonsdotter Johnson
father: Johan Jonsson
mother: Stina Nilsdotter Jonsson
1870 US Census, Colorado Territory, Boulder County, Left Hand

Johnson, Christine
b. abt 1820, NY
spouse: Joshua Johnson
1870 US Census, Colorado Territory, Boulder County, Left Hand

Johnson, Chrstina Larson
b. 10 Sept 1844, Sweden
d. 24 June 1912, Longmont, Boulder, CO
spouse: Andrew William Johnson
father: Lars Jonsson
mother: Kerstin Nilsdotter

Johnson, daughter of August
St Vrain Pioneers Assn Arrival Date: 1869

Johnson, David
b. abt 1837, NY
spouse: Amelia Johnson
1870 US Census, Colorado Territory, Boulder County, Left Hand

Johnson, Elizabeth
b. abt 1830, VA
spouse: Harvey Johnson
1870 US Census, Colorado Territory, Boulder County, St Vrain District

Johnson, Ella Cordelia Barney
b. 10 Oct 1865, White Rock, Boulder, Colorado Territory
d. 29 Mar 1922, Denver, CO
spouse: Andrew Lucien Johnson
father: William M Barney
mother: Malissa J Rannels Willson Barney
1870 US Census, Colorado Territory, Boulder County, St Vrain District

Johnson, Frank J
b. 4 Dec 1889
d. 14 Apr 1968
bd. Mountain View Memorial Park, Boulder, CO
spouse: Helen C Johnson
father: Nelson Magne Johnson
mother: Eva Parsons Johnson

Johnson, H
St Vrain Land Club Date: 1861 July 29

Johnson, Hannah
St Vrain Pioneers Assn Arrival Date: 1869

Johnson, Harvey/Henry
b. abt 1832, England
spouse: Elisabeth Johnson
1870 US Census, Colorado Territory, Boulder County, St Vrain District

Johnson, Joshua P
b. abt 1818, OH
d. 26 Sept 1897
bd. Niwot Cemetery, Niwot, Boulder, CO
spouse: Christine Johnson
St Vrain Pioneers Assn Arrival Date: 1863
1870 US Census, Colorado Territory, Boulder County, Left Hand

Johnson, Lottie
St Vrain Pioneers Assn Arrival Date: 1869

Johnson, Mrs A W
St Vrain Pioneers Assn Arrival Date: 1869

Johnson, Mrs August
spouse: August Johnson
St Vrain Pioneers Assn Arrival Date: 1869

Johnson, Mrs Swan
St Vrain Pioneers Assn Arrival Date: 1869

Johnson, Nathaniel D
b. abt 1860, IA
father: Joshua Johnson
mother: Christine Johnson
St Vrain Pioneers Assn Arrival Date: 1860
1870 US Census, Colorado Territory, Boulder County, Left Hand

Johnson, Peter J
b. 16 Dec 1833, Ryssby, Sweden
d. 30 Jan 1916, Boulder, CO
bd. Columbia Cemetery, Boulder, CO
spouse: Maga Stiena Nelson Johnson
St Vrain Pioneers Assn Arrival Date: 1868

Johnson, Susan J Thompson Barker Luther
b. 8 Nov 1834, Lunenberg, Essex, VT
d. 19 March 1921, Boulder, CO
bd. Green Mountain Cemetery, Boulder, CO
spouse: Thomas Cunningham Johnson, O A Luther, Andrew Barker

Johnson, Swan
St Vrain Pioneers Assn Arrival Date: 1869

Johnston, Estelle R Romigh
b. 10 June 1909, Omaha, Douglas, NE
d. 9 July 1979, Longmont, Boulder, CO
bd. Mountain View Cemetery, Longmont, Boulder, CO
spouse: Raymond Charles Johnston
father: Chester Arthur Romigh
mother: Lula May Newby Romigh

Johnston, Raymond Charles
b. 10 Nov 1907, Longmont, Boulder, CO
d. 11 July 1982
bd. Mountain View Cemetery, Longmont, Boulder, CO
spouse: Estelle R Romigh Johnston

St Vrain Valley Pioneers

father: George Washington Johnston
mother: Margaret A Lucas Johnston

Johnston, Zelda Ruth Biederman
b. Oct 1891, Weld, CO
d. 1967, Longmont, Boulder, CO
bd. Mountain View Cemetery, Longmont, Boulder, CO
spouse: Solomon Lee Johnston
father: Joseph Biderman, Jr
mother: Rosetta Mayfield Biederman

Jones, Daniel
b. abt 1841, PA
spouse: Margaret Jones
1870 US Census, Colorado Territory, Weld County, St Vrain District

Jones, Elisabeth
b. abt 1819, Wales
spouse: William P Jones
1870 US Census, Colorado Territory, Boulder County, Left Hand

Jones, family of James
father: James F Jones
mother: Sarah Catherine Jones
St Vrain Pioneers Assn Arrival Date: 1859

Jones, Florence
b. abt 1864, Colorado Territory
father: Daniel Jones
mother: Margaret Jones
1870 US Census, Colorado Territory, Weld County, St Vrain District

Jones, J N
St Vrain Pioneers Assn Arrival Date: 1860

Jones, J Y
St Vrain Land Club (M687) Date: 1859 Oct 13

Jones, James
b. abt 1866, Colorado Territory
father: Daniel Jones
mother: Margaret Jones
1870 US Census, Colorado Territory, Weld County, St Vrain District
Jones, James F
spouse: Sarah Catherine Jones
St Vrain Pioneers Assn Arrival Date: 1859

Jones, James N
b. 1 Jan 1837, Fayette, PA
d. 11 June 1888, Longmont, Boulder, CO
bd. Mountain View Cemetery, Longmont, Boulder, CO
spouse: Mary Bailey Jones
1870 US Census, Colorado Territory, Boulder County, St Vrain District

Jones, John
b. Nov 1869, Colorado Territory
father: James N Jones
mother: Mary Jones
1870 US Census, Colorado Territory, Boulder County, St Vrain District

Jones, Lewella Montana Orvis
b. 10 May 1862, Colorado Territory
d. 25 July 1945, Petaluma, Sonoma, CA
spouse: Hiram Randolf Jones
father: Harrison Fletcher Orvis
mother: Joanna C Corbin Orvis
1870 US Census, Colorado Territory, Boulder County, St Vrain District

Jones, Margaret
b. abt 1839, Sweden
spouse: Daniel Jones
1870 US Census, Colorado Territory, Weld County, St Vrain District

Jones, Mary
b. abt 1849, OH
spouse: James N Jones
1870 US Census, Colorado Territory, Boulder County, St Vrain District

Jones, Mrs J N
spouse: J N Jones
St Vrain Pioneers Assn Arrival Date: 1862

Jones, Reese
b. abt 1860, WI
d. Oct 1908, CA
father: William P Jones
mother: Elisabeth Jones
1870 US Census, Colorado Territory, Boulder County, Left Hand

Jones, Sarah Catherine
b. abt 1846, IA
spouse: James F Jones
St Vrain Pioneers Assn Arrival Date: 1859

Jones, Watkin
b. abt 1858, WI
father: William P Jones
mother: Elisabeth Jones
1870 US Census, Colorado Territory, Boulder County, Left Hand

Jones, William
b. abt 1856, WI
father: William P Jones
mother: Elisabeth Jones
1870 US Census, Colorado Territory, Boulder County, Left Hand

Jones, William P
b. abt 1818, Wales
d. 30 Sept 1873, Left Hand, Boulder, CO
bd. Columbia Cemetery, Boulder, CO
spouse: Elisabeth Jones
1870 US Census, Colorado Territory, Boulder County, Left Hand

Jones, William W
St Vrain Pioneers Assn Arrival Date: 1859

Jordan, Jacob
b. abt 1842, Switzerland
1870 US Census, Colorado Territory, Boulder County, Left Hand

K

Kearns, James K
St Vrain Pioneers Assn Arrival Date: 1870

Kearns, Mrs James K
St Vrain Pioneers Assn Arrival Date: 1870

Keatley, Joseph
St Vrain Pioneers Assn Arrival Date: 1867

Keen, Amos
b. abt 1852, NE Terr
1870 US Census, Colorado Territory, Boulder County, St Vrain District

Keen, James
b. abt 1828, ME
1870 US Census, Colorado Territory, Boulder County, St Vrain District

Keen, John F
b. abt 1839
d. 23 Jan 1880
bd. Hygiene Cemetery, Hygiene, Boulder, CO
spouse: Anna D Gilman Keen
St Vrain Pioneers Assn Arrival Date: 1864
1870 US Census, Colorado Territory, Boulder County, St Vrain District

Keep, Hattie A Mills Potter Calkins
b. 18 June 1843
d. 8 Aug 1923, MI
bd. Rice Cemetery, What Cheer, Keokuk, IA
spouse: Potter, Calkins, Asa Hugh Keep
father: Ezra James Mills
mother: Dorothy Wood Mills
St Vrain Pioneers Assn Arrival Date: 1868

Keith, John
b. abt 1840, OH
1870 US Census, Colorado Territory, Weld County, St Vrain District

Kelley, Ronald Clay
b. 1 Aug 1958
d. 29 Nov 1981
bd. Foothills Garden of Memory, Longmont, Boulder, CO
mother: JoAnne Thomas Kelley

Kellogg, Agnes Euphemia Greenly
b. 1 Feb 1858, Lockport, Will, IL
d. 13 Sept 1893, Fruita, Mesa, CO
spouse: Marvin Erford Kellogg
father: Jesse Greenly
mother: Malissa Greenly
1870 US Census, Colorado Territory, Boulder County, St Vrain District

Kelly, Abraham
b. abt 1866, Colorado Territory
father: William Kelly
mother: Chrissie Kelly
1870 US Census, Colorado Territory, Weld County, St Vrain District

Kelly, Chrissie
b. abt 1830, TN
spouse: William Kelly

St Vrain Valley Pioneers

1870 US Census, Colorado Territory, Weld County, St Vrain District

Kelly, David
b. abt 1851, IN
father: William Kelly
mother: Chrissie Kelly
1870 US Census, Colorado Territory, Weld County, St Vrain District

Kelly, Georgiana
b. abt 1866, Colorado Territory
father: William Kelly
mother: Chrissie Kelly
1870 US Census, Colorado Territory, Weld County, St Vrain District

Kelly, James W
b. abt 1858, IN
father: William Kelly
mother: Chrissie Kelly
1870 US Census, Colorado Territory, Weld County, St Vrain District

Kelly, Mary A
b. abt 1869, Colorado Territory
father: William Kelly
mother: Chrissie Kelly
1870 US Census, Colorado Territory, Weld County, St Vrain District

Kelly, Mary J
b. abt 1856, IN
father: William Kelly
mother: Chrissie Kelly
1870 US Census, Colorado Territory, Weld County, St Vrain District

Kelly, William
b. abt 1818, KY
spouse: Chrissie Kelly
1870 US Census, Colorado Territory, Weld County, St Vrain District

Kelly, William N
b. abt 1835, NY
1860 US Census, Nebraska Territory, Platte River

Kelly, William Q
b. abt 1864, Colorado Territory
father: William Kelly
mother: Chrissie Kelly
1870 US Census, Colorado Territory, Weld County, St Vrain District

Kelsay, Harriet Westcott Sheppard
b. 1816, NJ
d. 1 Feb 1901
bd. Kossler Ranch, Boulder, CO
spouse: James S Kelsay
1870 US Census, Colorado Territory, Boulder County, St Vrain District

Kelsay, James Sheppard
b. 30 Sept 1815, Cohansey, Cumberland, NJ
d. 2 Feb 1877, Boulder, CO
bd. Kossler Ranch, Boulder, CO
spouse: Harriet Westcott Sheppard Kelsay
father: Daniel Kelsay
mother: Hannah B Sheppard Kelsay
1870 US Census, Colorado Territory, Boulder County, St Vrain District

Kelsay, Joseph Lafayette
b. 10 Apr 1857, Edwardsville, Mason, IL
d. 25 Sept 1924, Weed, Siskiyou, CA
spouse: Martha Ellen Marcus Kelsay; Lenora Turner Kelsay
father: James Sheppard Kelsay
mother: Harriet Westcott Sheppard Kelsey
1870 US Census, Colorado Territory, Boulder County, St Vrain District

Kempton, Francis Henry
b. 2 Apr 1863, Georgetown, Clear Creek, Colorado Territory
d. 5 Jan 1922, Longmont, Boulder, CO
bd. Mountain View Cemetery, Longmont, CO
father: James Kempton
mother: Delphine Casteline Day Kempton

Kempton, James
d. 11 Mar 1911, Longmont, CO
St Vrain Pioneers Assn Arrival Date: 1870

Kempton, Mrs D C
St Vrain Pioneers Assn Arrival Date: 1864

Kempton, Mrs James
b. abt 1840
d. 23 Jan 1911, Longmont, CO
St Vrain Pioneers Assn Arrival Date: 1870

Kent, Catherine Maddux
b. 24 Mar 1843, Vallier, Wert, OH
d. 11 Mar 1907
bd. Green Lawn Cemetery, Rich Hill, Bates, MO
spouse: Jesse Harrison Kent
father: Peter Maddux
mother: Jemina Stults Maddux Armstrong
St Vrain Pioneers Assn Arrival Date: [not recorded]

Kesner, Mary Downer
b. 1885
d. 1967
bd. Mountain View Cemetery, Longmont, Boulder, CO
spouse: Henry James Kesner
father: Francis Mott Downer
mother: Mabel Clare Fox Downer

Key, Eliza Alice Beasley
b. 23 June 1859, Prairie, Schuyler, MO
d. 1 May 1945, Longmont, Boulder, CO
bd. Burlington Cemetery, Longmont, Boulder, CO
spouse: George Franklin Key
father: James Jackson Beasley
mother: Eliza Jones Beasley
St Vrain Pioneers Assn Arrival Date: 1863

Key, George Frank
b. 28 Mar 1841
d. 24 Dec 1895
bd. Burlington Cemetery, Longmont, Boulder, CO
spouse: Alice Key
St Vrain Pioneers Assn Arrival Date: 1866

Kimbers, Ama
b. abt 1854, PA
father: Andrew Kimbers
mother: Savilla Kimbers
1870 US Census, Colorado Territory, Boulder County, St Vrain District

Kimbers, Andrew
b. abt 1834, PA
spouse: Savilla Kimbers
1870 US Census, Colorado Territory, Boulder County, St Vrain District

Kimbers, Savilla
b. abt 1835, PA
1870 US Census, Colorado Territory, Boulder County, St Vrain District

King, H C
St Vrain Land Club Date: 1861 May 16

King, H E
St Vrain Land Club Date: 1861 Feb 15

Kinney, Edward Prentiss
b. 30 Apr 1839, Prattsburg, Steuben, NY
d. 12 Feb 1870, Burlington, Boulder, Colorado Territory
bd. Burlington Cemetery, Longmont, Boulder, CO
spouse: Tryphenia Baker Hutchin Kinney Smith
father: Norman Kinney
mother: Clarissa Prentiss Kinney
St Vrain Pioneers Assn Arrival Date: 1860

Kipp, Johnson
b. abt 1840, OH
1870 US Census, Colorado Territory, Boulder County, St Vrain District

Knaus, Clemens
b. 21 Nov 1843, Hohenzollern, Germany
d. 8 Jan 1914, Niwot, Boulder, CO
bd. Burlington Cemetery, Longmont, Boulder, CO
spouse: Eliza Alice Greub Bader Knaus
St Vrain Pioneers Assn Arrival Date: 1866
1870 US Census, Colorado Territory, Boulder County, Left Hand

Knaus, Daniel
b. 1 Mar 1890, Niwot, Boulder, CO
d. 9 Apr 1980, Longmont, Boulder, CO
bd. Mountain View Memorial Park, Boulder, CO
spouse: Lillian Almedia Wederquist Knaus; Rozella LaVerghn Rimer Knaus
father: Clemens Knaus
mother: Eliza Alice Greub Bader Knaus

Knaus, Earl Clemens
b. 21 Feb 1905, Niwot, Boulder, CO
d. 8 Oct 1998, Boulder, CO
bd. Mountain View Memorial Park, Boulder, CO
spouse: Sylvia Esther Finleon Knaus
father: Clemens Edward Knaus
mother: Katherine Ethel Green Knaus

St Vrain Valley Pioneers

Knaus, Eliza Alice Greub Bader
b. 4 Mar 1851, Berne Lotzvil, Switzerland
d. 10 Jan 1935, Niwot, Boulder, CO
bd. Burlington Cemetery, Longmont, Boulder, CO
spouse: Nicholas Earnest Bader, Clemens Knaus
father: Rudolph Greub
mother: Elizabeth Affolter Greub
St Vrain Pioneers Assn Arrival Date: 1864
1870 US Census, Colorado Territory, Boulder County, Left Hand

Knaus, Frederick
b. 19 Feb 1886, Niwot, Boulder, CO
d. 12 Apr 1982, Longmont, Boulder, CO
bd. Mountain View Cemetery, Longmont, Boulder, CO
spouse: Mildred Barnett Dodd Knaus
father: Clemens Knaus
mother: Eliza Alice Greub Bader Knaus

Knaus, Katherine Ethel Green
b. 30 Aug 1885
d. 27 Apr 1968
bd. Burlington Cemetery, Longmont, Boulder, CO
spouse: Clemens Edward Knaus
father: Ephaim Stout Green
mother: Louisa Lucretia Brown Green Massey

Knaus, Mildred Dodd
b. 14 Oct 1896
d. 6 Oct 1967
bd. Mountain View Cemetery, Longmont, Boulder, CO
spouse: Fred Knaus
father: J Harvey Dodd
mother: Mary E Dawson Dodd

Knaus, Sylvia Esther Finleon
b. 10 Jan 1908, Idaho Springs, Clear Creek, CO
d. 10 July 1981, Denver, CO
bd. Mountain View Memorial Park, Boulder, CO
spouse: Earl Clemens Knaus
father: Patrick Joseph Finleon
mother: Jessie May Benson Finleon

Kneale, Georgia Hatfield
St Vrain Pioneers Assn Arrival Date: 1860

Kneale, Idell Marie
b. 1894
d. 1968
bd. Mountain View Cemetery, Longmont, Boulder, CO

Kneen, James
b. abt 1832, GA
1860 US Census, Nebraska Territory, Platte River

Knoop, John
b. 30 Mar 1809, OH
d. 20 Aug 1886
1870 US Census, Colorado Territory, Boulder County, St Vrain District

Knutson, Betty Jane
b. 8 June 1920
d. 11 Nov 1967
bd. Foothills Garden of Memory, Longmont, Boulder, CO
spouse: William Russell Knutson

Knutson, Charles Herman
b. 28 June 1878, Douglass, NE
d. Mar 1967
bd. Mountain View Cemetery, Longmont, Boulder, CO
spouse: Emma F Gould Knutson
mother: Annie Christena Paulson Nelson

Knutson, Warren
b. 14 Aug 1921
d. 13 Nov 1981
bd. Foothills Garden of Memory, Longmont, Boulder, CO
spouse: Betty Jane Knutson
father: Charles Herman Knutson
mother: Emma F Gould Knutson

Kohler, Frederick W
b. 24 Oct 1832, Saxony, Germany
d. 13 Oct 1904, Boulder, CO
bd. Columbia Cemetery, Boulder, CO
spouse: Rosetta Viele Kohler
father: Frederick Kohler
mother: Christina Kohler
St Vrain Pioneers Assn Arrival Date: 1859

Kohler, Rosetta Viele
b. 14 Oct 1848, Stephenson, IL
d. 25 Oct 1919, Boulder, CO
bd. Columbia Cemetery, Boulder, CO
spouse: Frederick W Kohler, Sr
father: James Boyd Viele

mother: Lucinda Emerson Viele
St Vrain Pioneers Assn Arrival Date: 1859

L

Lacroy, Varus
b. abt 1839, Canada
1870 US Census, Colorado Territory, Boulder County, St Vrain District

Lagerman, Frederick
St Vrain Ditch Owner: Lagerman Supply Ditch No. 80, 14 Nov 1879

Lagrasse, John
b. abt 1838, NY
1870 US Census, Colorado Territory, Boulder County, St Vrain District

Lake, Arther
b. abt 1847, OH
1870 US Census, Colorado Territory, Weld County, St Vrain District

Lamb, Caroline
b. abt 1820, England
1860 US Census, Nebraska Territory, Platte River

Lamb, Elijah J
St Vrain Pioneers Assn Arrival Date: 1860

Lamb, Elizabeth
b. abt 1844, England
1860 US Census, Nebraska Territory, Platte River

Lamb, Ella
b. abt 1858, WI
1860 US Census, Nebraska Territory, Platte River

Lamb, F
b. abt 1854, England
1860 US Census, Nebraska Territory, Platte River

Lamb, Frederick
b. abt 1831, England
1860 US Census, Nebraska Territory, Platte River

Lamb, Thomas
b. abt 1848, England
1860 US Census, Nebraska Territory, Platte River

Lamberson, A
St Vrain Land Club (M687) Date: 1861 Apr 3

Lamson, Louise
b. abt 1841, NY
1870 US Census, Colorado Territory, Boulder County, St Vrain District

Lane, Albert D
b. 1842
d. 1938
bd. Fairmount Cemetery, Denver, CO
spouse: Mary E Lane
St Vrain Pioneers Assn Arrival Date: 1867

Lang, Joseph
b. abt 1845, IN
1870 US Census, Colorado Territory, Boulder County, St Vrain District

Langford, Mr
St Vrain Pioneers Assn Arrival Date: 1859

Lanier, Charles
St Vrain Pioneers Assn Arrival Date: 1866

Larison, George M
b. 12 Oct 1830, Westmoreland, PA
d. 12 June 1897, Boulder, CO
bd. Columbia Cemetery, Boulder, CO

Laroche, Medor
b. abt 1845, Canada
1870 US Census, Colorado Territory, Boulder County, St Vrain District

Larson, Andrew Peter
b. 1831, Sweden
d. 3 Oct 1904
bd. Columbia Cemetery, Boulder, CO

Larson, John
St Vrain Pioneers Assn Arrival Date: 1869

Larson, Mrs John
spouse: John Larson
St Vrain Pioneers Assn Arrival Date: 1869

Larson, Mrs Pete
spouse: Pete Larson
St Vrain Pioneers Assn Arrival Date: 1869

Larson, Pete
St Vrain Pioneers Assn Arrival Date: 1869

Lartson, George
b. abt 1833, PA
1870 US Census, Colorado Territory, Boulder County, St Vrain District

St Vrain Valley Pioneers

Larwing, Harley
St Vrain Land Club Date: 1861 May 29

Latham, G C/O
St Vrain Land Club Date: 1861 Apr 17

Latto, J A
St Vrain Land Club Date: 1861 Aug 15

Latto, S G
St Vrain Land Club Date: 1861 Aug 15

Laughlin, John
b. 1883
d. 7 Nov 1967
bd. Green Mountain Cemetery, Boulder, CO
spouse: Maude Gooding Laughlin
father: William Laughlin
mother: Mary Aiken Laughlin Burt

Laws, Ida Mae Dow
b. 9 June 1855, Prince William, VA
d. 1896, Los Angeles, CA
spouse: William Harrison Laws
father: James E Dow
mother: Charlotte Moore Dow
1870 US Census, Colorado Territory, Boulder County, St Vrain District

Lawson, Hester
b. abt 1864, IA
father: John Lawson
mother: Mary Lawson
1870 US Census, Colorado Territory, Boulder County, St Vrain District

Lawson, John W
b. abt 1835, NY
spouse: Mary Lawson
1870 US Census, Colorado Territory, Boulder County, St Vrain District

Lawson, Mary
b. abt 1840, IN
spouse: John Lawson
1870 US Census, Colorado Territory, Boulder County, St Vrain District
Lawson, William
b. abt 1862, IN
father: John Lawson
mother: Mary Lawson
1870 US Census, Colorado Territory, Boulder County, St Vrain District

Lea, Alfred Erskine
b. 25 Mar 1845, Cleveland, Bradley, TN
d. 16 Aug 1909, Los Angeles, CA
bd. Lee's Summit Historical Cemetery, MO, Jackson
spouse: Hersa A Coberly Lea, Emma Rice Wilson Lea
father: Pleasant John Graves Lea
mother: Lucinda Frances Callaway Lea
1870 US Census, Colorado Territory, Boulder County, St Vrain District

Leahy, Caroline Leach Brown Hill
b. 20 Sept 1834, NY
d. 23 Apr 1917, Boulder, CO
bd. Columbia Cemetery, Boulder, CO
spouse: Nathan Brown; Thomas J Hill; John C Leahy
father: Joseph Leach
mother: Lucy Leach
1870 US Census, Colorado Territory, Boulder County, St Vrain District

Lee, John Braxton
b. 11 Dec 1839, Vernon, Jennings, IN
d. 24 Feb 1919, Pueblo, CO
spouse: Margaret Ann Miller Lee
father: Joseph Lee
mother: Malinda Lee
1870 US Census, Colorado Territory, Boulder County, St Vrain District

Lee, Margaret Ann Miller
b. 9 May 1851, Greenbrier, WV
d. 17 June 1908, Cortez, Montezuma, CO
spouse: John Braxton Lee
father: Michael Christ Miller
mother: Isabel Agnes Honaker Miller Armstrong
1870 US Census, Colorado Territory, Boulder County, St Vrain District

Lee, Marion
St Vrain Pioneers Assn Arrival Date: 1858

Lee, William
b. abt 1842, NY
spouse: Mary A Hart Lee
1870 US Census, Colorado Territory, Boulder County, St Vrain District

St Vrain Valley Pioneers

Leech, D H
 b. abt 1836, PA
 1860 US Census, Nebraska Territory, Platte River

Leggett, Augusta Mary Hinman
 b. 3 Mar 1843, Coshocton, OH
 d. 27 Jan 1929, Boulder, CO
 bd. Columbia Cemetery, Boulder, CO
 spouse: Jeremiah Leggett
 father: Porter Timothy Hinman
 mother: Mary A Smith Hinman
 St Vrain Pioneers Assn Arrival Date: 1866

Leggett, Jeremiah
 b. 16 May 1837, Licking, OH
 d. 4 Sept 1916, Boulder, CO
 bd. Columbia Cemetery, Boulder, CO
 spouse: Augusta Mary Hinman Leggett
 father: James Leggett
 mother: Elizabeth Younger Leggett
 St Vrain Pioneers Assn Arrival Date: 1869

Leonard, Horace
 b. abt 1833, VT
 spouse: Emma Leonard
 St Vrain Pioneers Assn Arrival Date: 1859

Leshky, F
 b. abt 1831, Saxony, Germany
 1860 US Census, Nebraska Territory, Platte River

Lewis, Henry E
 b. abt 1838, OH
 1870 US Census, Colorado Territory, Weld County, St Vrain District

Lewis, Mattie
 d. 1929
 spouse: John D Lewis

Lewis, William J
 Troy District Land Club Claim Date: 1861 Mar 22

Leyner, Mary
 spouse: Peter A Leyner
 St Vrain Pioneers Assn Arrival Date: 1860

Leyner, Peter A
 b. 16 Nov 1822, Holland
 d. 13 Nov 1907
 bd. Columbia Cemetery, Boulder, CO
 spouse: Mary Leyner
 St Vrain Pioneers Assn Arrival Date: 1860
 1860 US Census, Nebraska Territory, Altona

Likely, H M
 b. abt 1834, IN
 1860 US Census, Nebraska Territory, Platte River

Lippold, Henry
 b. abt 1848, Saxony, Germany
 1870 US Census, Colorado Territory, Boulder County, St Vrain District

Lockhard, Ira
 St Vrain Pioneers Assn Arrival Date: 1860
 St Vrain Ditch Owner: Hayseed Ditch No. 1, 1 Jan 1860

Longdon, Jesse
 St Vrain Pioneers Assn Arrival Date: 1864

Longdon, William
 St Vrain Pioneers Assn Arrival Date: 1864

Lormer, James
 b. abt 1816, NJ
 spouse: Lydia Lormer
 1870 US Census, Colorado Territory, Boulder County, St Vrain District

Lormer, Lydia
 b. abt 1816, PA
 spouse: James Lormer
 1870 US Census, Colorado Territory, Boulder County, St Vrain District

Lorton, Thomas
 b. abt 1835, IL
 St Vrain Pioneers Assn Arrival Date: 1858

Louders, Peter J
 St Vrain Land Club (M687) Date: 1861 July 4

Lovejoy, Catherine Wakely Allen
 b. abt 1841, Streator, LaSalle, IL
 d. June 1871, Boulder, Colorado Territory
 spouse: Elijah V Lovejoy
 father: Perkins Allen
 mother: Roxena Sagal Allen
 St Vrain Pioneers Assn Arrival Date: 1867

Lovejoy, Elijah V
 b. 22 Aug 1833, NY
 d. 21 Sept 1918, Berthoud, Larimer, CO
 bd. Greenlawn Cemetery, Larimer, CO
 spouse: Katherine Wakely Allen Lovejoy, Mrs Wolfe Lovejoy, Mary Godfrey Lovejoy
 St Vrain Pioneers Assn Arrival Date: 1859

St Vrain Valley Pioneers

Lovell, Clarissa
b. abt 1858, MN
father: Lyman Lovell
mother: Louisa J Lovell
1870 US Census, Colorado Territory, Boulder County, St Vrain District

Lovell, Eliza
b. abt 1863, MN
father: Lyman Lovell
mother: Louisa J Lovell
1870 US Census, Colorado Territory, Boulder County, St Vrain District

Lovell, George
b. abt 1863, MN
father: Lyman Lovell
mother: Louisa J Lovell
1870 US Census, Colorado Territory, Boulder County, St Vrain District

Lovell, Louisa J
b. abt 1843, IN
spouse: Lyman Lovell
1870 US Census, Colorado Territory, Boulder County, St Vrain District

Lovell, Lyman
b. abt 1819, OH
spouse: Louisa J Lovell
1870 US Census, Colorado Territory, Boulder County, St Vrain District

Lovell, Melinda C
b. abt 1866, MN
father: Lyman Lovell
mother: Louisa J Lovell
1870 US Census, Colorado Territory, Boulder County, St Vrain District

Lovell, Oliver
b. abt 1856, MN
father: Lyman Lovell
mother: Louisa J Lovell
1870 US Census, Colorado Territory, Boulder County, St Vrain District

Lovell, Sheridan
b. Nov 1869, MN
father: Lyman Lovell
mother: Louisa J Lovell
1870 US Census, Colorado Territory, Boulder County, St Vrain District

Lovell, Sherman
b. Nov 1869, MN
father: Lyman Lovell
mother: Louisa J Lovell
1870 US Census, Colorado Territory, Boulder County, St Vrain District

Lovett, Joseph
b. abt 1847, England
1870 US Census, Colorado Territory, Boulder County, St Vrain District

Low, Eugene S
b. abt 1845, ME
1870 US Census, Colorado Territory, Boulder County, Left Hand

Lowe, P G
St Vrain Land Club (M687) Date: 1859 Oct 6

Lowe, Roger S
b. abt 1820, ME
d. by 1876
St Vrain Land Club Date: 1861 Aug 9

Loy, Emma
b. abt 1860, IL
father: William Loy
mother: Rosina Loy
1870 US Census, Colorado Territory, Boulder County, St Vrain District

Loy, Hattie
b. abt 1857, IL
father: William Loy
mother: Rosina Loy
1870 US Census, Colorado Territory, Boulder County, St Vrain District

Loy, Inez
b. abt 1862, IL
father: William Loy
mother: Rosina Loy
1870 US Census, Colorado Territory, Boulder County, St Vrain District

Loy, Mary
b. abt 1858, IL
father: William Loy
mother: Rosina Loy

1870 US Census, Colorado Territory, Boulder County, St Vrain District

Loy, Rosina
b. abt 1831, NY
spouse: William Loy
1870 US Census, Colorado Territory, Boulder County, St Vrain District

Loy, William
b. abt 1820, NY
spouse: Rosina Loy
1870 US Census, Colorado Territory, Boulder County, St Vrain District

Lucas, George W
b. abt 1844, KY
1870 US Census, Colorado Territory, Weld County, St Vrain District

Luis, Arthur C
b. abt 1834, NY
spouse: Harriet Luis
1860 US Census, Nebraska Territory, Platte River

Luis, Harriet
b. abt 1841, England
spouse: Arthur C Luis
1860 US Census, Nebraska Territory, Platte River

Luther, Mr
St Vrain Pioneers Assn Arrival Date: 1860

Luther, Samuel
St Vrain Pioneers Assn Arrival Date: 1867

Luther, Samuel O
b. abt 1844, RI
1870 US Census, Colorado Territory, Weld County, St Vrain District

Lycan, James
St Vrain Pioneers Assn Arrival Date: [not recorded]

Lykins, Ann Gilman Keen
spouse: John Keen, David Johnson Lykins
St Vrain Pioneers Assn Arrival Date: 1869

Lykins, David Johnson
b. abt 1851, IL
spouse: Ann Gillman Keen Lykins
St Vrain Pioneers Assn Arrival Date: 1859
1870 US Census, Colorado Territory, Boulder County, St Vrain District

Lynn, John
b. abt 1830, NY
1860 US Census, Nebraska Territory, Platte River

Lytle, George C
b. 27 Oct 1824, Washington Twp, Delaware, OH
d. 24 Sept 1897
bd. Columbia Cemetery, Boulder, CO
spouse: Mary Wood Lytle; Mary Jane Smith McAllister Lytle
father: James Lytle
mother: Mary Sturdevant Lytle
1870 US Census, Colorado Territory, Boulder County, St Vrain District

M

Mack, Henry
b. 28 Nov 1843, OH
d. 22 Oct 1885
bd. Gold Hill Cemetery, Gold Hill, Boulder, CO
spouse: Nellie Mack; Annie M Huberty Mack
1870 US Census, Colorado Territory, Boulder County, St Vrain District

Mack, Nellie
b. abt 1842, WI
spouse: Henry Mack
1870 US Census, Colorado Territory, Boulder County, St Vrain District

Maddux, Dallas D
b. abt 1857, Coldwater, Branch, MI
father: Peter Maddux
mother: Jemina Stults Maddux
St Vrain Pioneers Assn Arrival Date: [not recorded]

Maddux, Israel Oliver
b. 22 July 1859, Coldwater, Branch, MI
d. 9 Nov 1944, Las Vegas, San Miguel, NM
spouse: Ludia Jane Rutherford Maddux; Beatrice Crouch Maddux
father: Peter Maddux
mother: Jemina Stults Maddux
St Vrain Pioneers Assn Arrival Date: [not recorded]

St Vrain Valley Pioneers

Maddux, James Thomas
spouse: Mary Elizabeth Shock Maddux
father: Peter Maddux
mother: Jamima Stults Maddux Armstrong
St Vrain Pioneers Assn Arrival Date: [not recorded]

Maddux, Jemima
spouse: Peter Maddux
St Vrain Pioneers Assn Arrival Date: [not recorded]

Maddux, John Stultz
b. 24 Dec 1844, Vallier, Wert, OH
d. 20 Sept 1912, Denver, CO
bd. Riverside Cemetery, Denver, CO
spouse: Sophie Teresa Robinson Maddux
father: Peter Maddux
mother: Jemina Stults Maddux Armstrong
St Vrain Pioneers Assn Arrival Date: [not recorded]

Maddux, Peter
b. abt 1818, Pickaway, OH
d. Feb 1878, San Antonio, Bexar, TX
spouse: Jemina Stults Maddux Armstrong
father: James T Maddux
mother: Sarah Watson Maddux
St Vrain Pioneers Assn Arrival Date: [not recorded]

Magni, Swan
St Vrain Ditch Owner: Richardson Ditch No. 64, 15 June 1874

Mahoney, Annie Kennicott
b. abt 1849, NY
spouse: John Mahoney
1870 US Census, Colorado Territory, Boulder County, St Vrain District

Mahoney, Dennis
b. abt 1848, NY
spouse: Clara Burch Mahoney
1870 US Census, Colorado Territory, Weld County, St Vrain District

Mahoney, John
b. 1833, MI
d. 14 Mar 1888
bd. Columbia Cemetery, Boulder, CO
spouse: Annie Kennicott Mahoney
1870 US Census, Colorado Territory, Boulder County, St Vrain District

Maier, Elsie Rockwell
b. 1899
d. 1967
bd. Mountain View Cemetery, Longmont, Boulder, CO
spouse: John C Maier
father: Moses Benedict Rockwell
mother: Alice Amelia Sizer Rockwell

Maier, John C
b. 1899
d. 1967
bd. Mountain View Cemetery, Longmont, Boulder, CO
spouse: Elsie Rockwell Maier
father: John Maier
mother: Lillie May Casey Maier

Maloihill, Cynthia
b. abt 1849, OH
spouse: John Maloihill
1870 US Census, Colorado Territory, Weld County, St Vrain District

Maloihill, Frank
b. abt 1869, Colorado Territory
father: John Maloihill
mother: Cynthia Maloihill
1870 US Census, Colorado Territory, Weld County, St Vrain District

Maloihill, John
b. abt 1838, Canada
spouse: Cynthia Maloihill
1870 US Census, Colorado Territory, Weld County, St Vrain District

Manners, Harvey
b. 18 July 1821, Linden, Montgomery, IN
d. 31 Dec 1900, Denver, Adams, CO
bd. Mountain View Cemetery, Longmont, Boulder, CO
spouse: Sarah Oppy Manners
father: James Manners
mother: Letticia Hight Manners
St Vrain Pioneers Assn Arrival Date: 1864

St Vrain Valley Pioneers

Manners, Sarah Oppy
  b. 14 May 1825, Adams, OH
  d. 29 Sept 1899, Denver, Adams, CO
  bd. Mountain View Cemetery, Longmont, Boulder, CO
  spouse: Harvey Manners
  father: David Oppy
  mother: Elizabeth Edwards Oppy
  St Vrain Pioneers Assn Arrival Date: 1864

Manners, T M
  St Vrain Pioneers Assn Arrival Date: 1863

Mariam, John N
  b. abt 1840, MA
  1870 US Census, Colorado Territory, Boulder County, Left Hand

Maris, Herbert
  St Vrain Land Club Date: 1861

Marlough, E
  b. abt 1839, Canada
  1860 US Census, Nebraska Territory, Platte River

Marquardt, Emma E Bennett
  b. 6 July 1853
  d. 29 June 1934
  bd. Columbia Cemetery, Boulder, CO
  spouse: Frank Marquardt
  St Vrain Pioneers Assn Arrival Date: 1869

Marquette, Frank A
  St Vrain Ditch Owner: Smead Ditch No. 13, 1 Oct 1862

Marshall, family of Joseph
  St Vrain Pioneers Assn Arrival Date: 1859

Marshall, Joseph M
  St Vrain Pioneers Assn Arrival Date: 1859

Marshall, Mrs Joseph
  St Vrain Pioneers Assn Arrival Date: 1859

Martin, B
  b. abt 1833, MO
  spouse: M Martin
  1860 US Census, Nebraska Territory, Platte River

Martin, David
  b. abt 1832, NY
  1870 US Census, Colorado Territory, Boulder County, St Vrain District

Martin, Elisabeth
  b. abt 1855, IA
  spouse: Hamilton C Martin
  1870 US Census, Colorado Territory, Boulder County, St Vrain District

Martin, Emory
  b. abt 1835, PA
  d. 21 Mar 1917
  bd. Columbia Cemetery, Boulder, CO
  spouse: Lucinda Martin, Mary Helen Gillman Hempstead Martin
  1870 US Census, Colorado Territory, Boulder County, St Vrain District

Martin, Frank
  b. abt 1853, IA
  father: B Martin
  mother: M Martin
  1860 US Census, Nebraska Territory, Platte River

Martin, H Cree
  St Vrain Pioneers Assn Arrival Date: 1860

Martin, Hamilton C
  b. abt 1843, WV
  spouse: Elisabeth Martin
  1870 US Census, Colorado Territory, Boulder County, St Vrain District

Martin, Hellen
  b. abt 1864, IA
  father: Emory Martin
  mother: Lucinda Martin
  1870 US Census, Colorado Territory, Boulder County, St Vrain District

Martin, Izora
  b. abt 1866, IA
  father: Emory Martin
  mother: Lucinda Martin
  1870 US Census, Colorado Territory, Boulder County, St Vrain District

Martin, Julia
  b. abt 1851, IA
  father: Emory Martin
  mother: Lucinda Martin
  1870 US Census, Colorado Territory, Boulder County, St Vrain District

St Vrain Valley Pioneers

Martin, Lucinda
  b. abt 1841, IA
  spouse: Emory Martin
  1870 US Census, Colorado Territory, Boulder County, St Vrain District

Martin, M
  b. abt 1830, OH
  spouse: B Martin
  1860 US Census, Nebraska Territory, Platte River

Martin, Mary M Davis
  b. abt 1859, IA
  d. Feb 1912, Fort Collins, CO
  father: Joseph Davis
  mother: Alliean Davis
  1870 US Census, Colorado Territory, Boulder County, St Vrain District

Martin, Mrs H Cree
  St Vrain Pioneers Assn Arrival Date: 1868

Martin, William C
  b. abt 1844, NY
  1870 US Census, Colorado Territory, Boulder County, St Vrain District

Martin, William J
  b. abt 1842, OH
  1870 US Census, Colorado Territory, Boulder County, St Vrain District

Maser, Henry H
  b. abt 1836, PA
  1870 US Census, Colorado Territory, Boulder County, St Vrain District

Mason, George M
  b. abt 1822, OH
  spouse: Lucinda Mason
  1870 US Census, Colorado Territory, Boulder County, St Vrain District

Mason, George W
  St Vrain Pioneers Assn Arrival Date: 1860

Mason, Horace G
  b. abt 1854, IA
  father: George M Mason
  mother: Lucinda Mason
  1870 US Census, Colorado Territory, Boulder County, St Vrain District

Mason, James R
  b. abt 1849, KY
  d. abt 15 Aug 1912, Masonville, Larimer, CO
  spouse: Mary Mason
  St Vrain Pioneers Assn Arrival Date: 1863
  St Vrain Ditch Owner: Hayseed Ditch No. 2, 31 July 1860
  1870 US Census, Colorado Territory, Boulder County, St Vrain District

Mason, Lucinda
  b. abt 1821, KY
  spouse: George M Mason
  1870 US Census, Colorado Territory, Boulder County, St Vrain District

Mason, Martha
  b. abt 1859, IA
  father: George M Mason
  mother: Lucinda Mason
  1870 US Census, Colorado Territory, Boulder County, St Vrain District

Mason, Mary Ann Maddux
  b. 9 Jan 1849, Coldwater, Branch, MI
  spouse: Charles Mason
  father: Peter Maddux
  mother: Jemina Stults Maddux Armstrong
  St Vrain Pioneers Assn Arrival Date: [not recorded]

Mason, Mrs Geo W
  spouse: George W Mason
  St Vrain Pioneers Assn Arrival Date: 1860

Mason, Stephen F
  b. abt 1852, KY
  spouse: Clara Barnaby Mason
  1870 US Census, Colorado Territory, Boulder County, St Vrain District

Mason, William
  b. abt 1853, KY
  1870 US Census, Colorado Territory, Boulder County, St Vrain District

Mason, William S
  Franklin Township Land Club Claim Date: 1860 Feb 11

St Vrain Valley Pioneers

Mathews, Andrew Scott
 b. 1819, PA
 d. 22 June 1911, Longmont, CO
 bd. Mountain View Cemetery, Longmont, CO

Mathews, Bella
 b. abt 1844, NY
 spouse: Daniel Mathews
 1870 US Census, Colorado Territory, Boulder County, St Vrain District

Mathews, Daniel
 b. abt 1844, NY
 spouse: Bella Mathews
 1870 US Census, Colorado Territory, Boulder County, St Vrain District

Mathews, Orson P
 d. 28 June 1919, Denver, CO
 bd. Lakeside Cemetery, Loveland, Larimer, CO
 spouse: Emma Matthews
 St Vrain Land Club Date: 1861

Mattera, Louis
 b. abt 1848, Canada
 1870 US Census, Colorado Territory, Boulder County, St Vrain District

Matthews, Emma H
 b. abt 1851, IL
 spouse: Orson P Matthews
 St Vrain Pioneers Assn Arrival Date: 1860
 1870 US Census, Colorado Territory, Boulder County, St Vrain District

Matthews, Martha M Brush
 b. abt 1849, IA
 spouse: Milton Matthews
 St Vrain Pioneers Assn Arrival Date: 1864
 1870 US Census, Colorado Territory, Boulder County, Left Hand

Matthews, Milton
 b. 6 Feb 1837, Indianapolis, Marion, IN
 d. 26 Sept 1924, Longm,ont, Boulder, CO
 bd. Mountain View Cemetery, Longmont, Boulder, CO
 spouse: Martha M Brush Matthews
 St Vrain Pioneers Assn Arrival Date: 1865

Matthews, Newton
 b. Nov 1843, IN
 d. 3 Oct 1926, Old Soldiers' Home, Sawtelle, Los Angeles, CA
 bd. Loma Vista Memorial Park, Fullerton, Orange, CA
 spouse: Margaret Mathews

Matthews, Orson P
 b. abt 1843, IN
 spouse: Emma H Matthews
 St Vrain Pioneers Assn Arrival Date: 1860
 1870 US Census, Colorado Territory, Boulder County, St Vrain District

Mattingly, J C
 b. abt 1832, KY
 1860 US Census, Nebraska Territory, Platte River

Maxwell, James Philip
 b. 20 June 1839, Bigfoot, Walworth, WI
 d. 6 May 1929, Boulder, CO
 bd. Columbia Cemetery, Boulder, CO
 spouse: Franceila Orrill Smith Maxwell
 father: James Alexander Maxwell
 mother: Susan Vreeland Clark Maxwell

Mayfield, A R
 b. abt 1834, KY
 spouse: Samantha Mayfield
 1870 US Census, Colorado Territory, Weld County, St Vrain District

Mayfield, Charlotte
 b. abt 1861, IL
 father: A R Mayfield
 mother: Samantha Mayfield
 1870 US Census, Colorado Territory, Weld County, St Vrain District

Mayfield, daughter of E B Mayfield
 father: E B Mayfield
 St Vrain Pioneers Assn Arrival Date: 1861

Mayfield, Delia
 b. abt 1862, Colorado Territory
 father: A R Mayfield
 mother: Samantha Mayfield
 1870 US Census, Colorado Territory, Weld County, St Vrain District

Mayfield, E B
 St Vrain Pioneers Assn Arrival Date: 1859

St Vrain Valley Pioneers

Mayfield, Florence
b. abt 1866, Colorado Territory
father: A R Mayfield
mother: Samantha Mayfield
1870 US Census, Colorado Territory, Weld County, St Vrain District

Mayfield, Harman
b. abt 1869, Colorado Territory
father: A R Mayfield
mother: Samantha Mayfield
1870 US Census, Colorado Territory, Weld County, St Vrain District

Mayfield, John
b. abt 1868, Colorado Territory
father: A R Mayfield
mother: Samantha Mayfield
1870 US Census, Colorado Territory, Weld County, St Vrain District

Mayfield, Mrs E B
spouse: E B Mayfield
St Vrain Pioneers Assn Arrival Date: 1861

Mayfield, Samantha
b. abt 1836, OH
spouse: A R Mayfield
1870 US Census, Colorado Territory, Weld County, St Vrain District

Mayfield, Thomas Green
b. 22 Dec 1839, Casey, Butler, KY
d. 15 Feb 1908, Long Beach, Los Angeles, CA
bd. Mountain View Cemetery, Longmont, Boulder, CO
spouse: Catherine Mildred Cooke Mayfield
father: John Franklin Mayfield
mother: Lucinda Miller Mayfield
St Vrain Pioneers Assn Arrival Date: 1861
1870 US Census, Colorado Territory, Weld County, St Vrain District

Maynard, James
b. abt 1840, MD
1870 US Census, Colorado Territory, Boulder County, St Vrain District

McBride, R E
St Vrain Land Club Date: 1861 Dec 1

McBride, Robert
b. abt 1834, OH
1870 US Census, Colorado Territory, Boulder County, St Vrain District

McCall, Clara
b. abt 1867, Colorado Territory
father: Thomas McCall
mother: Eliza McCall
1870 US Census, Colorado Territory, Boulder County, St Vrain District

McCall, Eliza Jones
b. 1838, Wales/PA
d. 1912
bd. Lyons Cemetery, Lyons, Boulder, CO
spouse: Thomas McCall
St Vrain Pioneers Assn Arrival Date: 1860
1870 US Census, Colorado Territory, Boulder County, St Vrain District

McCall, Nathaniel H
b. 7 Feb 1840
d. 20 Jan 1899
bd. Columbia Cemetery, Boulder, CO

McCall, Thomas
b. 1830, OH
d. 1 Aug 1885
bd. Hygiene Cemetery, Hygiene, Boulder, CO
spouse: Eliza McCall
St Vrain Pioneers Assn Arrival Date: 1860
Franklin Township Land Club Claim Date: 1860 June 25

McCall, Thomas
b. 25 Oct 1869, Colorado Territory
d. 24 May 1923, South Fork Ranch, 16 mi west of Lyons, Boulder, CO
bd. Lyons Cemetery, Lyons, Boulder, CO
father: Thomas McCall
mother: Eliza Jones McCall
1870 US Census, Colorado Territory, Boulder County, St Vrain District

McCall, Wilber
b. abt 1868, Colorado Territory
father: Thomas McCall
mother: Eliza McCall
1870 US Census, Colorado Territory, Boulder County, St Vrain District

St Vrain Valley Pioneers

McCamey, Ida H Black
b. 1855
d. 25 July 1925, Longmont, Boulder, CO
spouse: Charles M McCamey
mother: Georgiana Simons Black Rice

McCarey, Charles
b. abt 1869, Colorado Territory
father: Van W McCarey
mother: Ellen McCarey
1870 US Census, Colorado Territory, Boulder
  County, St Vrain District

McCarey, Ellen
b. abt 1851
spouse: Van W McCarey
1870 US Census, Colorado Territory, Boulder
  County, St Vrain District

McCarey, Van W
b. abt 1841, IN
spouse: Ellen McCarey
1870 US Census, Colorado Territory, Boulder
  County, St Vrain District

McCaslin, Ada
b. abt 1867, Colorado Territory
father: Mathew McCaslin
mother: Miranda McCaslin
1870 US Census, Colorado Territory, Boulder
  County, St Vrain District

McCaslin, Lowry
b. abt 1869, Colorado Territory
father: Mathew McCaslin
mother: Miranda McCaslin
1870 US Census, Colorado Territory, Boulder
  County, St Vrain District

McCaslin, Mary Helen Montgomery
b. 8 July 1867, St Vrain, Boulder, CO
d. 22 Sept 1956, Longmont, Boulder, CO
bd. Mountain View Cemetery, Longmont,
  Boulder, Co
spouse: Matthew Lowry McCaslin
father: William Adolphus Montgomery
mother: Mary Jane Munger Montgomery
1870 US Census, Colorado Territory, Boulder
  County, St Vrain District

McCaslin, Matthew Lowry
b. 16 Feb 1822, Venango, PA
d. 12 Feb 1913, Hygiene, Boulder, CO
spouse: Miranda Haggerty McCaslin
father: Andrew McCaslin
mother: Catherine Mary Lowry McCaslin
St Vrain Pioneers Assn Arrival Date: 1858
St Vrain Land Club Date: 1861 Sept 3
St Vrain Ditch Owner: Chapman and McCaslin
  Ditch No. 9, 10 Mar 1862
1870 US Census, Colorado Territory, Boulder
  County, St Vrain District

McCaslin, Matthew Lowry
b. 31 Oct 1862, Boulder, Colorado Territory
d. 7 Jan 1936, Boulder, CO
spouse: Mary Helen Montgomery McCaslin
father: Mathew Lowry McCaslin
mother: Miranda Haggerty McCaslin
1870 US Census, Colorado Territory, Boulder
  County, St Vrain District

McCaslin, Miranda Haggerty
b. 8 May 1837, Venango, PA
d. 1 Aug 1908, Hygiene, Boulder, CO
spouse: Matthew Lowry McCaslin
father: James S Haggerty
mother: Sarah Webster Haggerty
St Vrain Pioneers Assn Arrival Date: 1859
1870 US Census, Colorado Territory, Boulder
  County, St Vrain District

McCaslin, Walter Lowrie
b. 1869, Colorado Territory
d. 22 Oct 1926, Longmont, Boulder, CO
bd. Mountain View Cemetery, Longmont,
  Boulder, CO
father: Mathew McCaslin
mother: Miranda McCaslin

McCaslin, Wilder D
b. 1896
d. 28 Apr 1967
bd. Mountain View Cemetery, Longmont,
  Boulder, CO
spouse: Ethel H O'Connor McCaslin
father: Matthew Lowry McCaslin
mother: Mary Helen Montgomery McCaslin

St Vrain Valley Pioneers

McClain, Thomas D
St Vrain Land Club Date: 1861 Feb 15

McCliver, Daniel
b. abt 1835, ME
1870 US Census, Colorado Territory, Boulder County, St Vrain District

McCormick, John
St Vrain Pioneers Assn Arrival Date: 1867

McCormick, William H
St Vrain Pioneers Assn Arrival Date: 1870

McCory, Ellen
b. abt 1851, MA
spouse: Vandaver W McCory
St Vrain Pioneers Assn Arrival Date: 1863

McCory, Vandaver W
b. 4 Jan 1842, IN
d. 1 Dec 1888
bd. Hygiene Cemetery, Hygiene, Boulder, CO
spouse: Ellen McCory
St Vrain Pioneers Assn Arrival Date: 1860
St Vrain Ditch Owner: Davis & Downing Ditch No. 33, 1 Nov 1866

McCun [McCune?]
Franklin Township Land Club Claim Date: 1860 Feb 11

McDermid, Hugh
b. 24 July 1846
d. 3 Feb 1933, Hygiene, Boulder, CO
bd. Hygiene Cemetery, Hygiene, Boulder, CO
St Vrain Pioneers Assn Arrival Date: 1869

McDermot, Hans
b. abt 1845, Canada
1870 US Census, Colorado Territory, Boulder County, St Vrain District

McDonald, Charles/Cordlus
b. Scotland
d. 20 Feb 1888, Erie, CO
bd. South Boulder Cemetery, Boulder, CO
St Vrain Pioneers Assn Arrival Date: 1869

Mcelany, William
St Vrain Land Club Date: 1861 Aug 15

McFadden, Charles
b. 25 Oct 1846, Keokuk, Lee, IA
d. 18 Mar 1914, Arvada, Jefferson, CO
bd. Crown Hill Cemetery, Wheat Ridge, Jefferson, CO
spouse: Margaret Mallon McFadden

McFarland, S
b. abt 1834, OH
1860 US Census, Nebraska Territory, Platte River

McGee, George
b. abt 1839, PA
1860 US Census, Nebraska Territory, Platte River

McGeen, John H
St Vrain Land Club Date: 1861 Mar 5

McGinn, Clementine Margaret DeBacker Blake
b. abt 1834, Belgium
d. 11 Apr 1899
bd. South Boulder Cemetery, Boulder, CO
spouse: Karle Blake, James McGinn
St Vrain Pioneers Assn Arrival Date: 1864

McGinnis, William
b. abt 1835, PA
1860 US Census, Nebraska Territory, Platte River

McGruder, James
b. abt 1844, IA
1870 US Census, Colorado Territory, Boulder County, St Vrain District

McIntosh, Angelina Stuart
b. 13 Dec 1839, Illinois City, Rock Island, IL
d. 25 Apr 1927, Boulder, Boulder, CO
bd. Columbia Cemetery, Boulder, CO
spouse: Lemuel McIntosh
father: Alanson Hancock Stuart
mother: Mary Jane Everhart Stuart

McIntosh, Elizabeth A Bailey
b. abt 1853, Ashland, IA
d. 25 Sept 1883, Jamestown, Boulder, CO
bd. Columbia Cemetery, Boulder, CO
spouse: Joseph P McIntosh
father: John Campbell Bailey
mother: Elizabeth Platt Bailey
St Vrain Pioneers Assn Arrival Date: 1866

McIntosh, George Robin
b. 12 Oct 1837, Portage, OH
d. 22 Oct 1924, Longmont, Boulder, CO
bd. Mountain View Cemetery, Longmont, Boulder, CO

spouse: Amanda Jane Lee Noble McIntosh
father: John McIntosh
mother: Jerusha Ferris McIntosh
St Vrain Pioneers Assn Arrival Date: 1859
1870 US Census, Colorado Territory, Boulder County, St Vrain District

McIver, Mrs Robert
spouse: Robert McIver
St Vrain Pioneers Assn Arrival Date: 1865

McIver, Robert W
St Vrain Pioneers Assn Arrival Date: 1865

McKam, Horatio
b. abt 1841, OH
spouse: Lydia McKam
1870 US Census, Colorado Territory, Weld County, St Vrain District

McKam, Lewis A
b. abt 1867, Colorado Territory
father: Horatio McKam
mother: Lydia McKam
1870 US Census, Colorado Territory, Weld County, St Vrain District

McKam, Lydia
b. abt 1850, IA
spouse: Horatio McKam
1870 US Census, Colorado Territory, Weld County, St Vrain District

McKan, William
b. abt 1869, Colorado Territory
father: Horatio McKam
mother: Lydia McKam,
1870 US Census, Colorado Territory, Weld County, St Vrain District

McKay, William
b. abt 1839, KY
1860 US Census, Nebraska Territory, Platte River

McKeirnan, A Holt
b. 1879
d. Sept 1968,
bd. Mountain View Cemetery, Longmont, Boulder, CO
spouse: Alice Day McKeirnan
father: John McKeirnan
mother: Jennie McKeirnan

McKinner, James
b. abt 1835, IL
1870 US Census, Colorado Territory, Boulder County, Left Hand

McKissick, Alice M
b. abt 1868, Colorado Territory
father: John McKissick
mother: Mary J McKissick
1870 US Census, Colorado Territory, Weld County, St Vrain District

McKissick, Anderson
St Vrain Pioneers Assn Arrival Date: 1859

McKissick, John
b. abt 1840, PA
spouse: Mary J McKissick
St Vrain Pioneers Assn Arrival Date: 1858
1870 US Census, Colorado Territory, Weld County, St Vrain District

McKissick, Mary J
b. abt 1844, IL
spouse: John McKissick
St Vrain Pioneers Assn Arrival Date: 1858
1870 US Census, Colorado Territory, Weld County, St Vrain District

McKissick, Nettie
b. abt 1867, Colorado Territory
father: John McKissick
mother: Mary J McKissick
1870 US Census, Colorado Territory, Weld County, St Vrain District

McKissick, Oliver
b. abt 1866, Colorado Territory
father: John McKissick
mother: Mary J McKissick
1870 US Census, Colorado Territory, Weld County, St Vrain District

McKissick, Thomas
b. abt 1831, PA
1870 US Census, Colorado Territory, Weld County, St Vrain District

McMahar, William
b. abt 1839, OH
1860 US Census, Nebraska Territory, Platte River

St Vrain Valley Pioneers

McMannis, Thomas
 b. abt 1835, Ireland
 1870 US Census, Colorado Territory, Boulder County, St Vrain District

McMien, James
 b. abt 1845, MO
 1870 US Census, Colorado Territory, Boulder County, St Vrain District

McMillin, J W
 St Vrain Land Club Date: 1861 June 1

McMuth, Andrew
 b. abt 1846, OH
 1870 US Census, Colorado Territory, Boulder County, St Vrain District

McNeil, Orman
 b. abt 1838, OH
 1870 US Census, Colorado Territory, Boulder County, St Vrain District

McPhillips, G Edwin
 b. 22 Dec 1870
 d. 13 Feb 1967
 bd. Mountain View Cemetery, Longmont, Boulder, CO
 spouse: MaryEdith McPhillips

McWearny, P
 b. abt 1832, Ireland
 1860 US Census, Nebraska Territory, Platte River

Mead, William
 St Vrain Land Club Date: 1861 Apr 19

Meek, William
 Franklin Township Land Club Claim Date: 1860 June 24
 St Vrain Land Club Date: 1860 June 24

Meeks, Bill
 St Vrain Pioneers Assn Arrival Date: 1859

Meeks, Joe
 St Vrain Pioneers Assn Arrival Date: 1859

Meglemre, Clyde Edward
 b. 6 Oct 1983, Bridgeport, Morrill, NE
 d. 6 Aug 1961, Longmont, Boulder, CO
 bd. Mountain View Cemetery, Longmont, Boulder, CO
 spouse: Elma Williams Meglemre
 father: John Edward Meglemre
 mother: Sarah Alsyra Richardson Meglemre

Meglemre, Elma Williams
 b. 6 Apr 1901
 d. 14 Dec 1981
 bd. Mountain View Cemetery, Longmont, Boulder, CO
 spouse: Clyde Edward Meglemre
 father: Joseph H Williams
 mother: Abbie May White Williams

Meikle, Kate L Burke Gallagher
 b. 1 Dec 1868, Colorado Territory
 d. 18 Mar 1903, Boulder, CO
 bd. Columbia Cemetery, Boulder, CO
 spouse: James Gallagher; George Meikle
 father: August G Burke
 mother: Mary J Harding Burke
 1870 US Census, Colorado Territory, Boulder County, Left Hand

Merrell, Tina
 b. abt 1847, ME
 1870 US Census, Colorado Territory, Boulder County, St Vrain District

Merriman, John Freeman
 b. 4 May 1838, Pittsburgh, Allegheny, PA
 d. 31 Aug 1875, Longmont, Boulder, CO
 bd. Burlington Cemetery, Longmont, Boulder, CO
 spouse: Mary Jane Baylor Merriman
 father: John Merriman
 mother: Ruth Reese Merriman
 St Vrain Pioneers Assn Arrival Date: 1870

Messer, Marie Hauck
 b. 13 June 1870, Boulder, Colorado Territory
 d. 25 May 1927, Jefferson, CO
 bd. Crown Hill Cemetery, Wheat Ridge, Jefferson, CO
 spouse: Messer
 father: Robert August Hauck
 mother: Ernestine Lange Hauck

Metcalf, Eli P
 b. 15 Mar 1842, Gilsum, Cheshire, NH
 d. 16 May 1904, Boulder, CO
 bd. Columbia Cemetery, Boulder, CO
 spouse: Margaret Mitchell Metcalf
 father: Zenas Decatur Metcalf

mother: Martha Hill Temple Metcalf
1870 US Census, Colorado Territory, Boulder County, St Vrain District

Miggins, G
b. abt 1834, MS
1860 US Census, Nebraska Territory, Platte River

Miller, Alfred
b. abt 1859, KS Terr
mother: Rosa Miller
1860 US Census, Nebraska Territory, Platte River

Miller, Arthur
b. abt 1862, IA
father: Johnson Miller
mother: Letitia Miller
St Vrain Pioneers Assn Arrival Date: 1864

Miller, Charles
b. abt 1836, Canada
1860 US Census, Nebraska Territory, Platte River

Miller, Clarence
b. abt 1864, IA
father: Johnson Miller
mother: Letitia Miller
St Vrain Pioneers Assn Arrival Date: 1864

Miller, Daniel W
b. abt 1845, OH
1870 US Census, Colorado Territory, Boulder County, St Vrain District

Miller, David Wallace
b. 13 Sept 1844, OH
d. 11 Dec 1907, Longmont, Boulder, CO
bd. Mountain View Cemetery, Longmont, Boulder, CO
spouse: Isabelle Douglas Hadley Miller
father: Beatty Miller
mother: Margaret McKee Miller
St Vrain Pioneers Assn Arrival Date: 1865

Miller, Ellen Clark
spouse: John H Miller
St Vrain Pioneers Assn Arrival Date: 1866

Miller, Emma L
spouse: George C Miller
St Vrain Pioneers Assn Arrival Date: 1862

Miller, George C
b. 15 Apr 1840, NY
d. 5 Jan 1902, Longmont, Boulder, CO
bd. Mountain View Cemetery, Longmont, Boulder, CO
spouse: Emma L Taylor Miller
St Vrain Pioneers Assn Arrival Date: 1866

Miller, George L
b. abt 1869, Colorado Territory
d. 11 Feb 1929
father: Lafayette Miller
mother: Mary E Foote Miller

Miller, J A
St Vrain Ditch Owner: Denio & Taylor Ditch No. 28, 15 July 1865

Miller, John H
b. abt 1802
d. 7 Jan 1871
bd. Burlington Cemetery, Longmont, Boulder, CO
spouse: Ellen Clark Miller
St Vrain Pioneers Assn Arrival Date: 1863
1870 US Census, Colorado Territory, Boulder County, St Vrain District

Miller, John Michael
b. 26 July 1862, MO
d. 13 Feb 1942
spouse: Mary Sophia Swanson Miller
father: Michael Christ Miller
mother: Isabel Agnes Honaker Miller Armstrong
1870 US Census, Colorado Territory, Boulder County, St Vrain District

Miller, John S
b. abt 1837, OH
d. 5 July 1882
bd. Hygiene Cemetery, Hygiene, Boulder, CO
spouse: Sarah E Miller
St Vrain Pioneers Assn Arrival Date: 1860
1870 US Census, Colorado Territory, Boulder County, St Vrain District

Miller, Johnson
b. abt 1838, IN
d. abt 1873, Boulder, CO
spouse: Letitia Miller
mother: Alvira Miller
St Vrain Pioneers Assn Arrival Date: 1864

St Vrain Valley Pioneers

Miller, Lafayette
b. 18 Mar 1840, IL
d. 28 May 1878
bd. Columbia Cemetery, Boulder, CO
spouse: Mary E Foote Miller
St Vrain Pioneers Assn Arrival Date: 1860

Miller, Letitia
b. abt 1841, IL
spouse: Johnson Miller
St Vrain Pioneers Assn Arrival Date: 1864

Miller, Mary E
b. abt 1869, Colorado Territory
father: John S Miller
mother: Sarah Miller
1870 US Census, Colorado Territory, Boulder County, St Vrain District

Miller, Mary E Foote
b. 3 Aug 1842, Geneseo, NY
d. 14 Nov 1921, Lafayette, Boulder, CO
bd. Columbia Cemetery, Boulder, CO
spouse: Lafayette Miller
father: John B Foote
mother: Sally Foote
St Vrain Pioneers Assn Arrival Date: 1860

Miller, Mary Isabella
b. 20 Mar 1865, MO
father: Michael Christ Miller
mother: Isabel Agnes Honaker Miller Armstrong
1870 US Census, Colorado Territory, Boulder County, St Vrain District

Miller, Mr
St Vrain Pioneers Assn Arrival Date: 1859

Miller, Mrs
St Vrain Pioneers Assn Arrival Date: 1859

Miller, Richard
b. abt 1851, IA
1870 US Census, Colorado Territory, Weld County, St Vrain District

Miller, Rosa
b. abt 1830, Baden, Germany
1860 US Census, Nebraska Territory, Platte River

Miller, Sarah Ellen
b. 3 Apr 1835, OH
d. 21 Sept 1920, Longmont, Boulder, CO
bd. Hygiene Cemetery, Hygiene, Boulder, CO
spouse: John S Miller
St Vrain Pioneers Assn Arrival Date: 1861
1870 US Census, Colorado Territory, Boulder County, St Vrain District

Miller, William T
b. abt 1829, WV
1870 US Census, Colorado Territory, Boulder County, St Vrain District

Miller, Willie W
b. abt 1867, Colorado Territory
father: John S Miller
mother: Sarah E Miller
1870 US Census, Colorado Territory, Boulder County, St Vrain District

Millice, Medora
b. 16 Mar 1876, Colorado Territory
d. 11 Aug 1967, Los Angeles, CA
bd. Mountain View Cemetery, Longmont, Boulder, CO
father: Amos Millice
mother: Orlenia Ann Barr Millice

Mills, Cornelia Phelps
b. abt 1848, IA
spouse: James Mills
1870 US Census, Colorado Territory, Weld County, St Vrain District

Mills, Edwin James
b. abt 1866, Colorado Territory
father: James Mills
mother: Cornelia Phelps Mills
1870 US Census, Colorado Territory, Weld County, St Vrain District

Mills, James
b. abt 1839, Ireland
spouse: Cornelia Phelps Mills
1870 US Census, Colorado Territory, Weld County, St Vrain District

Mills, Minnie E
b. abt 1869, Colorado Territory
father: James Mills
mother: Cornelia Phelps Mills
1870 US Census, Colorado Territory, Weld County, St Vrain District

St Vrain Valley Pioneers

Mills, William E
b. abt 1864, Colorado Territory
father: James Mills
mother: Cornelia Phelps Mills
1870 US Census, Colorado Territory, Weld County, St Vrain District

Milner, Sarah
St Vrain Pioneers Assn Arrival Date: 1864

Mishler, David
b. abt 1838, OH
1870 US Census, Colorado Territory, Boulder County, St Vrain District

Mitchell, A
b. abt 1831, Canada
1860 US Census, Nebraska Territory, Platte River

Mitchell, Bolus
b. abt 1843, Wurttemberg, Germany
d. 30 Aug 1923, Goshen, Elkhart, IN
1870 US Census, Colorado Territory, Boulder County, St Vrain District

Montgomery, Alexander W
b. 13 Jan 1840
d. 12 June 1931
bd. Lyons Cemetery, Lyons, Boulder, CO
spouse: Emma Ferguson Montgomery
St Vrain Pioneers Assn Arrival Date: 1862
St Vrain Ditch Owner: Montgomery Private Ditch No 12 1/2, 15 May 1862

Montgomery, Alexander Washington
b. 13 Jan 1840, York, VA
d. 12 June 1931, Colorado Springs, El Paso, CO
spouse: Mary Susan Elliott Montgomery
father: William Montgomery
mother: Mary E Dawson Montgomery
1870 US Census, Colorado Territory, Boulder County, St Vrain District

Montgomery, Benjamin Franklin
b. 18 Aug 1846, York, VA
d. 14 Apr 1932, Boulder, CO
bd. Columbia Cemetery, Boulder, CO
spouse: Mary Louise Hall Montgomery
father: William Montgomery
mother: Mary E Dawson Montgomery
1870 US Census, Colorado Territory, Boulder County, St Vrain District

Montgomery, Cyrus Wilton
b. 13 Sept 1850, Red Rock, Marion IA
d. 8 May 1935, Boulder, CO
bd. Columbia Cemetery, Boulder, CO
spouse: Nancy A Hedges
father: William Montgomery
mother: Mary E Dawson Montgomery
St Vrain Pioneers Assn Arrival Date: 1869
1870 US Census, Colorado Territory, Boulder County, St Vrain District

Montgomery, Emma Ferguson
b. 22 Apr 1855
d. 10 Oct 1912
bd. Lyons Cemetery, Lyons, Boulder, CO
spouse: Alexander W Montgomery
St Vrain Pioneers Assn Arrival Date: 1862

Montgomery, Frank
St Vrain Pioneers Assn Arrival Date: 1860

Montgomery, Mary Jane Munger
b. 16 June 1850, Keokuk, Lee, IA
d. 24 Mar 1929, Denver, CO
bd. Green Mountain Cemetery, Boulder, CO
spouse: William Adolphus Montgomery
father: Norton Munger
mother: Helen M M Hamlin Munger
1870 US Census, Colorado Territory, Boulder County, St Vrain District

Montgomery, Mrs Robert Bruce
St Vrain Pioneers Assn Arrival Date: 1863

Montgomery, Rebecca
spouse: William A Montgomery
St Vrain Pioneers Assn Arrival Date: 1861

Montgomery, Robert Bruce
b. abt 1835, Scotland
St Vrain Pioneers Assn Arrival Date: 1867

Montgomery, William A
b. 15 May 1842, PA
d. 3 Feb 1910, Weld, CO
bd. Mountain View Cemetery, Longmont, Boulder, CO
spouse: Rebecca Montgomery
St Vrain Pioneers Assn Arrival Date: 1861

Montgomery, William Adolphus
b. 26 Jan 1838, York, VA
d. 28 June 1911, Denver, CO

St Vrain Valley Pioneers

bd. Green Mountain Cemetery, Boulder, CO
spouse: Mary Jane Munger, Montgomery
father: William Montgomery
mother: Mary Elizabeth Dawson Montgomery
1870 US Census, Colorado Territory, Boulder County, St Vrain District

Mooney, Michael
b. abt 1842, Ireland
1870 US Census, Colorado Territory, Boulder County, St Vrain District

Moorby, Joshua
b. abt 1839, KY
1870 US Census, Colorado Territory, Boulder County, St Vrain District

Moore, J A
b. abt 1839, OH
1860 US Census, Nebraska Territory, Platte River

Moore, Mr
St Vrain Pioneers Assn Arrival Date: 1858

Moran, Casper
b. abt 1828, Switzerland
1860 US Census, Nebraska Territory, Platte River

Morgan, Andrew
b. abt 1844, IN
1870 US Census, Colorado Territory, Boulder County, St Vrain District

Morgan, D W
b. abt 1821, NY
1860 US Census, Nebraska Territory, Platte River

Morgan, Ivan Clifford
b. 1891
d. 1966
bd. Mitzpah Cemetery, Platteville, Weld, CO
spouse: Helen Alice Barkdoll Morgan

Morgan, Jesse A
b. abt 1847, IN
1870 US Census, Colorado Territory, Boulder County, St Vrain District

Morgan, Margaret Abernathy
b. 26 Oct 1881, Louisville, Boulder, CO
d. 9 June 1967, Boulder, CO
bd. Fairmount Cemetery, Denver, CO
spouse: William B Morgan
father: Samuel Abernathy
mother: Mary Jan Shepherd Abernathy

Mork, John J
b. 1847, Norway
d. 1925
bd. Fairmount Cemetery, Denver, CO
spouse: [the former] Miss Larson

Morkert, Saul
b. abt 1839, IN
1870 US Census, Colorado Territory, Boulder County, St Vrain District

Morris, Sarah Eunice Hutchinson Bucherdee
b. 6 Apr 1860, IA
d. 5 May 1950, Lyons, Boulder, CO
bd. Lyons Cemetery, Lyons, Boulder, CO
spouse: Fred C Bucherdee
father: Joseph Hutchinson
mother: Rhoda Elizabeth Violet Hutchinson
1870 US Census, Colorado Territory, Boulder County, St Vrain District

Morrison
b. abt 1808, NJ
1860 US Census, Nebraska Territory, Platte River

Morrison, James C
b. abt 1840, OH
spouse: Mary E Morrison
1870 US Census, Colorado Territory, Boulder County, St Vrain District

Morrison, Mary E
b. abt 1854, IA
spouse: James C Morrison
1870 US Census, Colorado Territory, Boulder County, St Vrain District

Morton, Henry H
b. 1885
d. 9 May 1968
bd. Lafayette Cemetery, Lafayette, Lafayette, Boulder, CO
father: Ralph Morton
mother: Elizabeth Morton

Morton, Mike
b. abt 1836, Ireland
1870 US Census, Colorado Territory, Weld County, St Vrain District

St Vrain Valley Pioneers

Mott, John
St Vrain Pioneers Assn Arrival Date: 1860

Mozier, Amelia
b. abt 1861, IA
father: Calvin Mozier
1870 US Census, Colorado Territory, Boulder County, St Vrain District

Mozier, Calvin
b. abt 1837, NY
spouse: Ellen Mozier
1870 US Census, Colorado Territory, Boulder County, St Vrain District

Mozier, Ellen
b. abt 1841, NY
spouse: Calvin Mozier
1870 US Census, Colorado Territory, Boulder County, St Vrain District

Mozier, Gilbert
b. abt 1859, IA
father: Calvin Mozier
mother: Ellen Mozier
1870 US Census, Colorado Territory, Boulder County, St Vrain District

Mozier, Rosella
b. abt 1867, Colorado Territory
father: Calvin Mozier
mother: Ellen Mozier
1870 US Census, Colorado Territory, Boulder County, St Vrain District

Muhme, Alfred
b. 9 Ded 1903
d. 30 Apr 1968
bd. Mountain View Cemetery, Longmont, Boulder, CO
spouse: Glenna Matthews Muhme
father: Fred William Muhme
mother: Minnie J Asmussen Muhme

Mulvihill, John
St Vrain Pioneers Assn Arrival Date: 1860
St Vrain Ditch Owner: Hayseed Ditch No. 1, 1 Jan 1860

Mulvihill, Mrs John
St Vrain Pioneers Assn Arrival Date: 1860

Mumford, Cora Electa Meeker
b. 29 Nov 1872
d. 7 Sept 1961
bd. Mountain View Cemetery, Longmont, Boulder, CO
spouse: Joseph Chandler Mumford

Mumford, Joseph Chandler
b. 9 May 1870, MA
d. 22 Jan 1945, Longmont, Boulder, CO
bd. Mountain View Cemetery, Longmont, Boulder, CO
spouse: Cora Electa Meeker Munford
father: W F Mumford
mother: Nellie Chandler Mumford Hall

Myer, John
b. abt 1842, Prussia
spouse: Lettie Johnson Myer
1870 US Census, Colorado Territory, Boulder County, St Vrain District

Myer, Lettie Johnson
b. abt 1838, Sweden
spouse: John Myer
1870 US Census, Colorado Territory, Boulder County, St Vrain District

Myers, Andrew R
b. abt 1833, IN
d. 27 Sept 1884, Grand Lake, CO
bd. Columbia Cemetery, Boulder, CO
spouse: Mary A Myers
1870 US Census, Colorado Territory, Boulder County, St Vrain District

Myers, Catherine
b. abt 1851, NY
mother: Mary Myers
1860 US Census, Nebraska Territory, Platte River

Myers, Cornelia
b. abt 1845, IL
spouse: George Myers
St Vrain Pioneers Assn Arrival Date: 1864
1870 US Census, Colorado Territory, Boulder County, St Vrain District

Myers, Elsa
b. abt 1865, Colorado Territory
father: George Myers
mother: Cornelia Myers

St Vrain Valley Pioneers

1870 US Census, Colorado Territory, Boulder County, St Vrain District

Myers, Etaile/Ettoil
b. abt 1869, Colorado Territory
father: Andrew R Myers
mother: Mary A Myers
1870 US Census, Colorado Territory, Boulder County, St Vrain District

Myers, Flora
b. abt 1867, Colorado Territory
father: George Myers
mother: Cornelia Myers
1870 US Census, Colorado Territory, Boulder County, St Vrain District

Myers, George
b. abt 1834, MI
spouse: Cornelia Myers
St Vrain Pioneers Assn Arrival Date: 1864
1870 US Census, Colorado Territory, Boulder County, St Vrain District

Myers, Jesse
b. abt 1868, Colorado Territory
father: Andrew Myers
mother: Mary A Myers
1870 US Census, Colorado Territory, Boulder County, St Vrain District

Myers, John
b. abt 1839, France
1860 US Census, Nebraska Territory, Platte River

Myers, John W
b. abt 1854, IA
father: Andrew Myers
mother: Mary A Myers
1870 US Census, Colorado Territory, Boulder County, St Vrain District

Myers, Mary
b. abt 1830, Ireland
1860 US Census, Nebraska Territory, Platte River

Myers, Mary A
b. abt 1839, IN
d. 27 Jan 1879, Boulder, CO
bd. Columbia Cemetery, Boulder, CO
spouse: Andrew R Myers
1870 US Census, Colorado Territory, Boulder County, St Vrain District

Myers, Myrtie J
b. abt 1869, Colorado Territory
father: George Myers
mother: Cornelia Myers
1870 US Census, Colorado Territory, Boulder County, St Vrain District

Myers, Reuben
b. abt 1858, IA
father: Andrew R Myers
mother: Mary A Myers
1870 US Census, Colorado Territory, Boulder County, St Vrain District

N

Neauxhurst, George
St Vrain Land Club (M687) Date: 1859 Dec 10

Neeley, John W
b. 6 June 1850
d. 9 Jan 1918
bd. Lafayette Cemetery, Lafayette, Boulder, CO
spouse: D F Neeley
St Vrain Pioneers Assn Arrival Date: 1868

Neeley, Mary E Caywood
b. 15 Oct 1861, Wapello, IA
spouse: William Neeley
father: William Wesley Caywood
mother: Katharine Donovan Newman Caywood
St Vrain Pioneers Assn Arrival Date: 1864
1870 US Census, Colorado Territory, Boulder County, Left Hand

Neeley, Robert
St Vrain Pioneers Assn Arrival Date: 1868

Nelson, August
b. 1841
d. 1915
bd. Ryssby Cemetery, Boulder, CO
spouse: Clara Soderberg Nelson
St Vrain Ditch Owner: Nelson Ditch No. 38, 1 Apr 1869

Nelson, Bengt Johan
b. 27 Nov 1836, Fallnakaveka, Sweden
d. 28 Apr 1888, Ryssby, Boulder, CO
bd. Ryssby Cemetery, Boulder, CO
spouse: Maria Peterson Nelson

St Vrain Valley Pioneers

Nelson, Johannes
b. 9 Jan 1836, Sweden
d. 2 Feb 1890
bd. Ryssby Cemetery, Boulder, CO

Nelson, John
St Vrain Pioneers Assn Arrival Date: 1869

Nelson, Louis
b. 1845
d. 1931
bd. Ryssby Cemetery, Boulder, CO
spouse: Anna Benson Nelson

Nelson, Mrs John
spouse: John Nelson
St Vrain Pioneers Assn Arrival Date: 1869

Neumeister, Louisa Barbara DeBacker
b. 22 May 1859, Iowa City, Johnson, IA
spouse: Emil Charles Neumeister
father: John Franciscus DeBacker
mother: Mary Fouse DeBacker
St Vrain Pioneers Assn Arrival Date: 1859

Newby, Bryant Nathaniel
b. 6 Jan 1853, Lathrop, Clinton, MO
d. 16 May 1937, Longmont, Boulder, CO
bd. Mountain View Cemetery, Longmont, Boulder, CO
spouse: Lillie Ada Hedges Newby; Anna Florence Cook Newby
father: Jeremiah N Newby
mother: Elizabeth Stonum Newby

Newnam, Edward B
b. 24 Oct 1833, MD
d. 27 Apr 1912, Denver, CO
bd. Fairmount Cemetery, Denver, CO
spouse: Sarah F Wiswall Newnam
St Vrain Pioneers Assn Arrival Date: 1868
1870 US Census, Colorado Territory, Boulder County, St Vrain District

Newnam, Sarah F
b. abt 1839, IL
spouse: Edward Mewnam
1870 US Census, Colorado Territory, Boulder County, St Vrain District

Nichols, James Bernard
b. 1906
d. 10 Jan 1981, Longmont, Boulder, CO
bd. Mountain View Cemetery, Longmont, Boulder, CO
spouse: Willa Ruth Rothrock Nichols
father: James Hampton Nichols
mother: Rosa Lee Nichols

Nichols, Willa Ruth Rothrock
b. 8 July 1900, Boulder, CO
d. June 1999, Boulder, CO
bd. Mountain View Cemetery, Longmont, Boulder, CO
spouse: James Bernard Nichols
father: William Henry Rothrock
mother: Clara Agness Dell Rothrock

Nicks, Catherine Fry
b. 24 Feb 1834, OH
d. 8 Feb 1908, Longmont, Boulder, CO
bd. Mountain View Cemetery, Longmont, Boulder, CO
spouse: William A Nicks, Sr
father: Jacob Fry
mother: Susana Wonstetler Fry
St Vrain Pioneers Assn Arrival Date: 1867

Nicks, Charles Wesley
b. 28 Apr 1858, Fidelity, Jersey, IL
d. 23 Dec 1926, Longmont, Boulder, CO
bd. Mountain View Cemetery, Longmont, Boulder, CO
spouse: Charlotte Thorp Nicks; Susan Anna Nicks
father: William A Nicks, Sr
mother: Catherine Fry Nicks
St Vrain Pioneers Assn Arrival Date: 1867

Nicks, Edward A
b. 26 July 1862, Fidelity, Jersey, IL
d. 8 Aug 1940, Longmont, Boulder, CO
spouse: Annie Elizabeth Knorr Nicks
father: William A Nicks, Sr
mother: Catherine Fry Nicks
St Vrain Pioneers Assn Arrival Date: 1867

Nicks, James Samuel
b. 28 Dec 1864, Fidelity, Jersey, IL
d. 4 Oct 1924, Longmont, Boulder, CO
bd. Mountain View Cemetery, Longmont, Boulder, CO
spouse: Ida Irene Gardner Nicks; Emma Frank Van Etten Nicks

St Vrain Valley Pioneers

father: William A Nicks, Sr
mother: Catherine Fry Nicks
St Vrain Pioneers Assn Arrival Date: 1867

Nicks, John H
b. 24 May 1856, Fidelity, Jersey, IL
d. 7 Jan 1911, Longmont, Boulder, CO
bd. Mountain View Cemetery, Longmont, Boulder, CO
spouse: Louia M Twiss Nicks
father: William A Nicks, Sr
mother: Catherine Fry Nicks
St Vrain Pioneers Assn Arrival Date: 1867

Nicks, Raymond Knorr
b. 4 Oct 1894, Longmont, Boulder, CO
d. 18 July 1967, Longmont, Boulder, CO
bd. Mountain View Cemetery, Longmont, Boulder, CO
spouse: Leona Hertha Nicks
father: Edward A Nicks
mother: Annie Elizabeth Knorr Nicks

Nicks, William A
b. 5 Aug 1867, Ottawa, Franklin, KS
d. 5 Feb 1944, Boulder, CO
bd. Mountain View Cemetery, Longmont, Boulder, CO
spouse: Jennie M Kearns Nicks
father: William A Nicks, Sr
mother: Catherine Fry Nicks
St Vrain Pioneers Assn Arrival Date: 1867

Nicks, William A
b. 20 Dec 1815, England
d. 22 Mar 1889
bd. Mountain View Cemetery, Longmont, Boulder, CO
spouse: Catherine Fry Nicks
St Vrain Pioneers Assn Arrival Date: 1867

Noblet, Mrs Samuel L
spouse: Samuel L Noblet
St Vrain Pioneers Assn Arrival Date: 1869

Noblet, Samuel L
St Vrain Pioneers Assn Arrival Date: 1869

Noblit, Bertha
b. abt 1867, Colorado Territory
father: Samuiel G Noblit
mother: Rhoda A Noblit
1870 US Census, Colorado Territory, Boulder County, St Vrain District

Noblit, Emma
b. abt 1861, KS Terr
father: Samuel G Noblit
mother: Rhoda A Noblit
1870 US Census, Colorado Territory, Boulder County, St Vrain District

Noblit, Henry
b. abt 1864, KS
father: Samuel G Noblit
mother: Rhoda A Noblit
1870 US Census, Colorado Territory, Boulder County, St Vrain District

Noblit, Rhoda A
b. abt 1859, KS Terr
father: Samuel G Noblit
mother: Rhoda A Noblit
1870 US Census, Colorado Territory, Boulder County, St Vrain District

Noblit, Rhoda A
b. abt 1828, IL
spouse: Samuel G Noblit
1870 US Census, Colorado Territory, Boulder County, St Vrain District

Noblit, Samuel G/L/T
b. abt 1820, PA
spouse: Rhoda A Noblit
1870 US Census, Colorado Territory, Boulder County, St Vrain District

Noblit, Samuel S/L/N
b. abt 1846, TX
father: Samuel G Noblit
mother: Rhoda A Noblit
1870 US Census, Colorado Territory, Boulder County, St Vrain District

Norris, A D
b. abt 1846, IA
1870 US Census, Colorado Territory, Weld County, St Vrain District

Norton, Henry Clay
St Vrain Pioneers Assn Arrival Date: 1860

Nuckolls, C
St Vrain Land Club (M687) Date: 1859 Oct 12

St Vrain Valley Pioneers

Nygren, Carl Arthur
b. 24 July 1910, Canfield, Boulder, CO
d. 29 Dec 1967, Longmont, Boulder, CO
bd. Hygiene Cemetery, Hygiene, Boulder, CO
spouse: Reathel O Martindale Nygren Bernard
father: John Nygren
mother: Mary Etta Buell Nygren

O

Oakley, Frank
b. abt 1835, NY
1860 US Census, Nebraska Territory, Platte River

Oard, Elizabeth Stewart
b. abt 1808
d. 11 July 1883
bd. Mountain View Cemetery, Longmont, Boulder, CO
spouse: William Oard Sr
St Vrain Pioneers Assn Arrival Date: 1868

Ochs, Alma R Anderson
b. 1898
d. 1967
bd. Mountain View Cemetery, Longmont, Boulder, CO
spouse: Henry Ochs
father: John Hugo Anderson
mother: Carolina Anderson

Olander, Martin O
b. 8 May 1883
d. 17 May 1968
bd. Mountain View Cemetery, Longmont, Boulder, CO
spouse: Olivia A Olander
father: August Persson Olander
mother: Hannah Johnsson Olander

Oliphant, Emma Louis Knaus
b. 2 May 1888, Longmont, Boulder, CO
d. 12 Sept 1967, Chatfield, Navarro, TX
bd. Chatfield Cemetery, Chatfield, Navarro, TX
spouse: Matt Finch Oliphant
father: Clemens Knaus
mother: Eliza Alice Greub Bader Knaus

Olmstead, George
b. abt 1847
1870 US Census, Colorado Territory, Boulder County, St Vrain District

Olney, Willis E
b. Aug 1866, Garnett, Anderson, KS
d. 19 Jan 1922, Denver, CO
bd. Crown Hill Cemetery, Wheat Ridge, Jefferson, CO
spouse: Mattie A Slater Olney
father: Isaac E Olney
mother: Adelia E Millard Waugh Olney

Orahood, Albina Amelia Godding
b. abt 1852, WI
d. bef 1874?
spouse: William M Orahood
1870 US Census, Colorado Territory, Weld County, St Vrain District

Orahood, William M
b. 30 Apr 1845
d. 28 Nov 1874
spouse: Albina Amelia Godding; Estella M Austin Orahood
1870 US Census, Colorado Territory, Weld County, St Vrain District

Orey, Justice
b. abt 1820, France
1870 US Census, Colorado Territory, Boulder County, St Vrain District

Orvis, Harrison Fletcher
b. 5 Jan 1835, Gainesville, Genessee, NY
d. 27 Mar 1920, Ingalls, Payne, OK
spouse: Joanna C Corbin Orvis, Susan A McNitt Orvis
father: Francis Orvis
mother: Zeruah Miller Orvis
1870 US Census, Colorado Territory, Boulder County, St Vrain District

Orvis, John Perrin
b. abt 1858, IA
d. 1920
spouse: Aldhedine H Powell Orvis
father: Harrison Fletcher Orvis
mother: Joanna C Corbin Orvis

St Vrain Valley Pioneers

1870 US Census, Colorado Territory, Boulder County, St Vrain District

Orvis, Lewis Frederick
b. 12 May 1855, WI
d. 25 Mar 1929, Ridgeway, Ouray, CO
father: Harrison Fletcher Orvis
mother: Joanna C Corbin Orvis
1870 US Census, Colorado Territory, Boulder County, St Vrain District

Osborne, William B
St Vrain Pioneers Assn Arrival Date: 1860

Osman, Henry
b. abt 1832, PA
1860 US Census, Nebraska Territory, Platte River

Ott, Louisa Dailey
b. 29 Mar 1868, Boulder Creek, Boulder, CO
d. 1 May 1956, Los Angeles, CA
spouse: Daniel M Ott
father: Dennis Dailey
mother: Juliette McDonald Green Dailey
1870 US Census, Colorado Territory, Weld County, St Vrain District

Overton, John H
b. abt 1832, PA
St Vrain Land Club (M687) Date: 1859 Dec 10
1860 US Census, Nebraska Territory, Platte River

Owens, Amanda
b. abt 1842, IN
spouse: Hugh Owens
St Vrain Pioneers Assn Arrival Date: [not recorded]
1870 US Census, Colorado Territory, Boulder County, Left Hand

Owens, Carrie E
b. abt 1860, IL
father: Hugh Owens
mother: Amanda Owens
1870 US Census, Colorado Territory, Boulder County, Left Hand

Owens, Hugh
b. abt 1839, OH
bd. Jamestown, Cemetery, Jamestown, Boulder, CO
spouse: Amanda Owens
St Vrain Pioneers Assn Arrival Date: [not recorded]
1870 US Census, Colorado Territory, Boulder County, Left Hand

Owens, John Frank
b. abt 1865, Colorado Territory
father: Hugh Owens
mother: Amanda Owens
1870 US Census, Colorado Territory, Boulder County, Left Hand

Owens, Mary V
b. abt 1867, Colorado Territory
father: Hugh Owens
mother: Amanda Owens
1870 US Census, Colorado Territory, Boulder County, Left Hand

P

Packard, John
b. abt 1850, MI
1870 US Census, Colorado Territory, Boulder County, St Vrain District

Page, William
b. abt 1834, NY
1860 US Census, Nebraska Territory, Platte River

Palmer, John
St Vrain Pioneers Assn Arrival Date: 1869

Pancost, Charles Sydney
b. 31 Dec 1833, Ashtabula, OH
d. 2 Aug 1900, Boulder, CO
bd. Valmont Cemetery, Boulder, CO
spouse: Ella Clodfelter Pancost
St Vrain Pioneers Assn Arrival Date: 1859

Pancost, Ella Clodfelter
b. 30 Nov 1850
d. 7 Oct 1929, Boulder, CO
bd. Valmont Cemetery, Boulder, CO
spouse: Charles Sydney Pancost
father: Augustus C Glotfelter
mother: Frances Eliza Kehler Clodfelter
St Vrain Pioneers Assn Arrival Date: 1859

Pancost, Lawrence Neal
b. 18 Feb 1881, Boulder, CO
d. 22 Aug 1967, Boulder, CO

bd. Green Mountain Cemetery, Boulder, CO
spouse: Theresa Rose Fuxa Jaros Pancost

Parish, George F
b. abt 1847, AL
1870 US Census, Colorado Territory, Boulder County, Left Hand

Parker, Family
St Vrain Pioneers Assn Arrival Date: 1859

Parker, N D
Troy District Land Club Claim Date: 1860 July 17

Parrington, Charles
b. abt 1842, CT
1870 US Census, Colorado Territory, Boulder County, Left Hand

Parsons, Clara
b. abt 1869, Colorado Territory
father: William Parsons
mother: Mary Parsons
1870 US Census, Colorado Territory, Boulder County, St Vrain District

Parsons, Frank
b. abt 1858, WI
spouse: Eliza Parsons
father: William Parsons
mother: Mary Parsons
1870 US Census, Colorado Territory, Boulder County, St Vrain District

Parsons, Mary
b. abt 1840, NY
d. 11 Feb 1912, Mineral Wells, TX
spouse: William L Parsons
St Vrain Pioneers Assn Arrival Date: 1863
1870 US Census, Colorado Territory, Boulder County, St Vrain District

Parsons, Robert
b. abt 1834, Sweden
1870 US Census, Colorado Territory, Boulder County, St Vrain District

Parsons, William
b. abt 1830, Ireland/England
spouse: Mary Parsons
1870 US Census, Colorado Territory, Boulder County, St Vrain District

Patrick, Thomas W
spouse: Fannie Colton Patrick
St Vrain Pioneers Assn Arrival Date: 1859

Patterson, James
St Vrain Land Club (M687) Date: 1859 Oct 13

Patterson, William R
Troy District Land Club Claim Date: 1860 Oct 4

Paul, Henry C
b. abt 1840, PA
d. 19 Mar 1873, Middle Boulder, Boulder, CO
bd. Nederland Cemetery?, Nederland, Boulder, CO
1870 US Census, Colorado Territory, Boulder County, St Vrain District

Pease, Mrs Simon
spouse: Simon Pease
St Vrain Pioneers Assn Arrival Date: 1863

Pease, Simon
St Vrain Pioneers Assn Arrival Date: 1863

Peck, Susan Edmund Walthall
b. 21 Nov 1833, Danville, Hendricks, IN
d. 24 Dec 1909, Boulder, CO
bd. Fairmount, Denver, CO
spouse: Thomas Samuel Peck
father: Samuel White Walthall
mother: Rebecca Ann Johns Walthall
St Vrain Pioneers Assn Arrival Date: 1859
1870 US Census, Colorado Territory, Boulder County, St Vrain District

Peck, Thomas Samuel
b. 22 Oct 1829, Hendricks, IN
d. 17 Mar 1898, Longmont, Boulder, CO
bd. Mountain View Cemetery, Longmont, Boulder, CO
spouse: Susan Edmund Walthall Peck
father: George S Peck
mother: Lucinda Samuell Peck
St Vrain Pioneers Assn Arrival Date: 1859
St Vrain Ditch Owner: Peck & Metcalf Ditch No. 36, 16 May 1867
1870 US Census, Colorado Territory, Boulder County, St Vrain District

Peck, Uriah L
b. 22 Oct 1825, Westminster, Windham, VT
d. 18 Mar 1897, Home Lake, Monte Vista, CO

bd. Mountain View Cemetery, Longmont, Boulder, CO
spouse: Mary Jane Peck
father: Uriah Peck
mother: Asenath Powers Peck
Troy District Land Club Claim Date: 1860 Aug 10
St Vrain Land Club Date: 1861 July 31

Pell, William Gibbons
b. 10 Aug 1820, Dunham, Missisquoi, Quebec, Canada
d. 21 Sept 1900, Boulder, CO
bd. Columbia Cemetery, Boulder, CO
spouse: Eliza Parker Pell, Ellen H Bergeron Pell
father: William Gibbons Pell
mother: Angelica Anna VanAntwerp Pell
St Vrain Pioneers Assn Arrival Date: 1859

Penister, John P
b. abt 1843, OH
1870 US Census, Colorado Territory, Boulder County, Left Hand

Penister, Perry
b. abt 1843, OH
1870 US Census, Colorado Territory, Boulder County, Left Hand

Pennock
St Vrain Land Club Date: 1861 Jan 30

Pennock, Chester Chandler
b. 30 Apr 1850, Norfolk, St Lawrence, NY/Rockford, IL
d. 7 Aug 1922, Boulder, CO
bd. Mountain View Cemetery, Longmont, Boulder, CO
father: Andrew Jackson Pennock
mother: Henrietta Eliza Chandler Pennock

Pennock, E C
St Vrain Pioneers Assn Arrival Date: 1862

Pennock, Glen Wildman
b. 1 Jan 1898, OH
d. Aug 1966, Boulder, CO
bd. Mountain View Cemetery, Longmont, Boulder, CO
spouse: Homer Arthur Pennock

Pennock, Jackson
St Vrain Pioneers Assn Arrival Date: 1860

Pennock, Porter Russell
b. 15 Sept 1834, Palmyra, Portage, OH
d. 30 Apr 1901, Longmont, Boulder, CO
spouse: Sabra Ellen Coffin Pennock
father: Russell Pennock
mother: Fannie Holmes Pennock
St Vrain Pioneers Assn Arrival Date: 1860

Pennock, Sabra Ellen Coffin
b. 6 Jan 1841, Roxbury, Delaware, NY
d. 24 Aug 1913, Longmont, Boulder, CO
spouse: Porter Russell Pennock
father: Jacob Coffin
mother: Mary Ann Hull Coffin
St Vrain Pioneers Assn Arrival Date: 1862

Pennock, Vivian Russell
b. 8 May 1870, DeKalb, IL
d. 19 Aug 1921, Longmont, Boulder, CO
bd. Mountain View Cemetery, Longmont, Boulder, CO
spouse: Lillian Adelicia Large Pennock
father: Porter Russell Pennock
mother: Sabra Ellen Coffin Pennock

Perkins, George N
b. abt 1835, TN
spouse: Mary A Foy Perkins
1870 US Census, Colorado Territory, Boulder County, St Vrain District

Perkins, Mary Ann Foy
b. 19 Sept 1835, IN
d. 22 Mar 1919, Hygiene, Boulder, CO
bd. Hygiene Cemetery, Hygiene, Boulder, CO
spouse: George N Perkins
1870 US Census, Colorado Territory, Boulder County, St Vrain District

Perkins, Mary Worthington Duncan
b. 10 May 1860, Bond, IL
d. 1952, Boulder, Boulder, CO
bd. Mountain View Cemetery, Boulder, CO
spouse: William Henry Perkins
father: Elisha Duncan
mother: Mary Worthington Myatt Duncan
St Vrain Pioneers Assn Arrival Date: 1861
1870 US Census, Colorado Territory, Weld County, St Vrain District

St Vrain Valley Pioneers

Perrin, John C
b. 1838, PA
d. 30 Sept 1888
bd. Mountain View Cemetery, Longmont, Boulder, CO
spouse: Mary Jane Perrin
1870 US Census, Colorado Territory, Boulder County, St Vrain District

Perrin, M J
St Vrain Pioneers Assn Arrival Date: 1870

Perrin, Mrs M J
St Vrain Pioneers Assn Arrival Date: 1869

Perrin, William M
b. 1831, PA
d. 30 Sept 1888
bd. Mountain View Cemetery, Longmont, Boulder, CO
1870 US Census, Colorado Territory, Boulder County, St Vrain District

Peryam, Alice Rebecca Bailey
b. 8 Apr 1854, OH or IA
d. 17 Dec 1937, Encampment, Carbon, WY
spouse: William Thomas Peryam
father: John Campbell Bailey
mother: Elizabeth Platt Bailey
St Vrain Pioneers Assn Arrival Date: 1866
1870 US Census, Colorado Territory, Boulder County, St Vrain District
1870 US Census, Colorado Territory, Weld County, St Vrain District

Peters, Anson W
b. abt 1835, MO
St Vrain Pioneers Assn Arrival Date: [not recorded]

Peters, Julias
b. abt 1849, TN
1870 US Census, Colorado Territory, Boulder County, Left Hand

Peterson, Aaron
b. 11 Sept 1827, Ryssby, Sweden
d. 14 Feb 1896, Loveland, CO
bd. Ryssby Cenetery, Boulder, CO
spouse: Ella Peterson
St Vrain Ditch Owner: Spring Creek Ditch No. 52, 1 June 1872

Peterson, Peter
St Vrain Pioneers Assn Arrival Date: [not recorded]

Peterson, W H
b. abt 1838, OH
1860 US Census, Nebraska Territory, Platte River

Pie (see Pye)

Pie, Ellen
b. abt 1859, IA
father: Samuel Pie
mother: Frances Pie
1870 US Census, Colorado Territory, Boulder County, St Vrain District

Pie, Frances
b. abt 1843, IN
spouse: Samuel Pie
1870 US Census, Colorado Territory, Boulder County, St Vrain District

Pie, Isaac
b. abt 1869, Colorado Territory
father: Samuel Pie
mother: Frances Pie
1870 US Census, Colorado Territory, Boulder County, St Vrain District

Pie, Lede
b. abt 1864, MI
father: Samuel Pie
mother: Frances Pie
1870 US Census, Colorado Territory, Boulder County, St Vrain District

Pie, Samuel
b. abt 1836, NY
1870 US Census, Colorado Territory, Boulder County, St Vrain District

Platt, Bertha Ellen Davis
b. 29 Sept 1862, IA
d. 19 Sept 1915, Rapid City, Pennington, SD
spouse: Milo Ellsworth Platt
father: John Davis Jr
mother: Lucy S Lyman Davis
1870 US Census, Colorado Territory, Boulder County, St Vrain District

St Vrain Valley Pioneers

Platto, John F
b. abt 1845, OH
1870 US Census, Colorado Territory, Weld County, St Vrain District

Plumb, Ida E
b. abt 1857, WI
father: Sylvester J Plumb
mother: Louise Plumb Brock
St Vrain Pioneers Assn Arrival Date: 1859
1870 US Census, Colorado Territory, Weld County, St Vrain District

Plumb, Mae A
b. 12 May 1868, Erie, Weld, Colorado Territory
father: Sylvester J Plumb
mother: Louise Plumb Brock
1870 US Census, Colorado Territory, Weld County, St Vrain District

Plumb, Sylvester J
b. abt 1828, NY
bd. Pleasant View Ridge Cemetery, Weld, CO
spouse: Louise Plumb Brock
St Vrain Pioneers Assn Arrival Date: 1859
1870 US Census, Colorado Territory, Weld County, St Vrain District

Pool, William
b. abt 1830, NY
1860 US Census, Nebraska Territory, Platte River

Poor, George D
St Vrain Pioneers Assn Arrival Date: 1867

Porter, Charles
St Vrain Pioneers Assn Arrival Date: 1868

Porter, family of Charles
St Vrain Pioneers Assn Arrival Date: 1868

Porter, Mrs Charles
St Vrain Pioneers Assn Arrival Date: 1868

Powell, Aaron
b. abt 1808, KY
St Vrain Land Club Date: 1861 Feb 16

Powell, Anderson M
St Vrain Land Club Date: 1861 Aug 14

Powell, Andrew M
Vrain Land Club Date: 1861 Aug 14

Powell, Benjamin F
b. abt 1848, IN
mother: Eliza Powell
1870 US Census, Colorado Territory, Boulder County, St Vrain District

Powell, Daniel C
St Vrain Land Club Date: 1861 Aug 18

Powell, Eliza
b. abt 1814, OH
d. abt 1869, Boulder, CO
1870 US Census, Colorado Territory, Boulder County, St Vrain District

Powell, Houck Henry
b. 16 June 1887
d. 7 Sept 1968
bd. Mountain View Cemetery, Longmont, Boulder, CO
spouse: Dena A Powell
father: George Robert Powell
mother: Mary Alice Houck Powell

Powell, John R
St Vrain Pioneers Assn Arrival Date: 1868

Powell, Mason
St Vrain Land Club Date: 1861 May 29

Powell, Mrs John R
St Vrain Pioneers Assn Arrival Date: 1868

Powell, Tyler
b. abt 1846, IN
mother: Eliza Powell
1870 US Census, Colorado Territory, Boulder County, St Vrain District

Pratt, Azro B/V
b. abt 1837, PA
1870 US Census, Colorado Territory, Boulder County, St Vrain District

Preffer, Daniel
b. 18 Dec 1836, Canada
spouse: Elisabeth Jane Smith Preffer
St Vrain Pioneers Assn Arrival Date: [not recorded]
1860 US Census, Nebraska Territory, Altona
1870 US Census, Colorado Territory, Boulder County, Left Hand

St Vrain Valley Pioneers

Preffer, Elisabeth Jane Smith
b. 29 Mar 1852, Kent City, Kent, MI
d. 22 Dec 1940, Czar, Alberta, Canada
spouse: Daniel Preffer
father: James Monroe Smith
mother: Lorinda Burton Smith
St Vrain Pioneers Assn Arrival Date: 1868
1870 US Census, Colorado Territory, Boulder County, Left Hand

Preffer, Milly
b. Dec 1868, Colorado Territory
d. 23 Apr 1936, Orofino, Clearwater, ID
father: Daniel Preffer
mother: Elisabeth Preffer
1870 US Census, Colorado Territory, Boulder County, Left Hand

Price, Ivan
d. 3 Jan 1912, Boulder, CO
St Vrain Pioneers Assn Arrival Date: 1859

Prince, George
b. abt 1830, VA
1860 US Census, Nebraska Territory, Platte River

Prince, Helan Mary Lindsey
b. 6 Sept 1837, OH
d. 21 Feb 1898
bd. Lafayette Cemetery, Boulder, CO
spouse: Hiram Prince
St Vrain Pioneers Assn Arrival Date: 1864

Prince, Hiram H
b. 6 May 1824, Mobile, AL
d. 25 Feb 1921, Lafayette, Boulder, CO
bd. Lafayette Cemetery, Boulder, CO
spouse: Helan Mary Lindsay Prince
St Vrain Pioneers Assn Arrival Date: 1864

Prindle, Lanader
b. abt 1804, NY
d. 23 Oct 1893, Santa Cruz, CA
bd. Evergreen Cemetery, Santa Cruz, CA
spouse: Savannah Prindle
St Vrain Pioneers Assn Arrival Date: 1862
1870 US Census, Colorado Territory, Boulder County, St Vrain District

Prindle, Savannah
b. abt 1809, KY
spouse: Lanander Prindle
1870 US Census, Colorado Territory, Boulder County, St Vrain District

Pughe, Charles Edward
b. 14 Feb 1845, Aberystwyth, Ceredigion, Wales
d. 28 Apr 1927, Longmont, Boulder, CO
spouse: Mary Dorothy Davis Pughe
father: Tudor Pugh
mother: Mary Morgan Pugh
St Vrain Pioneers Assn Arrival Date: 1869

Pughe, Mary Dorothy Davis
b. 9 Mar 1849, Huntington, IN
d. 31 Aug 1944, Longmont, Boulder, CO
spouse: Charles Edward Pughe
St Vrain Pioneers Assn Arrival Date: 1869

Putnam, George
St Vrain Land Club Date: 1861 Aug 20

Pye (see Pie)

Pye
Vrain Ditch Owner: Smead & Pye Ditch No. 44, 1 May 1871

Pye, Samuel
St Vrain Pioneers Assn Arrival Date: 1863

R

Rabb, George W
b. 26 Mar 1845, Licking Co, OH
d. 21 Mar 1920, Los Angeles, CA
bd. Hollywood Cemetery, Los Angeles, CA
spouse: Harriet E Goodhue Rabb, Emma Jennings Rabb
Pioneers Association Arrival Date: 1870

Rafferty, Benjamin F/T
St Vrain Land Club Date: 1861 Aug 22

Ragan, Florence May Robbins
b. May 1861, MO
d. July 1918, Loveland, Larimer, CO
bd. Loveland Burial Park, Loveland, Larimer, CO
spouse: George W Ragan

Ragan, George W
b. 1843
d. 6 Apr 1921, Loveland, Larimer, CO
bd. Loveland Burial Park, Loveland, Larimer, CO
spouse: Florence May Robbins Ragan
St Vrain Pioneers Assn Arrival Date: 1863

St Vrain Valley Pioneers

Ramage, Benjamin Frank
  1870 US Census, Colorado Territory, Boulder County, St Vrain District

Randolph, S R
  St Vrain Land Club (M687) Date: 1861 Jan 12

Rannells, Benjamin Bay
  b. 26 Nov 1842, Athens, OH
  d. 23 Mar 1892, CO
  bd. Mountain View Cemetery, Longmont, Boulder, CO
  spouse: Ann E Hadley Rannells
  father: Samuel Flemming Rannells
  mother: Sarah Bay Rannells
  St Vrain Pioneers Assn Arrival Date: 1864

Rannells, John Ray
  b. 10 Mar 1850, Athens, OH
  d. 21 Apr 1928, Josephine, OR
  spouse: Lydia Jane Johnson Rannells
  father: Samuel Flemming Rannells
  mother: Sarah Bay Rannells
  St Vrain Pioneers Assn Arrival Date: 1864

Rannells, Mrs Newt
  spouse: Newt Rannells
  St Vrain Pioneers Assn Arrival Date: 1860

Rannells, Newt
  St Vrain Pioneers Assn Arrival Date: 1864

Rannells, Samuel Flemming
  b. 27 July 1812, Morgan, OH
  d. 12 Mar 1903, Longmont, Boulder, CO
  bd. Mountain View Cemetery, Longmont, Boulder, CO
  spouse: Sarah Bay Rannells
  father: William Rannells
  mother: Rhoda Burg Rannells
  St Vrain Pioneers Assn Arrival Date: 1859

Rannells, Sarah Bay
  b. 20 Sept 1811, Washington, PA
  d. 17 Mar 1896, Longmont, Boulder, CO
  bd. Mountain View Cemetery, Longmont, Boulder, CO
  spouse: Samuel Flemming Rannells
  father: Benjamin Franklin Bay
  mother: Greselda Grace Campbell Bay
  St Vrain Pioneers Assn Arrival Date: 1864

Rannells, William Newton
  b. 26 Oct 1840, Guernsey, OH
  d. 27 Dec 1906, Salubria, Washington, ID
  bd. Salubria Cemetery, Washington, ID
  spouse: Clarinda Ann Mason Rannels
  father: Samuel Flemming Rannells
  mother: Sarah Bay Rannells
  St Vrain Pioneers Assn Arrival Date: 1864

Rant, Louis
  b. abt 1833, France
  1860 US Census, Nebraska Territory, Platte River

Raynolds, Benjamin B
  b. abt 1864, OH
  father: Same Raynolds
  mother: Sarah Raynolds
  1870 US Census, Colorado Territory, Boulder County, St Vrain District

Raynolds, John
  b. abt 1850, OH
  father: Same Raynolds
  mother: Sarah Raynolds
  1870 US Census, Colorado Territory, Boulder County, St Vrain District

Raynolds, Same
  b. abt 1812, OH
  spouse: Sarah Raynolds
  1870 US Census, Colorado Territory, Boulder County, St Vrain District

Raynolds, Sarah
  b. abt 1812, OH
  spouse: Same Raynolds
  1870 US Census, Colorado Territory, Boulder County, St Vrain District

Raynolds, Sarah E
  b. abt 1854, MO
  father: Same Raynolds
  mother: Sarah Raynolds
  1870 US Census, Colorado Territory, Boulder County, St Vrain District

Read, Luman
  Franklin Township Land Club Claim Date: 1860 Feb 16
  St Vrain Land Club Date: 1860 Feb 1

St Vrain Valley Pioneers

Read, Thomas Marion
b. 9 Aug 1846
d. 1 Mar 1920
bd. Jamestown Cemetery, Jamestown, Jamestown, Boulder, CO
spouse: Hannah L Read
St Vrain Land Club Date: 1861

Reed, family of Reuben
St Vrain Pioneers Assn Arrival Date: [not recorded]

Reed, Mrs Reuben
St Vrain Pioneers Assn Arrival Date: [not recorded]

Reed, Reuben
St Vrain Pioneers Assn Arrival Date: [not recorded]

Reese, Catherine Cornelia Gifford
b. 19 Feb 1835, Greenwich, Huron, OH
d. 13 Oct 1911, Lyons, Boulder, CO
bd. Hygiene Cemetery, Hygiene, Boulder, CO
spouse: John Reese
St Vrain Pioneers Assn Arrival Date: 1864
1870 US Census, Colorado Territory, Boulder County, St Vrain District

Reese, John
b. 12 Jan 1831, Dillisburg, York, PA
d. 10 May 1887, Lyons, Boulder, CO
bd. Hygiene Cemetery, Hygiene, Boulder, CO
spouse: Catherine Cornelia Gifford Reese
father: Thomas Reese
mother: Mary Bentz Reese
St Vrain Pioneers Assn Arrival Date: 1859
1870 US Census, Colorado Territory, Boulder County, St Vrain District

Renner, John
St Vrain Ditch Owner: Renner Ditch No. 60, 1 May 1874

Reynolds, B F
St Vrain Land Club (M687) Date: 1861 Feb 16

Reynolds, Clara
b. abt 1849, IL
spouse: Newton Reynolds
1870 US Census, Colorado Territory, Boulder County, St Vrain District

Reynolds, Frank
St Vrain Land Club (M687) Date: 1860 Nov 12

Reynolds, Newton
b. abt 1841, OH
spouse: Clara Reynolds
1870 US Census, Colorado Territory, Boulder County, St Vrain District

Rhoades, Jerome B
b. abt 1815, PA
d. 15 Sept 1887
bd. Burlington Cemetery, Longmont, Boulder, CO
1870 US Census, Colorado Territory, Boulder County, St Vrain District

Rhodes, J F
St Vrain Land Club (M687) Date: 1860 Oct 23

Rice, Catherine Augusta Rowe
b. 31 Dec 1842, MA
d. 11 Mar 1918, Boulder, CO
bd. Mountain View Cemetery, Longmont, Boulder, CO
spouse: Rufus Rice
St Vrain Pioneers Assn Arrival Date: 1859

Rice, John J
b. 18 Nov 1837, MA
d. 23 Aug 1922, Longmont, Boulder, CO
bd. Mountain View Cemetery, Longmont, Boulder, CO
spouse: Georgianna Simmons Black Rice
father: Comfort Rice
mother: Lucinda Wood Rice
St Vrain Pioneers Assn Arrival Date: 1860
St Vrain Ditch Owner: Bonus Ditch No. 6, 30 Mar 1861
1870 US Census, Colorado Territory, Boulder County, St Vrain District

Rice, Mary Eliza Van Valkenburg
b. 1 Mar 1862, Montrose, Susquehanna, PA
d. 17 Dec 1910, Denver, CO
bd. Fairmount, Denver, CO
spouse: George Arthur Rice
father: Richard Jeptha Van Valkenburg
mother: Cordelia Briggs Van Valkenburg
1870 US Census, Colorado Territory, Boulder County, St Vrain District

St Vrain Valley Pioneers

Rice, Rufus
b. 15 Feb 1836, Worcester, MA
d. 20 Oct 1915, Longmont, Boulder, CO
bd. Mountain View Cemetery, Longmont, Boulder, CO
spouse: Catherine Augusta Rowe Rice
father: Comfort Rice
mother: Lucinda Wood Rice
St Vrain Pioneers Assn Arrival Date: 1859
Troy District Land Club Claim Date: 1860 Oct 16
1870 US Census, Colorado Territory, Boulder County, St Vrain District

Rice, Willie J
b. 13 Sept 1877, Rice Farm, Longmont, Boulder, CO
d. 11 July 1927, Brush, Morgan, CO
bd. Mountain View Cemetery, Longmont, Boulder, CO
spouse: Mollie L Owens Rice
father: John J Rice
mother: Georgiana Simons Black Rice

Rice, Winnifred
b. abt 1889
d. 6 Jan 1923, Longmont, Boulder, CO
spouse: Mr Rice

Richardson
St Vrain Ditch Owner: Richardson Ditch No. 64, 15 June 1874

Richardson, Araminta
b. abt 1867, IA
father: William Henry Richardson
mother: Henrietta Susan Montgomery Richardson

Richardson, Frederick
b. 23 May 1803, Waterford, Caledonia, VT
d. 11 Feb 1876, St Vrain, Boulder, CO
bd. Weisner Cemetery, Boulder, CO
spouse: Laura Campbell Brown Richardson; Elizabeth Nelson Richardson
father: Isaac Richardson
mother: Thankful Towne Richardson
St Vrain Pioneers Assn Arrival Date: 1863
1870 US Census, Colorado Territory, Boulder County, St Vrain District

Richardson, Isaac
b. 25 Sept 1836, Waterford, Caledonia, VT
d. 1882, Boulder, CO
bd. Weisner Cemetery?, Boulder, CO
father: Frederick Richardson
mother: Laura Campbell Brown Richardson
St Vrain Pioneers Assn Arrival Date: 1869

Richardson, William Henry
b. 13 May 1840, IN
d. 24 Oct 1898, Boulder, CO
bd. Green Mountain Cemetery, Boulder, CO
spouse: Henrietta Ssusan Richardson

Richart, George W
b. abt 1838, OH
spouse: Maranda Richart
St Vrain Pioneers Assn Arrival Date: 1862

Richart, Maranda
b. abt 1845, KY
spouse: George Richart
St Vrain Pioneers Assn Arrival Date: 1862

Richart, Maranda Robinson Caywood
b. 1 Nov 1843, Vicksburg, Fleming, KY
d. 15 Jan 1937, Fort Collins, Larimer, CO
spouse: George Washington Richart
father: William Wesley Caywood
mother: Katharine Donovan Newman Caywood
St Vrain Pioneers Assn Arrival Date: 1864

Richart, Mary Henriettie Shepherd Gates
b. 31 Aug 1857, Appanoose, IA
d. 20 Feb 1946, Niwot, Boulder, CO
bd. Niwot Cemetery, Niwot, Boulder, CO
spouse: Henry Lewellyn Gates, Thomas Richart
father: David Lewis Shepherd
mother: Mary Sophia Osborn Shepherd
St Vrain Pioneers Assn Arrival Date: 1861

Richart, Thomas
b. 4 Dec 1848, Webster, Scioto, OH
d. 24 Jan 1918, Niwot, Boulder, CO
bd. Niwot Cemetery, Niwot, Boulder, CO
spouse: Mary Henriettie Shepherd Richart
St Vrain Pioneers Assn Arrival Date: 1869

Ridgely, Henry
b. abt 1815, Hesse, Germany
1870 US Census, Colorado Territory, Boulder County, St Vrain District

Riley, William
b. abt 1837, NY
1860 US Census, Nebraska Territory, Platte River

Ripley, David
St Vrain Land Club Date: 1861 Apr 23

Ripley, Frank
St Vrain Land Club Date: 1861 Apr 23

Ripley, Mrs Frank
St Vrain Pioneers Assn Arrival Date: 1863

Rizmon, Charles
b. abt 1845, OH
1870 US Census, Colorado Territory, Boulder County, St Vrain District

Roberts, S
b. abt 1820, MS
1860 US Census, Nebraska Territory, Platte River

Robinson, Eliza
b. abt 1846, MO
spouse: Silas R Robinson
St Vrain Pioneers Assn Arrival Date: 1868
1870 US Census, Colorado Territory, Boulder County, Left Hand

Robinson, Fred Earl
b. 12 Mar 1872, Longmont, Boulder, CO
d. 26 June 1920, near Canfield, Boulder, CO
bd. Mountain View Cemetery, Longmont, Boulder, CO
spouse: Hattie L Howell Robinson
father: Silas R Robinson
mother: Eliza Robinson

Robinson, Henry
b. abt 1832, OH
1860 US Census, Nebraska Territory, Platte River

Robinson, James G
b. abt 1839, ME
St Vrain Pioneers Assn Arrival Date: 1859
Troy District Land Club Claim Date: 1861 Jan 28
St Vrain Land Club Date: 1861 Aug 28

Robinson, Silas R
b. 4 May 1844, IL
d. 11 Sept 1903
bd. Pleasant View Ridge Cemetery, Weld, CO
spouse: Eliza Robinson
St Vrain Pioneers Assn Arrival Date: 1868
1870 US Census, Colorado Territory, Boulder County, Left Hand

Robinson, William T
b. abt 1824, PA
1860 US Census, Nebraska Territory, Platte River

Roe, family of John
St Vrain Pioneers Assn Arrival Date: 1869

Roe, John
St Vrain Pioneers Assn Arrival Date: 1869

Roe, Mrs John
St Vrain Pioneers Assn Arrival Date: 1869

Rogers, Henry
b. 15 Dec 1833
d. 4 July 1906
bd. Columbia Cemetery, Boulder, CO
spouse: Eliza Thomas Rogers

Roland, Benjamin
b. abt 1838, MO
1860 US Census, Nebraska Territory, Platte River

Roland, James
b. abt 1858, NE Terr
1860 US Census, Nebraska Territory, Platte River

Roland, William
b. abt 1851, NE Terr
1860 US Census, Nebraska Territory, Platte River

Rolland, William
b. abt 1837, MO
1860 US Census, Nebraska Territory, Platte River

Romigh, Chester Arthur
b. 14 Apr 1883, Alma Catron, NM
d. 27 May 1962, Longmont, Boulder, CO
bd. Mountain View Cemetery, Longmont, Boulder, CO
spouse: Lula May Newby Romigh
father: James Baker Romigh
mother: Helen Sarah Fezell Romigh

Romigh, Lula May Newby
b. 13 Dec 1881, Longmont, Boulder, CO
d. 13 Jan 1947, Longmont, Boulder, CO
bd. Mountain View Cemetery, Longmont, Boulder, CO
spouse: Chester Arthur Romigh
father: Bryant Nathaniel Newby
mother: Lillie Ada Hedges Newby

St Vrain Valley Pioneers

Roosa, Harriet Potter Harmon
b. 28 July 1877, CO
d. 14 Mar 1968, Loveland, Larimer, CO
bd. Green Mountain Cemetery, Boulder, CO
spouse: Frank Montayne Roosa
father: George Dana Boardman Harmon
mother: Carrie Haylett Harmon

Rose, Sarah Alberta Caywood
b. 1 Apr 1859, Wapello, IA
spouse: George Rose
father: William Wesley Caywood
mother: Katharine Donovan Newman Caywood
St Vrain Pioneers Assn Arrival Date: 1864
1870 US Census, Colorado Territory, Boulder County, Left Hand

Rose, William H
Troy District Land Club Claim Date: 1860 July 17

Ross, J H
St Vrain Land Club Date: 1861 Apr 11

Ross, James C/G
St Vrain Land Club Date: 1861 Nov 21

Rothrock, Eliza Catherine Buford
b. abt 1850, MO
spouse: John Ramsey Rothrock
St Vrain Pioneers Assn Arrival Date: 1862

Rothrock, John Ramsey
b. 3 Mar 1834, Bellefonte, Centre, PA
d. 7 Apr 1915, Longmont, CO
bd. Mountain View Cemetery, Longmont, Boulder, CO
spouse: Eliza Catherine Buford Rothrock
father: Henry Rothrock
mother: Nancy A Ramsey Rothrock
St Vrain Pioneers Assn Arrival Date: 1858

Ruby, Orin G
St Vrain Land Club (M687) Date: 1861 Jan 18

Rungan
b. abt 1870, Colorado Territory
father: James Rungan
mother: Elenor Rungan
1870 US Census, Colorado Territory, Boulder County, St Vrain District

Rungan, Elenor
b. abt 1850, IL
spouse: James Rungan
1870 US Census, Colorado Territory, Boulder County, St Vrain District

Rungan, James
b. abt 1846, IN
spouse: Elenor Rungan
1870 US Census, Colorado Territory, Boulder County, St Vrain District

Rungan, Roetta
b. abt 1868, IA
father: James Rungan
mother: Elenor Rungan
1870 US Census, Colorado Territory, Boulder County, St Vrain District

Runyan, Aaron Miller
b. 10 Dec 1842, IN
d. 7 July 1922, Longmont, Boulder, CO
bd. Mountain View Cemetery, Longmont, Boulder, CO
spouse: Julia Runyan
father: Isaac Runyan
mother: Mary Jane Runyan
St Vrain Land Club Date: 1861 Apr 17

Runyan, G S
St Vrain Land Club Date: 1861 Sept 8

Runyan, Isaac
b. abt 1820, OH
d. 5 Feb 1896
bd. Hygiene Cemetery, Hygiene, Boulder, CO
spouse: Mary J Runyan
St Vrain Pioneers Assn Arrival Date: 1860
St Vrain Ditch Owner: Runyan Ditch No. 15, 1 May 1863
1870 US Census, Colorado Territory, Boulder County, St Vrain District

Runyan, J S
b. 17 Jan 1821
d. 6 Feb 1896
bd. Hygiene Cemetery, Hygiene, Boulder, CO
Franklin Township Land Club Claim Date: 1860 June 30

Runyan, Marietta
b. abt 1865, Colorado Territory
father: Isaac Runyan
mother: Mary J Runyan
1870 US Census, Colorado Territory, Boulder County, St Vrain District

Runyan, Mary J
b. 24 Jan 1824, OH
d. 26 Feb 1905
bd. Hygiene Cemetery, Hygiene, Boulder, CO
spouse: Isaac Runyan
St Vrain Pioneers Assn Arrival Date: 1860
1870 US Census, Colorado Territory, Boulder County, St Vrain District

Runyan, Rosanna
b. abt 1862, Colorado Territory
father: Isaac Runyan
mother: Mary J Runyan
1870 US Census, Colorado Territory, Boulder County, St Vrain District

Runyan, Thomas
b. abt 1856, IA
father: Isaac Runyan
mother: Mary J Runyan
St Vrain Pioneers Assn Arrival Date: 1860
1870 US Census, Colorado Territory, Boulder County, St Vrain District

Rutter, James G
b. Oct 1834, OH
d. 22 July 1921, Walla Walla, WA
spouse: Amanda M Bachelder Rutter
father: Andrew Rutter
mother: Susan Gibson Rutter

S

Safely, Alexander Fenwick
b. 30 June 1841, Saratoga, NY
d. 5 July 1914, Boulder, CO
bd. Green Mountain Cemetery, Boulder, CO
spouse: Martha 'Jennie' Anderson Parker Safely
father: Thomas Safely
mother: Henrietta Fenwick Safely
1870 US Census, Colorado Territory, Boulder County, St Vrain District

Safely, Grant R
b. 9 May 1868, Boulder, Colorado Territory
d. 11 Aug 1914, Sacramento, CA
spouse: Blythe Hunt Safely
father: Alexander Fenwick Safely
mother: Martha Jane Anderson Safely
1870 US Census, Colorado Territory, Boulder County, St Vrain District

Safely, Martha Jane Anderson Parker
b. 7 July 1839, PA
d. 9 Nov 1912, Boulder, CO
bd. Green Mountain Cemetery, Boulder, CO
spouse: Alexander Fenwick Safely
1870 US Census, Colorado Territory, Boulder County, St Vrain District

Sage
Franklin Township Land Club Claim Date: 1860 July 10

Samuels, C
b. abt 1823, IL
1860 US Census, Nebraska Territory, Platte River

Samworth, Charles
b. abt 1868, Colorado Territory
father: Joseph Samworth
mother: Mary A Samworth
1870 US Census, Colorado Territory, Weld County, St Vrain District

Samworth, Jonas V
b. abt 1866, Colorado Territory
father: Joseph Samworth
mother: Mary A Samworth
1870 US Census, Colorado Territory, Weld County, St Vrain District

St Vrain Valley Pioneers

Samworth, Joseph
b. abt 1840, England
spouse: Mary A Samworth
1870 US Census, Colorado Territory, Weld County, St Vrain District

Samworth, Mary A
b. abt 1848, OH
spouse: Joseph Samworth
1870 US Census, Colorado Territory, Weld County, St Vrain District

Sanburn, John
b. abt 1847, OH
1870 US Census, Colorado Territory, Weld County, St Vrain District

Sanders, Barclay
b. 4 Oct 1824, Cincinnati, OH
d. 15 Dec 1913, Boulder, CO
bd. Columbia Cemetery, Boulder, CO
spouse: Rebecca J Sanders; Elizabeth Bottoms Davis Sanders
father: Jonathan Sanders
St Vrain Land Club Date: 1861 June 24

Sanderson, William,
b. abt 1832 Norway
1860 US Census, Nebraska Territory, Platte River

Sanford, Ada Belle Flemming
b. 28 Oct 1858, IL
d. 22 Nov 1940, Fort Morgan, Morgan, CO
bd. Linn Grove Cemetery, Greeley, Weld, CO
spouse: Steward Sanford
father: George Archibald Flemming
mother: Margaret Gordon Flemming

Sanford, Steward
b. 27 Apr 1848, Whitmore Lake, Livingston, MI
d. 28 Jan 1928, Greeley, Weld, CO
bd. Linn Grove Cemetery, Greeley, Weld, CO
spouse: Ada Belle Flemming Sanford
1870 US Census, Colorado Territory, Weld County, St Vrain District

Savory, Clara H Barney
b. 16 Nov 1846, Cass, MI
d. 20 Mar 1923, Los Angeles, CA
bd. Columbia Cemetery, Boulder, CO
spouse: George F Savory
father: John Gibbon Ackley Barney

Sawdey, Edgar
b. abt 1844, NY
d. 29 May 1922, Los Angeles, CA
spouse: Emma C Williams Sawdy
father: Curtis Isaac Sawdey
mother: Harriet C Van Burger Sawdey
St Vrain Pioneers Assn Arrival Date: 1868

Sawdey, Harold J
b. 28 Feb 1910
d. 19 Feb 1968
bd. Mountain View Cemetery, Longmont, Boulder, CO
spouse: Edith Pearl Davies Sawdey Bickel
father: Ivan Ezekiel Sawdey
mother: Maude A Rice Sawdey

Sawdey, Maude A Rice
b. 25 Mar 1883, Longmont, Boulder, CO
d. 9 Mar 1968, Longmont, Boulder, CO
bd. Mountain View Cemetery, Longmont, Boulder, CO
spouse: Ivan Ezekiel Sawdey
father: Rufus Rice
mother: Kate Augusta Rowe Rice

Sawdey, Rufus Rice
b. 19 Jan 1903, Longmont, Boulder, CO
d. 4 Sept 1965, Longmont, Boulder, CO
bd. Mountain View Cemetery, Longmont, Boulder, CO
spouse: Gladys C Davies Sawdey
father: Ivan Ezekiel Sawdey
mother: Maude A Rice Sawdey

Scarff, Henry J
b. abt 1810, MD
d. 10 Sept 1870, Boulder, CO
spouse: Sarah D Scharff
1870 US Census, Colorado Territory, Boulder County, St Vrain District

Scarff, John F/P
b. abt 1840, MD
father: Henry J Scharff
mother: Sarah D Scharff
1870 US Census, Colorado Territory, Boulder County, St Vrain District

St Vrain Valley Pioneers

Scarff, Sarah D
 b. abt 1810, MD
 spouse: Henry J Scarff
 1870 US Census, Colorado Territory, Boulder County, St Vrain District

Schofield, Carrie Matthews
 b. 1871, Boulder, Colorado Territory
 d. Oct 1924, Brighton, Adams, CO
 bd. Elmwood Cemetery, Brighton, Adams, CO
 spouse: Leveret D Schofield
 father: Milton Matthews
 mother: Martha Matthews

Schofield, Rena Jane Chapman
 b. 1883
 d. 2 Sept 1981
 bd. Lafayette Cemetery, Boulder, CO
 spouse: William Osborn Schofield
 father: Lafayette Chapman
 mother: Ella Marie Springsteel Chapman

Schofield, William Osborn
 b. 1870
 d. 1955
 bd. Lafayette Cemetery, Boulder, CO
 spouse: Rena Jane Chapman Schofield
 father: William Henry Schofield, Sr
 mother: Mary Eliza Downing Schofield

Scholes, John J
 b. abt 1850, ME
 spouse: Diantha M Wite Young Scholes
 mother: Bettie Scholes Brierley
 1870 US Census, Colorado Territory, Boulder County, St Vrain District

Schwilke, Florence C Montgomery
 b. 1886
 d. 1962
 bd. Mountain View Cemetery, Longmont, Boulder, CO
 spouse: Albert Schwilke

Scobey, Esther J
 b. abt 1848, IL
 d. 24 Sept 1923
 spouse: Daniel M Scobey

Scogland, John Colvin
 b. 3 May 1904, CO
 d. 19 May 1968, CO
 bd. Green Mountain Cemetery, Boulder, CO
 spouse: Thesta Kennedy Scotland
 father: Albert Scogland, Sr
 mother: Maude Oline Colvin Scogland

Scott, Holland S
 b. abt 1833, PA
 d. 3 Aug 1913
 bd. Columbia Cemetery, Boulder, CO
 spouse: Mary L Young Scott
 St Vrain Pioneers Assn Arrival Date: 1860
 St Vrain Ditch Owner: Hayseed Ditch No. 1, 1 Jan 1860
 1870 US Census, Colorado Territory, Weld County, St Vrain District

Scott, J D
 b. abt 1816, NC
 spouse: Mary Scott
 St Vrain Pioneers Assn Arrival Date: 1859

Scott, John
 St Vrain Land Club Date: 1861 Dec 1

Scourfield, William S
 St Vrain Land Club (M687) Date: 1858 Nov 1

Scoville, Rebecca Alice Miller
 b. 26 Nov 1858, MO
 d. 3 May 1880, Weld, CO
 bd. Burlington Cemetery, Longmont, Boulder, CO
 spouse: George Aderson Scoville
 father: Michael Christ Miller
 mother: Isabel Agnes Honaker Miller Armstrong
 1870 US Census, Colorado Territory, Boulder County, St Vrain District

Searcy, Webb
 b. abt 1841, ME
 1860 US Census, Nebraska Territory, Platte River

Secor, Fannie
 b. abt 1870, Colorado Territory
 father: William Walker Secor
 mother: Nellie M Coffman Secor
 1870 US Census, Colorado Territory, Boulder County, St Vrain District

Secor, Lydia Franklin
 d. 1946/1947
 father: R I Franklin
 St Vrain Pioneers Assn Arrival Date: 1865

St Vrain Valley Pioneers

Secor, Mary Helen Coffman
b. abt 1846, IL
spouse: William Walker Secor
father: Jacob Coffman
mother: Mary P Stover Coffman
St Vrain Pioneers Assn Arrival Date: 1865
1870 US Census, Colorado Territory, Boulder County, St Vrain District

Secor, Milo G
b. abt 1868, Colorado Territory
father: William Walker Secor
mother: Mary Helen Coffman Secor
1870 US Census, Colorado Territory, Boulder County, St Vrain District

Secor, William Walker
b. abt 1840, NY
d. 19 Oct 1888
bd. Mountain View Cemetery, Longmont, Boulder, CO
spouse: Mary Helen Coffman Secor
St Vrain Pioneers Assn Arrival Date: 1860
1870 US Census, Colorado Territory, Boulder County, St Vrain District

Shanahan, Michael
b. 1818, Ireland
d. 26 Feb 1888, Marshall, CO
bd. South Boulder Cemetery, Boulder, CO
spouse: Mary Shanahan
St Vrain Pioneers Assn Arrival Date: 1862

Shanahan, Patrick
St Vrain Pioneers Assn Arrival Date: 1862

Shanahan, Timothy
b. 1790, Ireland
d. 1880
bd. South Boulder Cemetery, Boulder, CO
spouse: Winifred Dunn Shanahan
St Vrain Pioneers Assn Arrival Date: 1862

Shasha, F
b. abt 1830, IL
1860 US Census, Nebraska Territory, Platte River

Shaw, Ada Myers Doggett Caywood
d. 16 Apr 1920, Niwot, Boulder, CO
spouse: R F Caywood
St Vrain Pioneers Assn Arrival Date: 1864

Shaw, Joseph
b. abt 1827, MN
1870 US Census, Colorado Territory, Boulder County, St Vrain District

Shay, Joseph H
b. abt 1841, Austria
St Vrain Pioneers Assn Arrival Date: 1860
1870 US Census, Colorado Territory, Boulder County, St Vrain District

Shennan, Isaac
b. abt 1835, NY
1870 US Census, Colorado Territory, Boulder County, Left Hand

Sheppard, David
St Vrain Pioneers Assn Arrival Date: 1861

Sheppard, family of David
St Vrain Pioneers Assn Arrival Date: 1861

Sheppard, Mrs David
St Vrain Pioneers Assn Arrival Date: 1861

Sherman, Charles M
b. 1873
d. 1966
bd. Niwot Cemetery, Niwot, Boulder, CO

Short, Amanda J Mason
b. abt 1846, IL
spouse: Elisha Benjamin Short
St Vrain Pioneers Assn Arrival Date: 1860
1870 US Census, Colorado Territory, Boulder County, St Vrain District

Short, Elisha Benjamin
b. abt 1844, WI
d. 25 Nov 1923
spouse: Amanda J Mason Short
St Vrain Pioneers Assn Arrival Date: 1860
1870 US Census, Colorado Territory, Boulder County, St Vrain District

Short, Lillian
b. 2 Apr 1869, Hygiene, Boulder, Colorado Territory
father: Elisha Benjamin Short
mother: Amanda Mason Short
1870 US Census, Colorado Territory, Boulder County, St Vrain District

St Vrain Valley Pioneers

Shrode, Flora H Wolfer
b. 1887
d. 18 Feb 1968
bd. Green Mountain Cemetery, Boulder, CO
spouse: Vernon Franklin Shrode, Sr
father: Carl Frederick Wolfer
mother: Flora Wolfer

Sigler
b. abt 1836, NY
1860 US Census, Nebraska Territory, Platte River

Sigley, Fred C
b. 6 Dec 1854, Warren, OH
d. 25 Aug 1925, Longmont, Boulder, CO
bd. Mountain View Cemetery, Longmont, Boulder, CO
father: William B Sigley
mother: Diantha L Thompson Sigley

Simmons, W
b. abt 1838, NY
1860 US Census, Nebraska Territory, Platte River

Simons, John
b. abt 1836, MO
1860 US Census, Nebraska Territory, Platte River

Simpson, John M
b. abt 1843, ME
1870 US Census, Colorado Territory, Boulder County, St Vrain District

Sites, Esther J Smith Cook
b. 27 Sept 1841, MO
d. 2 July 1912
bd. Hygiene Cemetery, Hygiene, Boulder, CO
spouse: Aquilla Cook, William M Sites
St Vrain Pioneers Assn Arrival Date: 1865
1870 US Census, Colorado Territory, Boulder County, St Vrain District

Sites, William M
b. abt 1834, ME
d. 28 Apr 1894
bd. Hygiene Cemetery, Hygiene, Boulder, CO
spouse: Esther J Cook Sites
St Vrain Pioneers Assn Arrival Date: 1865
1870 US Census, Colorado Territory, Boulder County, St Vrain District

Slater, Marthe
b. July 1869, Colorado Territory
father: William C Slater
mother: Manerva J Caywood Slater Williams
1870 US Census, Colorado Territory, Boulder County, Left Hand

Slaughter, Benjamin H
b. abt 1839, OH
1870 US Census, Colorado Territory, Boulder County, St Vrain District

Slifer, Christina Coffman
b. abt 1835, OH
d. 18 Oct 1907, Longmont, Boulder, CO
spouse: Ezra G Slifer
father: Jacob Coffman
mother: Mary P Stover Coffman
St Vrain Pioneers Assn Arrival Date: 1864
1870 US Census, Colorado Territory, Boulder County, St Vrain District

Slifer, Ezra/Esrom G
b. 14 Feb 1834, MD
d. 1905
bd. Mountain View Cemetery, Longmont, Boulder, CO
spouse: Christina Coffman Slifer
St Vrain Pioneers Assn Arrival Date: 1864

Slocum, Rose Adele Cushman
b. 26 Oct 1869, Colorado Territory
d. 10 Feb 1959, Los Angeles, CA
spouse: Charles S Slocum
father: Alfred Cushman
mother: Elisabeth Jane Powell Cushman
1870 US Census, Colorado Territory, Boulder County, St Vrain District

Smail, Charles
b. abt 1846, Canada
1870 US Census, Colorado Territory, Boulder County, St Vrain District

Smail, Thomas
b. abt 1833, Canada
1870 US Census, Colorado Territory, Boulder County, St Vrain District
Smead, Chester Lyman
b. 22 Feb 1822, Waybridge, VT
d. 13 June 1915, Lyons, Boulder, CO

St Vrain Valley Pioneers

bd. Hygiene, Boulder, CO
spouse: Mary Ann Portwood Smead
St Vrain Pioneers Assn Arrival Date: 1860
St Vrain Ditch Owner: Montgomery Private Ditch No 12 1/2, 15 May 1862
1860 US Census, Nebraska Territory, Altona
1870 US Census, Colorado Territory, Boulder County, St Vrain District

Smead, Chester Lyman
b. 1849, IL
d. 29 Dec 1882
bd. Hygiene Cemetery, Hygiene, Boulder, CO
father: Chester Lyman Smead
mother: Mary Ann Smead
Troy District Land Club Claim Date: 1861 Apr 30
1860 US Census, Nebraska Territory, Altona
1870 US Census, Colorado Territory, Boulder County, St Vrain District

Smead, Emma
b. abt 1866, Colorado Territory
father: Chester Lyman Smead
mother: Mary Ann Smead
1870 US Census, Colorado Territory, Boulder County, St Vrain District

Smead, Marion
b. abt 1855, IL
father: Chester Lyman Smead
mother: Mary Ann Smead
1860 US Census, Nebraska Territory, Altona
1870 US Census, Colorado Territory, Boulder County, St Vrain District

Smead, Mary Ann Portwood
b. 1 Jan 1826, IL
d. 5 Sept 1906
bd. Hygiene Cemetery, Hygiene, Boulder, CO
spouse: Chester Lyman Smead
St Vrain Pioneers Assn Arrival Date: 1860
1860 US Census, Nebraska Territory, Altona
1870 US Census, Colorado Territory, Boulder County, St Vrain District

Smead, Oma
b. abt 1859, IL
father: Chester Lyman Smead
mother: Mary Ann Smead
1870 US Census, Colorado Territory, Boulder County, St Vrain District

Smead, Rufus
b. abt 28 June 1869, St Vrain, Boulder, CO
father: Chester Lyman Smead
mother: Mary Ann Smead
1870 US Census, Colorado Territory, Boulder County, St Vrain District

Smead, Warren
b. abt 1862, Colorado Territory
father: Chester Lyman Smead
mother: Mary Ann Smead
1870 US Census, Colorado Territory, Boulder County, St Vrain District

Smith, Abigale Ward
b. 18 Sept 1849, Waukesha, WI
d. 18 Aug 1931, Nye, Stillwater, MT
spouse: Francis Marion Smith
1870 US Census, Colorado Territory, Boulder County, St Vrain District

Smith, Ada B
b. abt 1869, Colorado Territory
father: Minton Smith
mother: Affa B Smith
1870 US Census, Colorado Territory, Weld County, St Vrain District

Smith Ada, Mary
b. 9 June 1869, Erie, Weld, Colorado Territory
d. 22 July 1929, Redwood City, CA
father: Albert Malenthin Smith
mother: Margaret Platt Bailey Smith
1870 US Census, Colorado Territory, Weld County, St Vrain District

Smith, Ada V
b. abt 1867, Colorado Territory
father: Justice B Smith
mother: Mary J Smith
1870 US Census, Colorado Territory, Boulder County, St Vrain District

Smith, Affa B
b. abt 1847, OH
spouse: Minton Smith
1870 US Census, Colorado Territory, Weld County, St Vrain District

St Vrain Valley Pioneers

Smith, Albert E
b. abt 1862, Colorado Territory
d. 27 June 1936, Vancouver, British Columbia, Canada
father: James Monroe Smith
mother: Lorinda Burton Smith
1870 US Census, Colorado Territory, Boulder County, St Vrain District

Smith, Albert Malenthin
b. 6 Oct 1844, Waukeesha, WI
d. 1 Aug 1897, Jamestown, Boulder, CO
bd. Columbia Cemetery, Boulder, CO
spouse: Margaret Platt Bailey Smith
father: Horace Flint P Smith
mother: Mary H Olinger Smith
1870 US Census, Colorado Territory, Weld County, St Vrain District

Smith, Alonzo
b. abt 1847, IL
1870 US Census, Colorado Territory, Boulder County, St Vrain District

Smith, Amos Ebenezer
b. abt 1851, NM
spouse: Emma J E Grund Smith
1870 US Census, Colorado Territory, Boulder County, St Vrain District

Smith, Andrew H
St Vrain Land Club (M687) Date: 1860 Nov 5

Smith, Azial
b. abt 1810, MA
d. 22 Apr 1880
bd. Hygiene Cemetery, Hygiene, Boulder, CO
spouse: Elizabeth Smith
1870 US Census, Colorado Territory, Boulder County, St Vrain District

Smith, Azial John
b. 25 Mar 1869, St Vrain Canyon, Boulder, CO
father: Justice B Smith
mother: Mary J Smith
1870 US Census, Colorado Territory, Boulder County, St Vrain District

Smith, Benjamin F
b. abt 1843, PA
spouse: Emma Smith
1870 US Census, Colorado Territory, Boulder County, St Vrain District

Smith, Byron A
b. 24 Dec 1903
d. 27 Dec 1980
bd. Hygiene Cemetery, Hygiene, Boulder, CO
spouse: Irene Millicent Smith
father: William Jesse Smith
mother: Sadie Janet Cochran Smith Maxson

Smith, C
b. abt 1838, Ireland
1860 US Census, Nebraska Territory, Platte River

Smith, Charles Curtis
b. abt 1850, WI
spouse: Matina Mae Steele Smith
St Vrain Pioneers Assn Arrival Date: 1865
1870 US Census, Colorado Territory, Boulder County, Left Hand

Smith, D K
St Vrain Pioneers Assn Arrival Date: 1869

Smith, Dan
St Vrain Pioneers Assn Arrival Date: 1864

Smith, Dan
St Vrain Pioneers Assn Arrival Date: 1866

Smith, Dexter
b. abt 1856, IA
spouse: Jennie Evans Smith
father: Aziel Smith
mother: Elisabeth Smith
1870 US Census, Colorado Territory, Boulder County, St Vrain District

Smith, Edward
b. abt 1866, Colorado Territory
d. 26 Nov 1901, Nye, Stillwater, MT
father: James Monroe Smith
mother: Lorinda Burton Smith
1870 US Census, Colorado Territory, Boulder County, St Vrain District

Smith, Elizabeth
b. abt 1812, OH
d. 8 June 1876
bd. Hygiene Cemetery, Hygiene, Boulder, CO
spouse: Azial Smith
1870 US Census, Colorado Territory, Boulder County, St Vrain District

St Vrain Valley Pioneers

Smith, Emma
b. abt 1854, IA
spouse: Benjamin Smith
1870 US Census, Colorado Territory, Boulder County, St Vrain District

Smith, Florence
b. abt 1868, Colorado Territory
father: Rudolphus Nelson Smith
mother: Josie Pendleton Smith
1870 US Census, Colorado Territory, Weld County, St Vrain District

Smith, Francis L
d. 28 Jan 1920, El Centro, CA
spouse: Mary Ellen Slaughter Smith

Smith, Francis Marion
b. 7 Oct 1844, Grand Rapids, Kent, MI
d. 18 Aug 1931, Seattle, King, WA
spouse: Abigail Ward Smith
father: James Monroe Smith
mother: Lorinda Burton Smith
1870 US Census, Colorado Territory, Boulder County, St Vrain District

Smith, Fred
b. abt 1866, Colorado Territory
father: Rudolphus Nelson Smith
mother: Josie Pendleton Smith
1870 US Census, Colorado Territory, Weld County, St Vrain District

Smith, Margaretha "Greta" Matilda Anderson
b. 27 Apr 1839, Tjalmo, Ostergotlands, Sweden
d. 31 Mar 1914, Longmont, CO
bd. Mountain View Cemetery, Longmont, Boulder, CO
spouse: Ezra Sandford Calkins, Daniel Smith
father: Magnus Anderson
mother: Elizabeth Bengtsson Anderson

Smith, Helen Marie Campbell
b. 15 June 1813
d. 11 Oct 1909
bd. Columbia Cemetery, Boulder, CO
spouse: Nelson Ketchum Smith
St Vrain Pioneers Assn Arrival Date: 1860

Smith, Herbert M
b. abt 1868, Colorado Territory
spouse: Minnie Janette Huntington
father: Walter H Smith
mother: Susan Connor Smith
1870 US Census, Colorado Territory, Boulder County, St Vrain District

Smith, I K
St Vrain Pioneers Assn Arrival Date: 1860

Smith, Isaac H
St Vrain Pioneers Assn Arrival Date: [not recorded]

Smith, James
b. abt 1840, OH
1870 US Census, Colorado Territory, Weld County, St Vrain District

Smith, James H Thomas
St Vrain Land Club Date: 1861 Nov 21

Smith, James M
b. abt 1864, IA
spouse: Anna Ackerman Smith
father: Justice B Smith
mother: Mary J Smith
1870 US Census, Colorado Territory, Boulder County, St Vrain District

Smith, James Monroe
b. abt 1816, NY
d. bef 1 Jan 1872, Larimer, CO?
spouse: Lorinda Burton Smith
1870 US Census, Colorado Territory, Boulder County, St Vrain District

Smith, John R
b. 18 May 1846, VA
d. 26 Apr 1906
bd. Mountain View Cemetery, Longmont, Boulder, CO
spouse: Priscilla A Smith
St Vrain Pioneers Assn Arrival Date: 1864

Smith, Josie Wilbur Pendleton
b. 17 Sept 1847, Elgin, IL
d. 14 Feb 1922
spouse: Rudolphus Nelson Smith
father: Frederick Pendleton
mother: Abbie Gardner Germaine Pendleton
1870 US Census, Colorado Territory, Weld County, St Vrain District

Smith, Justice Butler
 b. 18 June 1837, Capolis, MI
 d. 26 Mar 1926, Longmont, Boulder, CO
 bd. Hygiene Cemetery, Hygiene, Boulder, CO
 spouse: Mary Jane Smith
 St Vrain Pioneers Assn Arrival Date: 1860
 1870 US Census, Colorado Territory, Boulder County, St Vrain District

Smith, Lewis B
 b. abt 1857, IA
 father: Justice B Smith
 mother: Mary J Smith
 1870 US Census, Colorado Territory, Boulder County, St Vrain District

Smith, Lorinda Burton
 b. 18 June 1827, Andover, Windsor, VT
 d. 1889, Palouse, Whitman, WA
 spouse: James Monroe Smith
 1870 US Census, Colorado Territory, Boulder County, St Vrain District

Smith, Margaret
 b. abt 1846, OH
 spouse: Albert Smith
 1870 US Census, Colorado Territory, Weld County, St Vrain District

Smith, Margaret Platt Bailey
 b. 6 Apr 1846, Ashland, OH
 d. 26 Oct 1923, Longmont, Boulder, CO
 bd. Columbia Cemetery, Boulder, CO
 spouse: Albert Malenthin Smith
 father: John Campbell Bailey
 mother: Elizabeth Platt Bailey
 St Vrain Pioneers Assn Arrival Date: 1862

Smith, Mary Ella Slaughter
 spouse: Frances L Smith

Smith, Mary Jane
 b. 2 Nov 1836, IL
 d. 25 July 1902
 bd. Hygiene Cemetery, Hygiene, Boulder, CO
 spouse: Justice B Smith
 1870 US Census, Colorado Territory, Boulder County, St Vrain District

Smith, Mary S
 b. abt 1867, Colorado Territory
 father: Minton Smith
 mother: Affa B Smith
 1870 US Census, Colorado Territory, Weld County, St Vrain District

Smith, Matina Mae Steele
 b. 27 June 1855, Lodi, Columbia, WI
 d. 11 May 1934, Altona, Boulder, CO
 bd. Mountain View Cemetery, Longmont, Boulder, CO
 spouse: Charles Curtis Smith
 father: Edward Dunsha Steele
 mother: Phoebe Ann Evans Steele
 St Vrain Pioneers Assn Arrival Date: 1865
 1870 US Census, Colorado Territory, Boulder County, Left Hand

Smith, Michal
 St Vrain Land Club (M687) Date: 1860 June 22

Smith, Mike
 St Vrain Pioneers Assn Arrival Date: 1860

Smith, Miles
 b. abt 1837
 St Vrain Pioneers Assn Arrival Date: 1864

Smith, Milo
 St Vrain Pioneers Assn Arrival Date: 1863

Smith, Minton
 b. abt 1831, VT
 spouse: Affa B Smith
 1870 US Census, Colorado Territory, Weld County, St Vrain District

Smith, Mr
 St Vrain Land Club (M687) Date: 1860 Nov 5

Smith, Nelson Ketchum
 b. 16 Sept 1810
 d. 25 Dec 1894
 bd. Columbia Cemetery, Boulder, CO
 spouse: Helen Marie Campbell Smith
 St Vrain Pioneers Assn Arrival Date: 1860

Smith, Perry
 St Vrain Pioneers Assn Arrival Date: 1860

Smith, Rudolphus Nelson
 b. 20 Feb 1844, Vernon, Waukesha, WI
 d. 7 Oct 1923, Longmont, Boulder, CO
 bd. Mountain View Cemetery, Longmont, Boulder, CO
 spouse: Joanna Wilbur Pendleton Smith

father: Nelson Ketchum Smith
St Vrain Pioneers Assn Arrival Date: 1860
1870 US Census, Colorado Territory, Weld County, St Vrain District

Smith, Sanford Hess
b. Dec 1846, Jamestown, Ottawa, MI
d. 4 Feb 1909, CA
bd. Modesto Citizens Cemetery, Stanislaus, CA
spouse: Tryphena Josephine Kinney Smith
father: James Monroe Smith
mother: Lorinda Burton Smith
St Vrain Land Club (M687) Date: 1860 Mar 23
1870 US Census, Colorado Territory, Boulder County, St Vrain District

Smith, Susan Connor
b. abt 1845, VT
d. aft 1893
spouse: Walter H Smith
1870 US Census, Colorado Territory, Boulder County, St Vrain District

Smith, Theodore Monroe
b. 22 Aug 1850, Kent City, Kent, MI
d. 27 Sept 1931, Redmond, Deschutes, OR
spouse: Laura Belle Lynd Smith
father: James Monroe Smith
mother: Lorinda Burton Smith
1870 US Census, Colorado Territory, Boulder County, St Vrain District

Smith, W D
b. abt 1833, NY
1860 US Census, Nebraska Territory, Platte River

Smith, Walter H
b. abt 1844, IL
d. May 1893, San Diego, CA
spouse: Susan Connor Smith
father: Marinus Gilbert Smith
mother: Anna Maria Woodruff Smith
1870 US Census, Colorado Territory, Boulder County, St Vrain District

Smith, Walter M
b. abt 1846
d. 20 Aug 1920, Haystack, Boulder, CO
St Vrain Pioneers Assn Arrival Date: 1864

Smith, Wilber F
b. 26 Jan 1859, Traverse des Sioux, Nichollet, MN
d. 10 Jan 1948, Palouse, Whitman, WA
father: James Monroe Smith
mother: Lorinda Burton Smith
1870 US Census, Colorado Territory, Boulder County, St Vrain District

Smith, William
St Vrain Land Club Date: 1862 Jan 26

Smith, William T
b. abt 1826, Bavaria, Germany
1860 US Census, Nebraska Territory, Platte River

Smith, Winton
b. abt 1831
d. 21 Sept 1911

Smithy, John H
b. abt 1843, MO
1870 US Census, Colorado Territory, Boulder County, St Vrain District

Smitz, John
b. abt 1835, Bavaria
1870 US Census, Colorado Territory, Boulder County, St Vrain District

Snead, Laura Emeline Chapman
b. 15 Sept 1848, Ottumwa, Wapello, IA
d. 6 May 1931, Greeley, Weld, CO
bd. Hygiene Cemetery, Hygiene, Boulder, CO
spouse: James L Snead
father: Joshua E Chapman
mother: Martha P Chapman
1870 US Census, Colorado Territory, Boulder County, St Vrain District

Snell, Jacob
St Vrain Land Club (M687) Date: 1861 Jan 10

Snively, Family
St Vrain Pioneers Assn Arrival Date: [not recorded]

Snively, George E
b. abt 1846, Canada
1870 US Census, Colorado Territory, Boulder County, St Vrain District

Snively, Mr
St Vrain Pioneers Assn Arrival Date: [not recorded]

St Vrain Valley Pioneers

Snively, Mrs
bd. Berthoud, Larimer, CO
St Vrain Pioneers Assn Arrival Date: [not recorded]

Snow, James
b. abt 1825, MO
1870 US Census, Colorado Territory, Boulder County, St Vrain District

Snyder, Effie A
b. abt 1869, Colorado Territory
d. 1910
father: Hanson Snyder
mother: Susan Brenneman Snyder
1870 US Census, Colorado Territory, Boulder County, St Vrain District

Snyder, Hanson
b. 22 Aug 1834, Hartford, Trumbull, OH
d. 27 Oct 1879, Leadville, Lake, CO
bd. Columbia Cemetery, Boulder, CO
spouse: Susan Brenneman Snyder
father: John Snyder
mother: Anna Crow Snyder
1870 US Census, Colorado Territory, Boulder County, St Vrain District

Snyder, John
b. abt 1859, IA
d. 1938
father: Hanson Snyder
mother: Susan Brennaman Snyder
1870 US Census, Colorado Territory, Boulder County, St Vrain District

Snyder, Susan Breneman
b. 10 Nov 1831, PA
d. 16 July 1916, Seattle, King, WA
spouse: Hanson Snyder
father: Abraham Brenneman
mother: Mary A Redsecker Breneman
1870 US Census, Colorado Territory, Boulder County, St Vrain District

Snyder, Wilber
b. abt 1864, Colorado Territory
d. 1911
spouse: Anna Bosley Snyder
father: Hanson Snyder
mother: Susan Brenneman Snyder
1870 US Census, Colorado Territory, Boulder County, St Vrain District

Southard, Mrs Samuel
St Vrain Pioneers Assn Arrival Date: 1869

Southard, Samuel H
St Vrain Pioneers Assn Arrival Date: 1869

Spangler, Mary Katherine
b. 1961
d. 1966
bd. Mountain View Cemetery, Longmont, Boulder, CO

Spencer, George A
b. abt 1844, Canada
1870 US Census, Colorado Territory, Boulder County, St Vrain District

Spencer, Walter
St Vrain Pioneers Assn Arrival Date: [not recorded]

Sperber, George
b. 1842
d. 1926
bd. Mountain View Cemetery, Longmont, Boulder, CO

Springer, David
b. abt 1832, ME
spouse: Hannah Springer
1870 US Census, Colorado Territory, Boulder County, St Vrain District

Springer, Hannah L
b. abt 1847, IN
spouse: David Springer
1870 US Census, Colorado Territory, Boulder County, St Vrain District

Springer, James
b. abt 1869, Colorado Territory
father: David Springer
mother: Hannah Springer
1870 US Census, Colorado Territory, Boulder County, St Vrain District

Springsteel, Ella/Ellen M
b. abt 1866, IA
father: James Hiram Springsteel
mother: Martha Esther Geer Springsteel
1870 US Census, Colorado Territory, Boulder County, St Vrain District

St Vrain Valley Pioneers

Springsteel, Ida A
b. abt 1869, IL
father: James Hiram Springsteel
mother: Martha Esther Geer Springsteel
1870 US Census, Colorado Territory, Boulder County, St Vrain District

Springsteel, James Hiram
b. 24 Dec 1843, Clermont, OH
d. 4 Sept 1916, Boulder, CO
bd. Niwot Cemetery, Niwot, Boulder, CO
spouse: Martha Esther Geer Springsteel
father: Milo Springsteel
mother: Elizabeth Hutchinson Springsteel
St Vrain Pioneers Assn Arrival Date: [not recorded]
1870 US Census, Colorado Territory, Boulder County, St Vrain District

Springsteel, Martha Esther Geer
b. 21 Nov 1846, IL
d. 23 Aug 1915, Niwot, Boulder, CO
bd. Niwot Cemetery, Niwot, Boulder, CO
spouse: James Hiram Springsteel
father: Solomon Geer
mother: Nancy Phenix Geer
St Vrain Pioneers Assn Arrival Date: 1866
1870 US Census, Colorado Territory, Boulder County, St Vrain District

Springsteel, Mary/Nancy E
b. abt 1864, IL
father: James Hiram Springsteel
mother: Martha Esther Geer Springsteel
1870 US Census, Colorado Territory, Boulder County, St Vrain District

Springsteel, Sarah Elizabeth Hively
b. 5 Feb 1848, Warren, IL
d. 5 Jan 1908, Boulder, CO
bd. Niwot Cemetery, Niwot, Boulder, CO
spouse: Thomas Jefferson Springsteel

Springsteel, Thomas Jefferson
b. 5 May 1848, IN
d. 10 Feb 1892, Boulder, CO
bd. Niwot Cemetery, Niwot, Boulder, CO
spouse: Sarah Elizabeth Hively Springsteel
father: Milo Springsteel
mother: Elizabeth Hutchinson
St Vrain Pioneers Assn Arrival Date: [not recorded]

Squires, family of George
St Vrain Pioneers Assn Arrival Date: 1859

Squires, George Clark
b. 14 Nov 1842, Northampton, CT
d. 1 Oct 1909, Boulder, CO
bd. Columbia Cemetery, Boulder, CO
spouse: Juliette Hopkins Squires
father: Frederick Augustin Squires
mother: Maranda Wade Squires
St Vrain Pioneers Assn Arrival Date: 1859

Squires, Juliette Hopkins
b. Sept 1846, OH
d. 10 Nov 1910, Granby, Grand, CO
bd. Columbia Cemetery, Boulder, CO
spouse: George Clark Squires
father: Isaac Hopkins
mother: Sarah Hopkins
St Vrain Pioneers Assn Arrival Date: 1859

Squires, Theodore J
St Vrain Pioneers Assn Arrival Date: 1858

Stalner, Hiriam
b. abt 1838, OH
1870 US Census, Colorado Territory, Weld County, St Vrain District

Stanley, Flora/Mira E
b. abt 1870, Colorado Territory
father: James J Stanley
mother: Mary E Stanley
1870 US Census, Colorado Territory, Boulder County, St Vrain District

Stanley, G B
St Vrain Land Club Date: 1861 Apr 11

Stanley, James J
b. abt 1841, OH
spouse: Mary E Stanley
1870 US Census, Colorado Territory, Boulder County, St Vrain District

Stanley, Mary E
b. abt 1843, OH
spouse: James J Stanley
1870 US Census, Colorado Territory, Boulder County, St Vrain District

Stanley, Wilson
　b. abt 1800
　d. 1 June 1885
　bd. Jamestown Cemetery, Jamestown, Boulder, CO
　Franklin Township Land Club Claim Date: 1860 Feb 12

Starley, Jennie
　b. abt 1854, IA
　1870 US Census, Colorado Territory, Boulder County, St Vrain District

Starley, Wilson
　b. abt 1803, PA
　1870 US Census, Colorado Territory, Boulder County, St Vrain District

Starns, Byron H
　St Vrain Land Club Date: 1861

Steahan, William
　b. abt 1834, IN
　1860 US Census, Nebraska Territory, Platte River

Stebbins, William
　b. abt 1845, NY
　1870 US Census, Colorado Territory, Weld County, St Vrain District

Steck, James
　St Vrain Land Club (M687) Date: 1859 Oct 6

Steele, Douglas
　b. 14 Feb 1901
　d. 15 Mar 1981
　bd. Forest Lawn Memorial Park, Cypress, Orange, CA
　spouse: Hannah Elizabeth McGillivray Steele

Steele, Edward P
　St Vrain Pioneers Assn Arrival Date: 1859

Steele, Edward Phoebus
　b. 5 May 1859, Lodi, Columbia, WI
　d. 26 Nov 1940, Rock Springs, Sweetwater, WY
　spouse: Emma Belle Hoff Steele
　father: Edward Dunsha Steele
　mother: Phoebe Ann Evans Steele
　St Vrain Pioneers Assn Arrival Date: 1864
　1870 US Census, Colorado Territory, Boulder County, Left Hand

Steele, family of Edward P
　St Vrain Pioneers Assn Arrival Date: 1859

Steele, John Dunsha
　b. 2 Apr 1865, Lodi, Columbia, WI
　d. 11 Dec 1960, Left Hand, Boulder, CO
　bd. Niwot Cemetery, Niwot, Boulder, CO
　spouse: Blanche Estelle Bliven Steele
　father: Edward Dunsha Steele
　mother: Phoebe Ann Evans Steele
　St Vrain Pioneers Assn Arrival Date: 1864
　1870 US Census, Colorado Territory, Boulder County, Left Hand

Steele, Mrs Edward P
　St Vrain Pioneers Assn Arrival Date: 1859

Stephen, Joseph
　b. abt 1829, Prussia
　1870 US Census, Colorado Territory, Boulder County, St Vrain District

Stephens, F A
　b. abt 1815, IN
　1860 US Census, Nebraska Territory, Platte River

Stephens, J H
　b. abt 1831, NY
　1860 US Census, Nebraska Territory, Platte River

Stepp, Thomas O
　St Vrain Pioneers Assn Arrival Date: 1861

Stewart, Carter T
　St Vrain Pioneers Assn Arrival Date: 1864

Stewart, Charles
　b. abt 1833, VA
　1870 US Census, Colorado Territory, Boulder County, St Vrain District

Stewart, Walter E
　b. 4 Apr 1886
　d. 5 Oct 1967
　bd. Foothills Garden of Memory, Longmont, Boulder, CO
　spouse: Audrey Matilda Beers Stewart
　father: Jesse B Stewart
　mother: Susan Catherine Stanley Stewart

Stiles, Henry C
　b. 1824, NY
　d. 1905
　bd. Hygiene Cemetery, Hygiene, Boulder, CO

St Vrain Valley Pioneers

   spouse: Mary S Stiles
   St Vrain Pioneers Assn Arrival Date: 1862
Stiles, Mary S
   b. 1834, PA
   d. 1898
   bd. Hygiene Cemetery, Hygiene, Boulder, CO
   spouse: Henry C Stiles
   St Vrain Pioneers Assn Arrival Date: 1864
Stiles, Wellington
   b. abt 1858, IA
   spouse: Lillian Stiles
   father: Henry C Stiles
   mother: Mary S Stiles
   St Vrain Pioneers Assn Arrival Date: 1864
Stimson, family of William
   St Vrain Pioneers Assn Arrival Date: 1859
Stimson, Mrs William
   St Vrain Pioneers Assn Arrival Date: 1859
Stimson, William
   b. abt 1835, ME
   d. 17 June 1898
   bd. Columbia Cemetery, Boulder, CO
   St Vrain Pioneers Assn Arrival Date: 1859
Stites, Edward W
   b. abt 1858, IA
   father: Henry C Stites
   mother: Samantha Stites
   1870 US Census, Colorado Territory, Boulder County, St Vrain District
Stites, Henry C
   b. abt 1824, NY
   spouse: Samantha Stites
   1870 US Census, Colorado Territory, Boulder County, St Vrain District
Stites, Lilly
   b. abt 1867, Colorado Territory
   father: Henry C Stites
   mother: Samantha Stites
   1870 US Census, Colorado Territory, Boulder County, St Vrain District
Stites, Samantha
   b. abt 1833, PA
   spouse: Henry C Stites
   1870 US Census, Colorado Territory, Boulder County, St Vrain District

Stone, Alonzo
   b. abt 1839, Canada
   1860 US Census, Nebraska Territory, Platte River
Stone, Lewis/Louis
   St Vrain Land Club Date: 1861 Mar 25
Stoner, Mary Ann Hopkins Wellman
   b. 25 July 1839, OH
   d. 13 Apr 1923, Loveland, Larimer, CO
   spouse: Luther C Wellman; Peter Stoner
   father: Isaac Daniel Hopkins
   mother: Matilda Sarah D Henry Hopkins
   St Vrain Pioneers Assn Arrival Date: 1859
Stoner, Peter
   b. 12 July 1824, Stark Cty, OH
   d. 12 Dec 1909, Longmont, Boulder, CO
   bd. Hygiene Cemetery, Hygiene, Boulder, CO
   spouse: Anzo E Hannah Stoner, Mary Stoner
   St Vrain Ditch Owner: Zweck & Turner Ditch No. 21, 30 June 1864
Stotts, family of Joseph
   St Vrain Pioneers Assn Arrival Date: 1859
Stotts, Joseph
   St Vrain Pioneers Assn Arrival Date: 1859
Stotts, Lewis
   b. 4 Jan 1835, Adair, KY
   d. 11 Mar 1867, Boulder, CO
   bd. IA
   spouse: Mary Elizabeth Riddle Stotts Hake
   father: John R Stotts
   mother: Mary Schultz Stotts
   St Vrain Pioneers Assn Arrival Date: 1859
Stotts, Mrs Joseph
   St Vrain Pioneers Assn Arrival Date: 1859
Streeter, Reinzi
   b. abt 1838, PA
   father: Lydia Streeter
   St Vrain Pioneers Assn Arrival Date: 1868
   1870 US Census, Colorado Territory, Boulder County, St Vrain District
Strock, Amos C
   b. 6 Nov 1819, Canfield, Trumbull, OH
   d. 30 Dec 1888, Boulder, Boulder, CO
   bd. Hygiene Cemetery, Hygiene, Boulder, CO
   spouse: Elizabeth S Beattie Strock

1870 US Census, Colorado Territory, Boulder County, St Vrain District

Strock, David Breckenridge
b. 28 Aug 1853, MO
d. 11 June 1922
bd. Hygiene Cemetery, Hygiene, Boulder, CO
father: Amos C Strock
mother: Elizabeth S Beattie Strock

Strock, Frank L
b. 3 Apr 1847, OH
d. 1 Apr 1921
bd. Columbia Cemetery, Boulder, CO
spouse: Hattie Fleck Strock
1870 US Census, Colorado Territory, Boulder County, St Vrain District

Sturdevant, James
b. abt 1810, OH
1870 US Census, Colorado Territory, Boulder County, St Vrain District

Sublett John,
b. abt 1827 KY
1870 US Census, Colorado Territory, Boulder County, St Vrain District

Sutphen, Daniel
b. abt 1839, IN
St Vrain Pioneers Assn Arrival Date: [not recorded]

Swack, Annie A
b. abt 1869, Colorado Territory
father: George A Swack
mother: Mary Swack
1870 US Census, Colorado Territory, Boulder County, St Vrain District

Swack, George E
b. abt 1836, Prussia
spouse: Mary Swack
1870 US Census, Colorado Territory, Boulder County, St Vrain District

Swack, Mary
b. abt 1847, Switzerland
spouse: George E Swack
1870 US Census, Colorado Territory, Boulder County, St Vrain District

Swack, Mary E
b. abt 1867, Colorado Territory
father: George E Swack
mother: Mary Swack
1870 US Census, Colorado Territory, Boulder County, St Vrain District

Swallow, Isaac
St Vrain Land Club Date: 1861 Aug 29

Swan, Magna
b. abt 1846, Sweden
1870 US Census, Colorado Territory, Boulder County, Left Hand

Swanson, Annie Justine Andersson
b. 19 Aug 1876, Hjortsberga, Kronoberga Ian, Sweden
d. 19 Dec 1966, Berthoud, Larimer, CO
bd. Greenlawn Cemetery, Berthoud, Larimer, CO
spouse: Gume Salomon Swanson

Sylvester, Amos
b. abt 1833, IN
1860 US Census, Nebraska Territory, Platte River

Sylvester, Benjamin
b. abt 1833, ME
1860 US Census, Nebraska Territory, Platte River

T

Tales, H B
b. abt 1830, NY
1860 US Census, Nebraska Territory, Platte River

Talmadge, Carl J
d. 15 Nov 1926, Longmont, Boulder, CO

Tarbox, Mr
St Vrain Pioneers Assn Arrival Date: 1860

Tarbox, W
b. abt 1835, MS
1860 US Census, Nebraska Territory, Platte River

Taylor
St Vrain Ditch Owner: Denio & Taylor Extension Ditch No. 69, 1 June 1875

Taylor, Ann
b. abt 1838, OH
spouse: David C Taylor
St Vrain Pioneers Assn Arrival Date: 1860

St Vrain Valley Pioneers

Taylor, Charles
b. abt 1837, IL
1870 US Census, Colorado Territory, Boulder County, St Vrain District

Taylor, D H
St Vrain Land Club Date: 1861 June 23

Taylor, David C
b. abt 1832, OH
spouse: Ann Taylor
St Vrain Pioneers Assn Arrival Date: 1860
Franklin Township Land Club Claim Date: 1860 June 26
St Vrain Land Club Date: 1861 Apr 7

Taylor, family of John H
father: John H Taylor
St Vrain Pioneers Assn Arrival Date: 1862

Taylor, George M
b. abt 1844, KY
1870 US Census, Colorado Territory, Boulder County, St Vrain District

Taylor, James
b. abt 1844, Canada
d. Boulder, CO
spouse: Sophronie Taylor
1870 US Census, Colorado Territory, Boulder County, St Vrain District

Taylor, James H
b. abt 1832, Scotland
spouse: Rachel Taylor
1870 US Census, Colorado Territory, Boulder County, Left Hand

Taylor, James Monroe
b. 9 July 1843, IN
d. 2 Dec 1913, Boulder, CO
bd. Columbia Cemetery, Boulder, CO
spouse: Hattie A Bunce Taylor; Delilah Taylor
St Vrain Pioneers Assn Arrival Date: 1865
1870 US Census, Colorado Territory, Boulder County, Left Hand

Taylor, John H
St Vrain Pioneers Assn Arrival Date: 1862

Taylor, Mrs Frank
d. 1926

Taylor, Mrs James Monroe
St Vrain Pioneers Assn Arrival Date: 1865

Taylor, Mrs John H
spouse: John H Taylor
St Vrain Pioneers Assn Arrival Date: 1862

Taylor, Norval J
b. abt 1865, Colorado Territory
father: James H Taylor
mother: Rachel Taylor
1870 US Census, Colorado Territory, Boulder County, Left Hand

Taylor, Phizer G
St Vrain Land Club Date: 1861 May 21

Taylor, Rachel
b. abt 1838, OH
spouse: James H Taylor
1870 US Census, Colorado Territory, Boulder County, Left Hand

Taylor, Sophronie
b. abt 1850, VA
spouse: James Taylor
1870 US Census, Colorado Territory, Boulder County, St Vrain District

Taylor, Theophilus
d. bef 7 Oct 1876
spouse: Elizabeth Taylor
Troy District Land Club Claim Date: 1860 June 8

Taylor, Thomas J
b. abt 1840, IN
St Vrain Land Club Date: 1861 Aug 19
1870 US Census, Colorado Territory, Boulder County, Left Hand

Taylor, W J
St Vrain Land Club Date: 1861 Apr 1

Taylor, Warren
Troy District Land Club Claim Date: 1861 Oct 14
St Vrain Land Club Date: 1861 July 31

Taylor, Zoe Ann
b. abt 1868, Colorado Territory
father: James H Taylor
mother: Rachel Taylor
1870 US Census, Colorado Territory, Boulder County, Left Hand

St Vrain Valley Pioneers

Teater, Wesley
Franklin Township Land Club Claim Date: 1860 June 30

Teater/Teter, N
St Vrain Land Club Date: 1861 Apr 8

Telton, Elizabeth
b. abt 1858, MO
father: T L Telton
mother: Mary Telton
1860 US Census, Nebraska Territory, Platte River

Telton, Mary
b. abt 1835, IL
spouse: T L Telton
1860 US Census, Nebraska Territory, Platte River

Telton, T L
b. abt 1833, NY
1860 US Census, Nebraska Territory, Platte River

Temple, Edwin James
b. 22 June 1849, Youngstown, Warren, OH
d. 2 Feb 1929, Boulder, CO
bd. Columbia Cemetery, Boulder, CO
spouse: Nina Marie Smith Temple; Alice Hite Smothers Temple
father: James Edward Temple
mother: Rebecca Reid Temple
St Vrain Pioneers Assn Arrival Date: 1861

Templeton, Andrew
St Vrain Pioneers Assn Arrival Date: 1866

Terry, Frances Adeline Burbank
b. 20 Jan 1828, Enfield, Hartford, CT
d. 10 Dec 1928, Boulder, CO
bd. Mountain View Cemetery. Longmont, Boulder, CO
spouse: Seth Terry
father: John Burbank
mother: Sarah Sanderson Burbank

Thomas, Charles
b. abt 1862, IN
father: Clew Thomas
mother: Margaret Thomas
1870 US Census, Colorado Territory, Boulder County, St Vrain District

Thomas, Clemment
b. abt 1869, Colorado Territory
father: Clew Thomas
mother: Margaret Thomas
1870 US Census, Colorado Territory, Boulder County, St Vrain District

Thomas, Clew
b. abt 1830, OH
spouse: Margaret Thomas
1870 US Census, Colorado Territory, Boulder County, St Vrain District

Thomas, Frank
b. abt 1859, IN
father: Clew Thomas
mother: Margaret Thomas
1870 US Census, Colorado Territory, Boulder County, St Vrain District

Thomas, Izella.Rozella Mary
b. abt 1865, KY
father: Clew Thomas
mother: Margaret Thomas
1870 US Census, Colorado Territory, Boulder County, St Vrain District

Thomas, Jay
St Vrain Pioneers Assn Arrival Date: 1859

Thomas, Jesse
b. abt 1857, IN
father: Clew Thomas
mother: Margaret Thomas
1870 US Census, Colorado Territory, Boulder County, St Vrain District

Thomas, Maggie
b. Feb 1870, Colorado Territory
father: Clew Thomas
mother: Margaret Thomas
1870 US Census, Colorado Territory, Boulder County, St Vrain District

Thomas, Margaret
b. abt 1842, Ireland
spouse: Clew Thomas
1870 US Census, Colorado Territory, Boulder County, St Vrain District

Thomas, Minnie
b. abt 1867, Colorado Territory
father: Clew Thomas

St Vrain Valley Pioneers

mother: Margaret Thomas
1870 US Census, Colorado Territory, Boulder County, St Vrain District

Thomas, Mr
St Vrain Land Club (M687) Date: 1860 Oct 23

Thomas, Samuel
b. abt 1845, OH
1870 US Census, Colorado Territory, Boulder County, St Vrain District

Thomas, William J
b. Oct 1892
d. Oct 1967
bd. Mountain View Memorial Park, Boulder, CO
spouse: Livinia Thomas
father: William J Thomas, Sr
mother: Anna Waneka Thomas

Thompson, Edward
b. abt 1840, PA
d. 8 Oct 1877
bd. Columbia Cemetery, Boulder, CO
1870 US Census, Colorado Territory, Boulder County, St Vrain District

Thompson, G M
b. abt 1833, ME
1860 US Census, Nebraska Territory, Platte River

Thorn, Albert
St Vrain Land Club (M687) Date: 1860 Aug 28

Tiffany, Betsey M
b. 3 Apr 1826
d. 10 Jan 1911
bd. Mountain View Cemetery, Longmont, Boulder, CO
spouse: Alonzo Monroe Tiffany
father: Nathan Willard Waldron
mother: Sally Bibee Waldron
St Vrain Pioneers Assn Arrival Date: 1870

Tilson, Charles J
b. abt 1843, IN
spouse: C E Tilson

Tinnis, John
b. abt 1821, Canada
1870 US Census, Colorado Territory, Boulder County, St Vrain District

Titus, Albert C
St Vrain Ditch Owner: Titus & Goyn Ditch No. 72, 1 Apr 1878

Titus, Augustus
b. abt 1859, WI
father: John A Titus
mother: Hattie Titus
1870 US Census, Colorado Territory, Weld County, St Vrain District

Titus, Campbell
b. abt 1855, WI
father: John A Titus
mother: Hattie Titus
1870 US Census, Colorado Territory, Weld County, St Vrain District

Titus, Hattie
b. abt 1825, NY
spouse: John A Titus
1870 US Census, Colorado Territory, Weld County, St Vrain District

Titus, John A
b. abt 1823, NY
spouse: Hattie Titus
St Vrain Pioneers Assn Arrival Date: 1860
Troy District Land Club Claim Date: 1861 Jan 28
1870 US Census, Colorado Territory, Weld County, St Vrain District

Titus, Tim
St Vrain Pioneers Assn Arrival Date: 1860

Tobbes, James
b. abt 1834, NY
1860 US Census, Nebraska Territory, Platte River

Tobin, William
b. abt 1838, ME
1870 US Census, Colorado Territory, Boulder County, St Vrain District

Todd, William
b. abt 1833, KY
1860 US Census, Nebraska Territory, Platte River

Torry, Nash
b. abt 1809, NY
1870 US Census, Colorado Territory, Boulder County, St Vrain District

St Vrain Valley Pioneers

Tourtellot, Charles
b. abt 1867, Colorado Territory
father: James Buchanan Tourtellot
mother: Sarah A Smith Toutellot
1870 US Census, Colorado Territory, Boulder County, Left Hand

Tourtellot, James
b. 27 July 1868, Lefthand Creek, Boulder, Colorado Territory
father: James Buchanan Tourtellot
mother: Sarah A Smith Tourtellot
1870 US Census, Colorado Territory, Boulder County, Left Hand

Tourtellot, James Buchanan
b. 26 Mar 1841, Chepacket, Providence, RI
d. 7 Feb 1910, Boulder, CO
bd. Green Mountain Cemetery, Boulder, CO
spouse: Sarah A Smith Tourtellot
father: Jonathan Aborn Tourtellot
mother: Maria Wade Tourtellot
1870 US Census, Colorado Territory, Boulder County, Left Hand

Tourtellot, Jonathan Aborn
b. 15 Sept 1812, Gloucester, Providence, RI
d. 27 Jan 1870, Boulder, Colorado Territory
bd. Columbia Cemetery, Boulder, CO
spouse: Maria Wade Tourtellot
father: Jesse Tourtellot
mother: Ruth Steere Tourtellot
St Vrain Pioneers Assn Arrival Date: 1860

Tourtellot, Sarah Ann Smith
b. May 1848, Knox, IL
d. 1933, Boulder, CO
bd. Green Mountain Cemetery, Boulder, CO
spouse: James Buchanan Tourtellot
father: Marinus Gilbert Smith
mother: Anna Marie Woodruff Smith
1870 US Census, Colorado Territory, Boulder County, Left Hand

Tower, Elizabeth
b. abt 1838, OH
spouse: Gilbert Tower
1870 US Census, Colorado Territory, Boulder County, St Vrain District

Tower, Ella
b. abt 1861, Colorado Territory
father: Gilbert Tower
mother: Elizabeth Tower
1870 US Census, Colorado Territory, Boulder County, St Vrain District

Tower, Gilbert J
b. abt 1834, NY
spouse: Elizabeth Tower
St Vrain Pioneers Assn Arrival Date: 1858
St Vrain Land Club Date: 1861 May 20
1870 US Census, Colorado Territory, Boulder County, St Vrain District

Tower, J
St Vrain Land Club Date: 1861 July 29

Tower, Mary
b. abt 1863, Colorado Territory
father: Gilbert Tower
mother: Elizabeth Tower
1870 US Census, Colorado Territory, Boulder County, St Vrain District

Tracy, Amelia Cavey
b. abt 1850, England
spouse: Daniel C Tracy
St Vrain Pioneers Assn Arrival Date: 1868

Tracy, Daniel L
b. abt 1849, VT
spouse: Amelia Cavey Tracy
St Vrain Pioneers Assn Arrival Date: 1867
1870 US Census, Colorado Territory, Boulder County, Left Hand

Traxel, Jonathan
St Vrain Land Club Date: 1860 Feb 15

Trevarton, Emma Jane Collins Johns
b. Aug 1841, St Blazey, Cornwall, England
d. 18 Nov 1899, Cold Springs Ranch, Nederland, Boudler, CO
bd. Green Mountain Cemetery, Boulder, CO
spouse: John Henry Johns; Thomas John Trevarton
father: William Collins
mother: Mary Frances Roach Collins
St Vrain Pioneers Assn Arrival Date: 1867

St Vrain Valley Pioneers

True, Charles Carl
 b. abt 1833, Caledonia, VT
 d. 21 May 1894, Hygiene, Boulder, CO
 bd. Green Mountain Cemetery, Boulder, CO
 spouse: Lydia Ann Davis True
 father: Pearson R True
 mother: Jerusha Stoddard True
 St Vrain Pioneers Assn Arrival Date: 1860
 St Vrain Land Club Date: 1861 Apr 11
 St Vrain Ditch Owner: True & Webster Ditch No. 11, 1 Apr 1862
 1870 US Census, Colorado Territory, Boulder County, St Vrain District

True, Edwin Stoddard
 b. 5 July 1869, Colorado Territory
 d. 3 May 1960, Murtaugh, ID
 spouse: Elizabeth May Wellman True
 father: Charles Carl True
 mother: Lydia Ann Davis True
 1870 US Census, Colorado Territory, Boulder County, St Vrain District

True, Lydia Ann Davis
 b. abt 1851, IA or IN
 d. 1917, Boulder, CO
 spouse: Charles Carl True
 father: Joseph Davis
 mother: Alliean Ratliff Davis
 St Vrain Pioneers Assn Arrival Date: 1860
 1870 US Census, Colorado Territory, Boulder County, St Vrain District

Tucker, J H
 St Vrain Land Club Date: 1860 Feb 2

Tumbleson, John
 St Vrain Pioneers Assn Arrival Date: [not recorded]

Tumbleson, Thomas
 St Vrain Pioneers Assn Arrival Date: 1865

Turner, C
 b. abt 1834, PA
 1860 US Census, Nebraska Territory, Platte River

Turner, Peter C
 b. abt 1826, CT
 St Vrain Pioneers Assn Arrival Date: 1861

Turner, Tazwell Adolphus
 b. 1836, VA
 d. 1917
 bd. Hygiene Cemetery, Hygiene, Boulder, CO
 spouse: Maria Turner
 St Vrain Pioneers Assn Arrival Date: 1861
 St Vrain Ditch Owner: Zweck & Turner Ditch No. 21, 30 June 1864

Turrell, Amy Sophia Greenly
 b. 9 Nov 1852, IL
 spouse: James Henry Turrell
 father: Jesse Hamilton Greenly
 mother: Melissa Sophia Corwin Greenly
 1870 US Census, Colorado Territory, Boulder County, St Vrain District

Turrell, Judson W
 b. 26 Aug 1843, PA
 d. 21 Nov 1902, Longmont, Boulder, CO
 bd. Mountain View Cemetery, Longmont, Boulder, CO
 spouse: Mary V W Tiffany Turrell
 St Vrain Pioneers Assn Arrival Date: 1866

Turrell, Mary V W Tiffany
 b. abt 1850, PA
 spouse: Judson W Turrell
 St Vrain Pioneers Assn Arrival Date: 1866

Tyler, Clinton Monroe
 b. 16 Jan 1834, Livingston, NY
 d. 18 Mar 1886, Boulder, CO
 bd. Columbia Cemetery, Boulder, CO
 spouse: Sarah Emma Smith Tyler
 father: George W Tyler
 mother: Margaret (Lodoiska) Norton Tyler
 St Vrain Pioneers Assn Arrival Date: 1860

Tyler, Lee C
 b. abt 1875
 d. 6 Dec 1928, On the train home from MN

Tyler, Sarah Emma Smith
 b. 30 May 1835, Courtland, NY
 d. 14 Oct 1928, Boulder, CO
 bd. Columbia Cemetery, Boulder, CO
 spouse: Clinton Monroe Tyler
 father: Nelson Ketchum Smith
 mother: Helen MarieCampbell Smith
 St Vrain Pioneers Assn Arrival Date: 1860

U

Ullery, John R
b. abt 1832, OH
spouse: Mary Ullery
St Vrain Ditch Owner: Ullery Ditch No. 66, 1 July 1874

Urmson, John S
b. abt 1848, PA
d. 19 Aug 1883
bd. Mount Pleasant Ridge Cemetery, Weld, CO
1870 US Census, Colorado Territory, Boulder County, St Vrain District

Utter, Mary
b. abt 1795, VT
1870 US Census, Colorado Territory, Boulder County, St Vrain District

V

Valentine, J
b. abt 1834, OH
1860 US Census, Nebraska Territory, Platte River

Van Camp, Samuel
b. abt 1841
spouse: Candido Van Camp
St Vrain Pioneers Assn Arrival Date: [not recorded]

Van Meter, Mr
St Vrain Pioneers Assn Arrival Date: [not recorded]

Van Valkenburg, Cordelia Briggs
b. 10 Dec 1823, Nichols, Tioga, NY
d. 17 Jan 1914, Greeley, Weld, CO
bd. Fairmount Cemetery, Denver, CO
spouse: Richard J Van Valkenburg
St Vrain Pioneers Assn Arrival Date: 1866
1870 US Census, Colorado Territory, Boulder County, St Vrain District

Van Valkenburg, Galen B
b. 29 Nov 1847, NY
d. 6 Dec 1896
bd. Lafayette Cemetery, Boulder, CO
spouse: Phoebe A Slaughter Van Valkenburg
father: Richard Jeptha Van Valkenburg
mother: Cordelia Briggs Van Valkenburg
1870 US Census, Colorado Territory, Boulder County, St Vrain District

Van Valkenburg, Richard Jeptha
b. 16 Aug 1823, Schoharie, NY
d. 8 Sept 1912, Greeley, Weld, CO
bd. Fairmount Cemetery, Denver, CO
spouse: Cordelia Briggs Van Valkenburg
father: Edward Van Valkenburg
mother: Alice B Grinnell Van Valkenburg
St Vrain Pioneers Assn Arrival Date: 1865
1870 US Census, Colorado Territory, Boulder County, St Vrain District

Varney, Elmyra Bailey
b. 7 Feb 1856, IA
d. 10 Dec 1928, CO
bd. Crown Hill Cemetery, Wheatridge, CO
spouse: Nathan E Varney
father: John Campbell Bailey
mother: Elisabeth Platt Bailey
St Vrain Pioneers Assn Arrival Date: 1866
1870 US Census, Colorado Territory, Weld County, St Vrain District

Vasquez, A P
St Vrain Land Club (M687) Date: 1859 Oct 28

Vasquez, Louis
St Vrain Land Club (M687) Date: 1859 Oct 28

Viers, Carlten
b. abt 1864, Colorado Territory
1870 US Census, Colorado Territory, Boulder County, St Vrain District

Viers, Cora
b. abt 1862, IA
1870 US Census, Colorado Territory, Boulder County, St Vrain District

Virden, Georgina
b. abt 1858, NE Terr
father: John Virden
mother: Jane Virden
1870 US Census, Colorado Territory, Boulder County, St Vrain District

Virden, Jane Hunt
b. abt 1818, IL
d. 12 June 1885, Jamestown, Boulder, CO
bd. Columbia Cemetery, Boulder, CO

spouse: John Virden
1870 US Census, Colorado Territory, Boulder County, St Vrain District

Virden, John
b. abt 1816, KY
d. 1 May 1900, Boulder, CO
spouse: Jane Hunt Virden
St Vrain Ditch Owner: Zweck & Turner Ditch No. 21, 30 June 1864
1870 US Census, Colorado Territory, Boulder County, St Vrain District

Virden, John Wesley
b. 6 Mar 1842, Edwards, IL
d. 23 May 1906, Boulder, CO
bd. Columbia Cemetery, Boulder, CO
spouse: Nancy Jane Morrow Virden
father: John Virden
mother: Jane Hunt Virden
1870 US Census, Colorado Territory, Boulder County, St Vrain District

Virden, Martha
b. abt 1849, WI
father: John Virden
mother: Jane Hunt Virden
1870 US Census, Colorado Territory, Boulder County, St Vrain District

Virden, Martin S
b. abt 1854, IA
father: John Virden
mother: Jane Hunt Virden
1870 US Census, Colorado Territory, Boulder County, St Vrain District

Voake, Catherine
b. 25 June 1884, CO
d. 18 Jan 1968
bd. Mountain View Cemetery, Longmont, Boulder, Co
spouse: John Voake
father: George Martin Fuhrman
mother: Mary Elizabeth Nicks Furhman

Vrand, J
b. abt 1834, OH
1860 US Census, Nebraska Territory, Platte River

W

Wade, Noble R
b. 1843, OH
d. 11 July 1934, Denver, CO
bd. Fairmount Cemetery, Denver, CO
spouse: Rosie Millar Wade
St Vrain Pioneers Assn Arrival Date: 1865
1870 US Census, Colorado Territory, Weld County, St Vrain District

Wade, Rosie Millar
b. 9 Dec 1942, Oshkosh, WI
d. 1928, Denver, CO
bd. Fairmount Cemetery, Denver, CO
spouse: Noble Wade
father: Orlando Millar
mother: Mary B Newcombe Millar
St Vrain Pioneers Assn Arrival Date: 1865
1870 US Census, Colorado Territory, Weld County, St Vrain District

Wade, Willie
b. abt 1865, Colorado Territory
father: Noble Wade
mother: Rose Wade
1870 US Census, Colorado Territory, Weld County, St Vrain District

Waeneka, Henry Adolf
b. abt 1826, Prussia
d. 11 Oct 1896
bd. Lafayette Cemetery, Boulder, CO
St Vrain Pioneers Assn Arrival Date: 1861

Waeneka, 3 children of Adolf Waeneka
father: Adolf Waeneka
mother: Anna Waneeka
St Vrain Pioneers Assn Arrival Date: 1861

Waeneke, Adolph
b. abt 1857, CT
father: Henry Adolph Waeneke
mother: Anna Stretz Waeneke Wilsky Schneider
St Vrain Pioneers Assn Arrival Date: 1861

Waeneke, Anna
b. abt 1854, CT
father: Henry Adolph Waeneke
mother: Anna Stretz Waeneke Wilsky Schneider
St Vrain Pioneers Assn Arrival Date: 1861

Waeneke, William
b. abt 1859, CT
father: Henry Adolph Waeneke
mother: Anna Stretz Waeneke Wilsky Schneider
St Vrain Pioneers Assn Arrival Date: 1861

Wagner, Michael T
b. 19 May 1961
d. 2 Apr 1967
bd. Mountain View Memorial Park, Boulder, CO

Wagner, T F
Franklin Township Land Club Claim Date: [not recorded]

Wakely, Burton
St Vrain Land Club (M687) Date: 1860 Mar 1

Waldron, Charles P
b. abt 1843, NY
d. 8 Jan 1921, National Veterans Home, Sawtell, CA
spouse: Louise McMinn Waldron

Waldron, Louise McMinn
b. 31 Dec 1845, MI
d. 2 Mar 1911, Boulder, CO
bd. Columbia Cemetery, Boulder, CO
spouse: Charles P Waldron
father: Francis McMinn
mother: Marcia Beach McMinn

Walker, James Andrew
b. 7 June 1847, VA
d. 18 Jan 1922, Boulder, CO
bd. Green Mountain Cemetery, Boulder, CO
spouse: Phoebe Fidelia Skinner Walker
1870 US Census, Colorado Territory, Boulder County, Left Hand

Wallace, Lewis
b. abt 1824, New Brunswick, Canada
1870 US Census, Colorado Territory, Boulder County, St Vrain District

Walling, D W
St Vrain Pioneers Assn Arrival Date: 1859

Ward, Calvin W
b. abt 1832, NY
St Vrain Pioneers Assn Arrival Date: 1860

Ward, Warrington
b. abt 1854, WI
1870 US Census, Colorado Territory, Boulder County, St Vrain District

Warner, Wilson
b. abt 1851, PA
1870 US Census, Colorado Territory, Boulder County, St Vrain District

Warren, William
b. abt 1816, England
1870 US Census, Colorado Territory, Boulder County, St Vrain District

Washburn, Hiram Elliott
b. 11 Jan 1843, Waverly, OH
d. 25 Apr 1916, Boulder, CO
bd. Columbia Cemetery, Boulder, CO
spouse: Mary Ann Allen Washburn
father: John Washburn
mother: Elvira Elliott Washburn
1870 US Census, Colorado Territory, Weld County, St Vrain District

Washburn, Mary Ann Allen
b. abt 1852, WI
spouse: Hiram Elliot Washburn
father: Alonzo Nelson Allen
mother: Mary Harris Allen
St Vrain Pioneers Assn Arrival Date: 1863
1870 US Census, Colorado Territory, Boulder County, St Vrain District

Way, Ellen
b. abt 1853, IA
father: Enoch Way
mother: Perlina Caroline Stewart Way
St Vrain Pioneers Assn Arrival Date: 1864
1870 US Census, Colorado Territory, Boulder County, Left Hand

Way, Enoch
b. 10 May 1810, NC
d. 10 Feb 1888, Boulder, CO
bd. Burlington Cemetery, Longmont, Boulder, CO
spouse: Perlina Caroline Stewart Way
father: Joseph Way
mother: Margaret Moss Way
St Vrain Pioneers Assn Arrival Date: 1864
1870 US Census, Colorado Territory, Boulder County, Left Hand

St Vrain Valley Pioneers

Way, Francenus C
  b. abt 1856, IA
  father: Enoch Way
  mother: Perlina Caroline Stewart Way
  St Vrain Pioneers Assn Arrival Date: [not recorded]
  1870 US Census, Colorado Territory, Boulder County, Left Hand

Way, Perlina Carolina Stewart
  b. 25 Nov 1812, Indiana Territory
  d. 6 July 1886, Niwot, Boulder, CO
  bd. Burlington Cemetery, Longmont, Boulder, CO
  spouse: Enoch Way
  father: David Davis Stewart
  mother: Minnie Blackwell Stewart
  St Vrain Pioneers Assn Arrival Date: 1864
  1870 US Census, Colorado Territory, Boulder County, Left Hand

Way, Royal Clinton
  b. 15 Oct 1859, Blakesburg, Wapello, IA
  d. Yukon?
  spouse: Jessie A Wright Way
  father: Enoch Way
  mother: Perlina Caroline Steart Way
  1870 US Census, Colorado Territory, Boulder County, Left Hand

Wayne, William
  Troy District Land Club Claim Date: 1861 Mar 28

Weaver, George
  b. abt 1824, NY
  1860 US Census, Nebraska Territory, Platte River

Webb, Daniel
  b. abt 1842, OH
  1870 US Census, Colorado Territory, Boulder County, St Vrain District

Webb, Ovid Victor
  b. 8 Jan 1868, Libertyville, IL
  d. 4 July 1929, Estes Park, Larimer, CO
  bd. Mountain View Cemetery, Longmont, Boulder, CO
  spouse: Dora E Rowe Webb

Webster, George Washington
  b. 30 Oct 1834, Ashland, OH
  d. 6 Jan 1904, Hygiene, Boulder, CO
  bd. Hygiene Cemetery, Hygiene, Boulder, CO
  spouse: Mary Ellen Weisner Webster; Mary Ann Johnson
  father: John N Webster
  mother: Mary Maurer Webster
  St Vrain Pioneers Assn Arrival Date: 1860
  St Vrain Land Club Date: 1861 Apr 11
  St Vrain Ditch Owner: True & Webster Ditch No. 11, 1 Apr 1862
  1870 US Census, Colorado Territory, Boulder County, St Vrain District

Webster, Mary Ellen Harp Weisner
  b. 8 Mar 1840, Frederick, MD
  d. 22 Apr 1869, Hygiene, Boulder, Co
  bd. Hygiene Cemetery, Hygiene, Boulder, CO
  spouse: Norman Weisner;. George Washington Webster
  father: Daniel Harp
  mother: Mary Ann Zentmyer Harp
  St Vrain Pioneers Assn Arrival Date: 1864

Weese, Christopher Columbus
  b. 1846, Greene Co, IL
  d. 18 Apr 1916, Hygiene, CO
  bd. Hygiene Cemetery, Hygiene, Boulder, CO
  spouse: Malinda J Weese
  father: Samuel Weese
  mother: Rebecca Brackett Weese
  St Vrain Pioneers Assn Arrival Date: 1862
  St Vrain Land Club Date: 1862 Jan 23
  St Vrain Ditch Owner: Baker & Weese Ditch No. 24, 1 June 1865
  1870 US Census, Colorado Territory, Boulder County, St Vrain District

Weese, John
  b. 20 Dec 1841, IL
  d. 17 Apr 1912
  bd. Hygiene Cemetery, Hygiene, Boulder, CO
  spouse: Rozella Smith Weese
  father: Samuel Weese
  mother: Rebecca Brackett Weese
  St Vrain Pioneers Assn Arrival Date: 1859
  Franklin Township Land Club Claim Date: 1860 Feb 12
  1870 US Census, Colorado Territory, Boulder County, St Vrain District

Weese, Lizzie
  b. 31 Mar 1869, St Vrain, Boulder, CO
  father: John Weese
  mother: Rosella Smith Weese
  1870 US Census, Colorado Territory, Boulder County, St Vrain District

Weese, Rozella Smith
  b. 9 July 1848, Cass, MI
  d. 17 Mar 1925, Los Angeles, CA
  bd. Hygiene Cemetery, Hygiene, Boulder, CO
  spouse: John Weese
  St Vrain Pioneers Assn Arrival Date: 1865
  1870 US Census, Colorado Territory, Boulder County, St Vrain District

Weisner, Norman
  spouse: Mary Ellen Harp Weisner
  Franklin Township Land Club Claim Date: 1860 Feb 12
  St Vrain Land Club Date: 1862 Jan 23

Welch, David E
  b. abt 1838, MI
  d. 7 Jan 1897, Altona, Boulder, CO
  bd. Columbia Cemetery, Boulder, CO
  spouse: Hannah Nicholas Welch

Wellman, Electa Bennett
  b. abt 1843, PA
  d. 21 Jan 1884, Jamestown, Boulder, CO
  bd. Columbia Cemetery, Boulder, CO
  spouse: Henry Lewis Wellman
  father: Benjamin Bennett
  mother: Eliza Bennett
  St Vrain Pioneers Assn Arrival Date: 1859

Wellman, Henry Lewis
  b. 28 Dec 1821, New Milford, Susquehanna, PA
  d. 10 Dec 1895, Longmont, Boulder, CO
  bd. Columbia Cemetery, Boulder, CO
  spouse: Electa Bennett Wellman
  father: John Wellman
  mother: Polly Wade Wellman
  St Vrain Pioneers Assn Arrival Date: 1859

Wellman, Luther C
  b. 20 Mar 1826, New Milford, Susquehanna, PA
  d. 3 Feb 1897, Aspen, Pitkin, CO
  spouse: Mary Ann Hopkins Wellman
  father: John Wellman
  mother: Polly Wade Wellman
  St Vrain Pioneers Assn Arrival Date: 1859

Wellman, Roumelia Amelia Towner
  b. 8 Mar 1847, Hunter, Greene, NY
  d. 6 July 1922, Boulder, CO
  bd. Columbia Cemetery, Boulder, CO
  spouse: Sylvanus DeKalb Wellman
  father: Reuben E Towner
  mother: Lucinda Howard Towner
  St Vrain Pioneers Assn Arrival Date: 1859

Wellman, Sylvanus DeKalb
  b. 19 Sept 1834, New Milford, Susquehanna, PA
  d. 3 July 1896, Boulder, CO
  bd. Columbia Cemetery, Boulder, CO
  spouse: Roumelia Amelia Towner Wellman
  father: John Wellman
  mother: Polly Wade Wellman
  St Vrain Pioneers Assn Arrival Date: 1859

Wells, John B
  d. 1923, Chicago, IL

Wells, John H
  b. 28 Mar 1842, IL
  d. 16 Apr 1923, Chicago, IL
  bd. Fairmount Cemetery, Denver, CO
  spouse: Romelia Adeliza Smith Wells
  St Vrain Pioneers Assn Arrival Date: 1866
  1870 US Census, Colorado Territory, Boulder County, St Vrain District

Wemott, Stephen Smith
  St Vrain Land Club Date: 1861 Aug 27

Wheelock
  St Vrain Pioneers Assn Arrival Date: 1858

White, David
  b. abt 1840, PA
  spouse: Margaret White
  1870 US Census, Colorado Territory, Boulder County, St Vrain District

White, Dulcina Catherine Beasley
  b. 4 Dec 1853, MO
  d. 7 Oct 1944, Jefferson, CO
  spouse: Terrence White
  father: James Jackson Beasley
  mother: Eliza Jones Beasley
  St Vrain Pioneers Assn Arrival Date: 1863

St Vrain Valley Pioneers

White, George
b. abt 1843
d. 19 Oct 1923

White, Harry Duel
b. 28 Feb 1868, Niwot, Boulder, Colorado Territory
d. 17 June 1904, Longmont, Boulder, CO
spouse: Hattie Williams
father: John Guess White
mother: Rhoda Ann Van Camp White
1870 US Census, Colorado Territory, Boulder County, St Vrain District

White, John Guess
b. 20 Oct 1834, Carroll, OH
d. 10 Oct 1901, Boulder, CO
bd. Burlington Cemetery, Longmont, Boulder, CO
spouse: Rhoda Ann Van Camp White
father: John J White
mother: Sarah Deets White
St Vrain Pioneers Assn Arrival Date: 1867
1870 US Census, Colorado Territory, Boulder County, St Vrain District

White, Lee
b. abt 1869, Colorado Territory
father: David White
mother: Margaret White
1870 US Census, Colorado Territory, Boulder County, St Vrain District

White, Lyman Alonzo
b. 5 Mar 1835, South Hadley, Hampshire, MA
d. 5 Sept 1911, Longmont, CO
bd. Mountain View Cemetery, Longmont, Boulder, CO
father: Ralph White
mother: Ruth Stebbins Lyon White
St Vrain Pioneers Assn Arrival Date: 1862
1870 US Census, Colorado Territory, Boulder County, St Vrain District

White, Margaret
b. abt 1845, OH
spouse: David White
1870 US Census, Colorado Territory, Boulder County, St Vrain District

White, Orvil
b. abt 1867, Colorado Territory
father: David White
mother: Margaret White
1870 US Census, Colorado Territory, Boulder County, St Vrain District

White, Perry
b. 22 Feb 1820, Gallia, OH
d. 10 July 1885, 7 Miles West of Longmont
bd. Columbia Cemetery, Boulder, CO
spouse: Rachel Irvine White
St Vrain Pioneers Assn Arrival Date: 1860
St Vrain Land Club Date: 1861 Aug 29
1870 US Census, Colorado Territory, Boulder County, St Vrain District

White, Rachel Barlow Irvine
b. Feb 1823, Gallia, OH
d. 27 Dec 1910, Boulder, CO
bd. Columbia Cemetery, Boulder, CO
spouse: Perry White
father: John Irvine
St Vrain Pioneers Assn Arrival Date: 1860
1870 US Census, Colorado Territory, Boulder County, St Vrain District

White, Rhoda Ann Van Camp
b. 2 Dec 1842, OH
d. 6 Oct 1912, Longmont, Boulder, CO
bd. Burlington Cemetery, Longmont, Boulder, CO
spouse: John Guess White
St Vrain Pioneers Assn Arrival Date: 1867
1870 US Census, Colorado Territory, Boulder County, St Vrain District

White, Richard L
St Vrain Pioneers Assn Arrival Date: 1862

White, William
b. abt 1847, IL
1870 US Census, Colorado Territory, Boulder County, St Vrain District

White, William
b. abt 1836, PA
1860 US Census, Nebraska Territory, Platte River

White, William Lyman
b. Apr 1868, Benton, IA
d. Sept 1928, Boulder, CO
bd. Burlington Cemetery, Longmont, Boulder, CO

father: John Guess White
mother: Rhoda Ann Van Camp White
1870 US Census, Colorado Territory, Boulder County, St Vrain District

Whiteley, Mina Augusta Andrews
b. 29 Oct 1859, Galva, Henry, IL
d. 20 Aug 1923, Boulder, CO
bd. Columbia Cemetery, Boulder, CO
spouse: Monford Schley Whiteley
father: George Asa Andrews
mother: Mary Ann Ellsworth Andrews

Whiteside, William
b. abt 1841, IL
1870 US Census, Colorado Territory, Boulder County, St Vrain District

Whitnah, Matilda Groseclose
b. abt 1860, IA
spouse: Joseph C Whitnah
father: Peter Groseclose
mother: Helena Sophia Anderson Groseclose
1870 US Census, Colorado Territory, Weld County, St Vrain District

Wicks, James
b. abt 1837, OH
1860 US Census, Nebraska Territory, Platte River

Wigle, William
St Vrain Pioneers Assn Arrival Date: 1865

Williams, D H
St Vrain Land Club (M687) Date: 1860 May 4

Williams, Elijah R
b. abt 1834, NY
spouse: Nancy Williams
St Vrain Pioneers Assn Arrival Date: 1865
1870 US Census, Colorado Territory, Boulder County, Left Hand

Williams, family of Thomas E
St Vrain Pioneers Assn Arrival Date: 1870

Williams, George Washington
b. 10 Apr 1842, Columbia, Adair, KY
d. 9 Mar 1910, Sugarloaf, Boulder, CO
bd. Nederland Cemetery, Nederland, Boulder, CO
spouse: Ida Mae Orvis Williams
father: William Williams
mother: Mildred Carlton Rowe Williams
1870 US Census, Colorado Territory, Boulder County, St Vrain District

Williams, H N
St Vrain Pioneers Assn Arrival Date: 1860

Williams, Ida Mae Orvis
b. 15 Aug 1860, Russell Gulch, Gilpin, CO
d. 24 Aug 1904, Gordon Gulch, Boulder, CO
spouse: George Washington Williams
father: Harrison Fletcher Orvis
mother: Joanna C Corbin Orvis
1870 US Census, Colorado Territory, Boulder County, St Vrain District

Williams, James F
b. abt 1859, IA
father: Elijah R Williams
mother: Nancy Williams
1870 US Census, Colorado Territory, Boulder County, Left Hand

Williams, John
b. abt 1833, Ireland
St Vrain Pioneers Assn Arrival Date: 1869
1870 US Census, Colorado Territory, Boulder County, Left Hand

Williams, Joseph D
b. abt 1862, Colorado Territory
father: Elijah R Williams
mother: Charlotte Williams
1870 US Census, Colorado Territory, Boulder County, Left Hand

Williams, Manerva Jane Caywood Slater
b. 5 Mar 1850, Fleming, KY
d. 20 Aug, Denver, CO
spouse: William C Slater, Thomas Williamson
father: William Wesley Caywood
mother: Katharine Donovan Caywood
St Vrain Pioneers Assn Arrival Date: 1864
1870 US Census, Colorado Territory, Boulder County, Left Hand

Williams, Mrs Thomas E
spouse: Thomas E Williams
St Vrain Pioneers Assn Arrival Date: 1870

Williams, Nancy
b. abt 1838, IL
spouse: Elijah R Williams

St Vrain Valley Pioneers

1870 US Census, Colorado Territory, Boulder County, Left Hand

Williams, Scott,
St Vrain Land Club (M687) Date: 27 Jan 1861

Williams, Spencer
b. abt 1867, Colorado Territory
father: Elijah R Williams
mother: Nancy Williams
1870 US Census, Colorado Territory, Boulder County, Left Hand

Williams, Thomas Edward
b. 4 Mar 1845, Wilcox, AL
d. 2 June 1927, Longmont, Boulder, CO
bd. Riverside Cemetery, Fort Morgan, Morgan, CO
spouse: Minerva J Slater Williams
St Vrain Pioneers Assn Arrival Date: 1865

Williams, Urial,
St Vrain Ditch Owner: Davis & Downing Ditch No. 33, 1 Nov 1866

Williams, William
b. abt 1856, IL
father: Elijah R Williams
mother: Nancy Williams
1870 US Census, Colorado Territory, Boulder County, Left Hand

Williamson, Anna A
b. abt 1859, IA
father: Samuel Williamson
mother: Luvesta Williamson
St Vrain Pioneers Assn Arrival Date: 1864
1870 US Census, Colorado Territory, Boulder County, Left Hand

Williamson, Calester/Silester
b. abt 1868, Colorado Territory
father: Samuel Williamson
mother: Luvesta Williamson
1870 US Census, Colorado Territory, Boulder County, Left Hand

Williamson, Caroline/Paulina J
b. abt 1865, Colorado Territory
father: Samuel Williamson
mother: Luvesta Williamson
1870 US Census, Colorado Territory, Boulder County, Left Hand

Williamson, Cresia A
b. abt 1860, IA
father: Samuel Williamson
mother: Luvesta Williamson
St Vrain Pioneers Assn Arrival Date: 1864
1870 US Census, Colorado Territory, Boulder County, Left Hand

Williamson, Enoch T
b. abt 1862, IA
father: Samuel Williamson
mother: Luvesta Williamson
St Vrain Pioneers Assn Arrival Date: 1864
1870 US Census, Colorado Territory, Boulder County, Left Hand

Williamson, George Richard
b. 14 July 1824, Mercer, Butler, PA
d. 30 Jan 1911, Boulder, CO
bd. Green Mountain Cemetery, Boulder, CO
father: Thomas Williamson
mother: Sarah Elizabeth Fruit Williamson
St Vrain Pioneers Assn Arrival Date: 1859

Williamson, Luvesta A
b. 1838
d. Apr 1891
bd. Burlington Cemetery, Longmont, Boulder, CO
spouse: Samuel Williamson
St Vrain Pioneers Assn Arrival Date: 1864
1870 US Census, Colorado Territory, Boulder County, Left Hand

Williamson, Quincy
b. 1860
d. 1954
father: Samuel Williamson
mother: Luvesta Williamson
St Vrain Pioneers Assn Arrival Date: 1864

Williamson, Samuel
b. 19 Sept 1832, IN
d. 29 Sept 1923, Longmont, Boulder, CO
bd. Burlington Cemetery, Longmont, Boulder, CO
spouse: Luvesta Ann Way Wiliamson
father: Thomas Williamson, Sr
mother: Lumira Newman Williamson
St Vrain Pioneers Assn Arrival Date: 1864
1870 US Census, Colorado Territory, Boulder County, Left Hand

St Vrain Valley Pioneers

Williamson, Walter
b. abt 1870, Colorado Territory
father: Samuel Williamson
mother: Luvesta Williamson
St Vrain Pioneers Assn Arrival Date: [not recorded]
1870 US Census, Colorado Territory, Boulder County, Left Hand

Wilson, Alonzo N
b. abt 1834, OH
spouse: Pruda C Wilson
1860 US Census, Nebraska Territory, Altona
1870 US Census, Colorado Territory, Boulder County, St Vrain District

Wilson, Harriet
b. abt 1859, MN
father: Alonzo Wilson
mother: Pruda C Wilson
1860 US Census, Nebraska Territory, Altona
1870 US Census, Colorado Territory, Boulder County, St Vrain District

Wilson, James
b. abt 1863, Colorado Territory
father: Alonzo Wilson
mother: Pruda C Wilson
1870 US Census, Colorado Territory, Boulder County, St Vrain District

Wilson James B
b. abt 1839, OH
spouse: Mary Platt Wilson
St Vrain Pioneers Assn Arrival Date: [not found]

Wilson, Jane
b. abt 1869, Colorado Territory
father: Alonzo Wilson
mother: Pruda C Wilson
1870 US Census, Colorado Territory, Boulder County, St Vrain District

Wilson, John
b. abt 1833, Scotland
1860 US Census, Nebraska Territory, Platte River

Wilson, Pruda C
b. abt 1837, NY
spouse: Alonzo Wilson
1860 US Census, Nebraska Territory, Altona
1870 US Census, Colorado Territory, Boulder County, St Vrain District

Wilson, Seth J
b. abt 1840, IL
1870 US Census, Colorado Territory, Boulder County, Left Hand

Wilson, William
b. abt 1864, Colorado Territory
father: Alonzo Wilson
mother: Pruda C Wilson
1870 US Census, Colorado Territory, Boulder County, St Vrain District

Winegar, Elizabeth
b. abt 1847, Baden
spouse: Joseph Winegar
1870 US Census, Colorado Territory, Boulder County, St Vrain District

Winegar, Henry
b. abt 1867, Colorado Territory
father: Joseph Winegar
mother: Lizzie Winegar
1870 US Census, Colorado Territory, Boulder County, St Vrain District

Winegar, Joseph
b. abt 1822, Switzerland
spouse: Lizzie Winegar
1870 US Census, Colorado Territory, Boulder County, St Vrain District

Winegar, Joseph
b. abt 1866, Colorado Territory
father: Joseph Winegar
mother: Lizzie Winegar
1870 US Census, Colorado Territory, Boulder County, St Vrain District

Winegar, Rose
b. abt 1869, Colorado Territory
father: Joseph Winegar
mother: Lizzie Winegar
1870 US Census, Colorado Territory, Boulder County, St Vrain District

Winslow, George
St Vrain Pioneers Assn Arrival Date: 1868

St Vrain Valley Pioneers

Wise, Ada A
b. abt 1860, WI
father: J Oliver E Wise
mother: Adaline B Rogers Wise
St Vrain Pioneers Assn Arrival Date: 1870

Wise, Adaline B Rogers
b. 12 May 1827, Guensey, OH
d. 30 Aug 1907
bd. Mountain View Cemetery, Longmont, Boulder, CO
spouse: J Oliver E Wise
St Vrain Pioneers Assn Arrival Date: 1870

Wise, Dessie Matthews
St Vrain Pioneers Assn Arrival Date: 1869

Wise, J Oliver E
b. abt 1820, ME
spouse: Adaline B Rogers Wise
St Vrain Pioneers Assn Arrival Date: 1870

Wise, Joseph Oscar V
b. abt 1854, WI
spouse: Sarah A Beasley Wise
father: J Oliver E Wise
mother: Adaline B Rogers Wise
St Vrain Pioneers Assn Arrival Date: 1870

Wise, Oscar
b. abt 1854, WI
father: J Oliver E Wise
mother: Adaline B Rogers Wise
St Vrain Pioneers Assn Arrival Date: 1870

Wise, William
b. abt 1848, WI
father: J Oliver E Wise
mother: Adaline B Rogers Wise
St Vrain Pioneers Assn Arrival Date: 1870

Wise, William O
b. abt 1849
d. 21 Aug 1911, Canfield, CO

Wist, Frank
b. abt 1836, Baden
spouse: Katie Wist
1870 US Census, Colorado Territory, Boulder County, St Vrain District

Wist, John H
b. abt 1860, IL
father: Frank Wist
mother: Katie Wist
1870 US Census, Colorado Territory, Boulder County, St Vrain District

Wist, Katie
b. abt 1835, Baden
spouse: Frank Wist
1870 US Census, Colorado Territory, Boulder County, St Vrain District

Wist, Louisa
b. abt 1865, IL
father: Frank Wist
mother: Katie Wist
1870 US Census, Colorado Territory, Boulder County, St Vrain District

Wiswall, Bruce
d. Feb 1914, Denver, CO

Wiswall, Ella J Greenly
b. 5 Mar 1856
d. 24 Dec 1919
spouse: Farris Wiswall
St Vrain Pioneers Assn Arrival Date: 1869

Wiswall, Farris/Ferris
spouse: Ella J Greenly Wiswall
St Vrain Pioneers Assn Arrival Date: 1869

Witter, Daniel A
St Vrain Ditch Owner: Coffman Ditch No. 20, 30 May 1864

Wolcott, Edward Corning
b. 1 June 1862, Grinnell, Poweshiek, IA
d. 23 Oct 1940, Boulder, CO
bd. Green Mountain Cemetery, Boulder, CO
spouse: Sarah Josephine Guggenheim Wolcott, Samantha Wolcott, Elsie M Nelmes McNaughton Wolcott
father: Horace Alanson Wolcott
mother: Louisa Payson Bixby Wolcott Housel
1870 US Census, Colorado Territory, Boulder County, St Vrain District

Wolcott, Horace Alanson
b. 30 Oct 1821, OH
d. 22 Feb 1887
spouse: Louisa Payson Bixby Wolcott Housel
1870 US Census, Colorado Territory, Boulder County, St Vrain District

St Vrain Valley Pioneers

Wood, William
St Vrain Land Club Date: 1861 May 23

Woodbury, Charles H
b. abt 1844, NY
spouse: Louisa Runyan Woodbury
1870 US Census, Colorado Territory, Boulder County, St Vrain District

Woodbury, Louisa M Runyan
b. 26 Apr 1855, IN
d. 9 Sept 1933
bd. Hygiene Cemetery, Hygiene, Boulder, CO
spouse: Charles H Woodbury
father: Isaac Runyan
mother: Mary J Runyan
St Vrain Pioneers Assn Arrival Date: 1860
1870 US Census, Colorado Territory, Boulder County, St Vrain District

Woodcock, Wesley
b. 17 ct 1904, Niwot, Boulder, CO
d. 7 July 1968, Denver, CO
bd. South Routt Cemetery, Yampa, Routt, CO
spouse: Ruth Rebecca McKinney Woodcock
father: Charles Wesley Woodcock
mother: Louisa Estella Henry Woodcock

Woods, Charles L
St Vrain Pioneers Assn Arrival Date: 1865

Woodward, Robert J
b. abt 1837, NY
spouse: Amanda Woodward
St Vrain Pioneers Assn Arrival Date: 1860

Woodworth, Anna Maria Allen
b. abt 1837, MA
spouse: Henry C Woodworth
father: John Allen
mother: Ann Maria Allen
St Vrain Pioneers Assn Arrival Date: 1870

Wooley, David M
St Vrain Pioneers Assn Arrival Date: 1859

Workman, Alberta Dailey
b. abt 1865, Boulder Creek, Boulder, Colorado Territory
Sherman L Workman
father: Dennis Dailey
mother: Juliette McDonald Green Dailey
1870 US Census, Colorado Territory, Weld County, St Vrain District

Workman, William
b. abt 1827, KY
1870 US Census, Colorado Territory, Boulder County, St Vrain District

Worrell, Cora Mabelle Johnson
b. abt 1862, Colorado Territory
father: Harvey Johnson
mother: Elisabeth Johnson
1870 US Census, Colorado Territory, Boulder County, St Vrain District

Wright, Allen Kendrick
b. 15 May 1862, Pottawatomie, KS
d. 19 June 1948, Los Angeles, CA
bd. Sunnyside Cemetery, Long Beach, Los Angeles, CA
spouse: Emmeline Thomas Wright
father: Turner Wright
mother: Isabella Rhoten Wright
1870 US Census, Colorado Territory, Weld County, St Vrain District

Wright, Amos
d. 15 May 1929, Pueblo, CO
father: Turner Wright

Wright, Charles
b. abt 1848, IA
1870 US Census, Colorado Territory, Boulder County, St Vrain District

Wright, Elenor
b. abt 1867, Colorado Territory
father: Turner Wright
mother: Isabelle Wright
1870 US Census, Colorado Territory, Weld County, St Vrain District

Wright, Isabella Rhoten
b. 25 Oct 1827, OH
d. 14 Feb 1904, Denver, Arapahoe, CO
spouse: Turner Wright
St Vrain Pioneers Assn Arrival Date: 1860
1870 US Census, Colorado Territory, Weld County, St Vrain District

Wright, James Amos
b. abt 1858, IN
father: Turner Wright

mother: Isabella Wright
1870 US Census, Colorado Territory, Weld County, St Vrain District

Wright, Martha
b. abt 1854, IN
father: Turner Wright
mother: Isabella Wright
1870 US Census, Colorado Territory, Weld County, St Vrain District

Wright, Martin
b. abt 1834, Hanover, Germany
1860 US Census, Nebraska Territory, Platte River

Wright, Nancy J
b. abt 1864, Colorado Territory
father: Turner Wright
mother: Isabella Wright
1870 US Census, Colorado Territory, Weld County, St Vrain District

Wright, Turner
b. 4 Aug 1829, Davidson, NC
d. 4 Oct 1918, Denver, CO
spouse: Isabella Rhoten Wright
St Vrain Pioneers Assn Arrival Date: 1860
1870 US Census, Colorado Territory, Weld County, St Vrain District

Wyatt, Albert
b. abt 1845, KY
1870 US Census, Colorado Territory, Boulder County, St Vrain District

Y

Young, George X
d. Aug 1914, Oakland, CA
St Vrain Pioneers Assn Arrival Date: [not recorded]

Youngham, E J
b. abt 1824, PA
1860 US Census, Nebraska Territory, Platte River

Yount, Abram Knox
b. abt 1833, PA
d. 1876, Denver, Arapahoe, CO
spouse: Elvira Bethena Doolittle Yount
father: Gabriel Yount
mother: Mariah Elizabeth Wilson Yount
St Vrain Pioneers Assn Arrival Date: 1858

Z

Zachany, Emos
b. abt 1845, IA
1870 US Census, Colorado Territory, Weld County, St Vrain District

Zimmerman, George
St Vrain Pioneers Assn Arrival Date: 1868

Zimmerman, John
St Vrain Pioneers Assn Arrival Date: 1868

Zook, Sarah
b. 1881
d. 27 June 1968
bd. Mount Pleasant Cemetery, Erie, Weld, CO
spouse: Ira D Zook

Zweck, George
b. 6 Dec 1829, Germany
d. 24 Dec 1902
bd. Burlington Cemetery, Longmont, Boulder, CO
spouse: Mary Louise Greub Zweck
St Vrain Pioneers Assn Arrival Date: 1860
St Vrain Land Club Date: 1861 Aug 11
St Vrain Ditch Owner: Zweck & Turner Ditch No. 21, 30 June 1864
1870 US Census (see Sweck)

Zweck, Hallie
b. 13 July 1886
d. 27 Sept 1981
bd. Hygiene Cemetery, Hygiene, Boulder, CO
spouse: George Herbert Zweck

Zweck, Mary Louise Greub
b. 4 July 1848, Lotzvil, Bern, Switzerland
d. 29 Jan 1934, Longmont, Boulder, CO
bd. Burlington Cemetery, Longmont, Boulder, CO
spouse: George Zweck
father: Rudolph Greub
mother: Elizabeth Affolter Greub
St Vrain Pioneers Assn Arrival Date: 1864

Additional Colorado Research Titles

If you borrowed this copy from a library and would like to order a copy, please send a check or money order to: Iron Gate Publishing, P.O. Box 999, Niwot, CO 80544. Our research books are available online to institutions and individuals at Amazon.com and on our website:

www.irongate.com

Colorado's Historical Assets: A Research Guide for Genealogists, Local Historians and History Buffs Containing a Treasure Trove of Museums, Ghost Towns, Courthouses, Historic Homes and Hotels, along with the Libraries and Archives Holding Colorado's History
ISBN 978-1-68224-044-1 $35.00 + $5.00 S&H

Digging Up Dirt: The Gold Hill Cemetery, Gold Hill, Colorado
ISBN 978-1-68224-037-3 $34.95 + $5.00 S&H

Rocky Ford, Colorado—A Walk Past Local Doors: Businesses and Residences from the Fairgrounds to Reservoir Hill, US 50 Curve to Curve
ISBN 978-1-68224-025-0 $34.95 + $6.00 S&H

Walking Rocky Ford and the Arkansas Valley: A Tour of Rocky Ford, Colorado and Vicinity
ISBN 978-1-68224-180-6 $29.95 + $6.00 S&H

Colorado's Historical Assets: A Research Guide for Genealogists, Local Historians and History Buffs Containing a Treasure Trove of Museums, Ghost Towns, Courthouses, Historic Homes and Hotels, along with the Libraries and Archives Holding Colorado's History
ISBN 978-1-68224-044-1 $35.00 + $5.00 S&H

Digging Up Dirt: The Gold Hill Cemetery, Gold Hill, Colorado
ISBN 978-1-68224-037-3 $34.95 + $5.00 S&H

Rocky Ford, Colorado—A Walk Past Local Doors: Businesses and Residences from the Fairgrounds to Reservoir Hill, US 50 Curve to Curve
ISBN 978-1-68224-025-0 $34.95 + $6.00 S&H

Walking Rocky Ford and the Arkansas Valley: A Tour of Rocky Ford, Colorado and Vicinity
ISBN 978-1-68224-180-6 $29.95 + $6 S&H

Cemeteries and Remote Burials in Larimer County, Colorado, Volume I: The Poudre and North, Including the Laramie River Valley and Livermore
ISBN 978-1-68224-010-6 $44.95 + $5.00 S&H

Cemeteries and Remote Burials in Larimer County, Colorado, Volume II: South of the Poudre, Including Fort Collins, Loveland, and Berthoud
ISBN 978-1-68224-012-0 $41.95 + $5.00 S&H

Cemeteries and Remote Burials in Larimer County, Colorado, Volume III: Estes Park Area and the Rocky Mountain National Park, Including Park Property in Grand County
ISBN 978-1-68224-014-4 $23.95 + $5.00 S&H

Taxpayer Series
Boulder County, Colorado Taxpayers, 1866-1867: An Index
ISBN 978-1-68224-184-4 $11.95 + $5.00 S&H

Boulder County, Colorado Taxpayers, 1868-1869: An Index
ISBN 978-1-68224-186-8 $11.95 + $5.00 S&H

Boulder County, Colorado Taxpayers, 1870-1871: An Index
ISBN 978-1-68224-187-5 $11.95 + $5.00 S&H

Boulder County, Colorado Taxpayers, 1872-1873: An Index
 ISBN 978-1-68224-188-2 $11.95 + $5.00 S&H

Boulder County, Colorado Taxpayers, 1874: An Index
 ISBN 978-1-68224-189-9 $11.95 + $5.00 S&H

Boulder County, Colorado Taxpayers, 1875: An Index
 ISBN 978-1-68224-190-5 $11.95 + $5.00 S&H

Boulder County, Colorado Taxpayers Assessment Roll, 1872-1873: An Index
 ISBN 978-1-68224-191-2 $11.95 + $5.00 S&H

Boulder County, Colorado Taxpayers Assessment Roll, 1874: An Index
 ISBN 978-1-68224-192-9 $11.95 + $5.00 S&H

Boulder County, Colorado Taxpayers Assessment Roll, 1876: An Index
 ISBN 978-1-68224-193-6 $11.95 + $5.00 S&H

School District Series

Boulder County, Colorado School Census Records 1875–1885: An Annotated Index
 ISBN 978-1-68224-175-2 $35.95 + $5.00 S&H

Boulder County, Colorado School Census Records 1886–1890: An Annotated Index
 ISBN 978-1-68224-174-5 $45.95 + $5.00 S&H

Boulder County, Colorado School Census Records 1891–1895: An Annotated Index
 ISBN 978-1-68224-173-8 $55.95 + $6.00 S&H

Boulder County, Colorado School Census Records 1896–1900: An Annotated Index
 ISBN 978-1-68224-172-1 $65.95 + $6.00 S&H

Boulder County, Colorado District 1—Superior School Census Records 1876–1900: An Annotated Index
 ISBN 978-1-68224-114-1 $9.95 + $4.00 S&H

Boulder County, Colorado District 2—Shamrock School Census Records 1876–1900: An Annotated Index
 ISBN 978-1-68224-115-8 $9.95 + $4.00 S&H

Boulder County, Colorado District 3—Boulder School Census Records 1877–1900: An Annotated Index
 ISBN 978-1-68224-113-4 $35.95 + $6.00 S&H

Boulder County, Colorado District 4—Valmont School Census Records 1879–1900: An Annotated Index
 ISBN 978-1-68224-116-5 $9.95 + $4.00 S&H

Boulder County, Colorado District 5—Davidson School Census Records 1879–1900: An Annotated Index
 ISBN 978-1-68224-117-2 $9.95 + $4.00 S&H

Boulder County, Colorado District 6—Burlington School Census Records 1875–1900: An Annotated Index
 ISBN 978-1-68224-118-9 $9.95 + $4.00 S&H

Boulder County, Colorado District 7—Niwot School Census Records 1876–1900: An Annotated Index
 ISBN 978-1-68224-119-6 $14.95 + $4.00 S&H

Boulder County, Colorado District 8—Montgomery School Census Records 1879–1900: An Annotated Index
 ISBN 978-1-68224-120-2 $9.95 + $4.00 S&H

Boulder County, Colorado District 9—Pella School Census Records 1880–1900: An Annotated Index
 ISBN 978-1-68224-121-9 $9.95 + $4.00 S&H

Boulder County, Colorado District 10—Baseline School Census Records 1879–1900: An Annotated Index
 ISBN 978-1-68224-122-6 $11.95 + $4.00 S&H

Boulder County, Colorado District 11—Jamestown School Census Records 1879–1900: An Annotated Index
 ISBN 978-1-68224-123-3 $14.95 + $4.00 S&H

Boulder County, Colorado District 12—Ward School Census Records 1879–1900: An Annotated Index
ISBN 978-1-68224-124-0 $11.95 + $4.00 S&H

Boulder County, Colorado District 13—Bader School Census Records 1879–1900: An Annotated Index
ISBN 978-1-68224-125-7 $9.95 + $4.00 S&H

Boulder County, Colorado District 14—White Rock School Census Records 1879–1900: An Annotated Index
ISBN 978-1-68224-126-4 $9.95 + $4.00 S&H

Boulder County, Colorado District 15—Marshall School Census Records 1879–1900: An Annotated Index
ISBN 978-1-68224-127-1 $14.95 + $4.00 S&H

Boulder County, Colorado District 16—Pleasant View School Census Records 1883–1900: An Annotated Index
ISBN 978-1-68224-128-8 $11.95 + $4.00 S&H

Boulder County, Colorado District 17—Longmont School Census Records 1883–1900: An Annotated Index
ISBN 978-1-68224-129-5 $32.95 + $5.00 S&H

Boulder County, Colorado District 18—Middle Boulder School Census Records 1884–1900: An Annotated Index
ISBN 978-1-68224-130-1 $9.95 + $4.00 S&H

Boulder County, Colorado District 19—Caribou School Census Records 1879–1900: An Annotated Index
ISBN 978-1-68224-131-8 $11.95 + $4.00 S&H

Boulder County, Colorado District 20—Batchelder School Census Records 1884–1900: An Annotated Index
ISBN 978-1-68224-132-5 $9.95 + $4.00 S&H

Boulder County, Colorado District 21—Hygiene View School Census Records 1885–1900: An Annotated Index
ISBN 978-1-68224-133-2 $11.95 + $4.00 S&H

Boulder County, Colorado District 22—Altona School Census Records 1885–1900: An Annotated Index
ISBN 978-1-68224-134-9 $9.95 + $4.00 S&H

Boulder County, Colorado District 23—Armstrong School Census Records 1885–1900: An Annotated Index
ISBN 978-1-68224-135-6 $11.95 + $4.00 S&H

Boulder County, Colorado District 24—Gold Hill School Census Records 1885–1900: An Annotated Index
ISBN 978-1-68224-136-3 $11.95 + $4.00 S&H

Boulder County, Colorado District 25—Bashor School Census Records 1884–1900: An Annotated Index
ISBN 978-1-68224-137-0 $9.95 + $4.00 S&H

Boulder County, Colorado District 26—Ryssby School Census Records 1885–1900: An Annotated Index
ISBN 978-1-68224-138-7 $9.95 + $4.00 S&H

Boulder County, Colorado District 27—Wallstreet School Census Records 1886–1900: An Annotated Index
ISBN 978-1-68224-139-4 $9.95 + $4.00 S&H

Boulder County, Colorado District 28—Sunshine School Census Records 1885–1900: An Annotated Index
ISBN 978-1-68224-140-0 $9.95 + $4.00 S&H

Boulder County, Colorado District 29—Louisville School Census Records 1885–1900: An Annotated Index
ISBN 978-1-68224-141-7 $24.95 + $5.00 S&H

Boulder County, Colorado District 30—Pine Grove School Census Records 1885–1900: An Annotated Index
ISBN 978-1-68224-142-4 $9.95 + $4.00 S&H

Boulder County, Colorado District 31—Salina School Census Records 1884–1900: An Annotated Index
ISBN 978-1-68224-143-1 $11.95 + $4.00 S*H

Boulder County, Colorado District 32—Crisman School Census Records 1886–1900: An Annotated Index
ISBN 978-1-68224-144-8 $9.95 + $4.00 S&H

Boulder County, Colorado District 33—Silver Spruce School Census Records 1886–1900: An Annotated Index
ISBN 978-1-68224-145-5 $9.95 + $4.00 S&H

Boulder County, Colorado District 34—Sugarloaf School Census Records 1886–1900: An Annotated Index
    ISBN 978-1-68224-146-2 $9.95 + $4.00 S&H

Boulder County, Colorado District 35—Chapman School Census Records 1886–1900: An Annotated Index
    ISBN 978-1-68224-147-9 $9.95 + $4.00 S&H

Boulder County, Colorado District 36—Eldorado Springs School Census Records 1886–1900: An Annotated Index
    ISBN 978-1-68224-148-6 $9.95 + $4.00 S&H

Boulder County, Colorado District 37—Culver School Census Records 1885–1900: An Annotated Index
    ISBN 978-1-68224-149-3 $9.95 + $4.00 S&H

Boulder County, Colorado District 38—Magnolia School Census Records 1884–1900: An Annotated Index
    ISBN 978-1-68224-150-9 $9.95 + $4.00 S&H

Boulder County, Colorado District 39—Rowena School Census Records 1884–1900: An Annotated Index
    ISBN 978-1-68224-151-6 $9.95 + $4.00 S&H

Boulder County, Colorado District 40—Springdale School Census Records 1886–1900: An Annotated Index
    ISBN 978-1-68224-152-3 $9.95 + $4.00 S&H

Boulder County, Colorado District 41—Fairview School Census Records 1885–1900: An Annotated Index
    ISBN 978-1-68224-153-0 $9.95 + $4.00 S&H

Boulder County, Colorado District 42—Beasley School Census Records 1885–1900: An Annotated Index
    ISBN 978-1-68224-154-7 $9.95 + $4.00 S&H

Boulder County, Colorado District 43—Broomfield School Census Records 1884–1900: An Annotated Index
    ISBN 978-1-68224-155-4 $11.95 + $4.00 S&H

Boulder County, Colorado District 44—Potato Hill School Census Records 1885–1900: An Annotated Index
    ISBN 978-1-68224-156-1 $9.95 + $4.00 S&H

Boulder County, Colorado District 45—Pleasant View Ridge School Census Records 1885–1900: An Annotated Index
    ISBN 978-1-68224-157-8 $9.95 + $4.00 S&H

Boulder County, Colorado District 46—Canfield School Census Records 1880–1900: An Annotated Index
    ISBN 978-1-68224-158-5 $11.95 + $4.00 S&H

Boulder County, Colorado District 47—Lyons School Census Records 1885–1900: An Annotated Index
    ISBN 978-1-68224-159-2 $14.95 + $4.00 S&H

Boulder County, Colorado District 48—Nelson School Census Records 1886–1900: An Annotated Index
    ISBN 978-1-68224-160-8 $9.95 + $4.00 S&H

Boulder County, Colorado District 49—Bunce School Census Records 1886–1900: An Annotated Index
    ISBN 978-1-68224-161-5 $9.95 + $4.00 S&H

Boulder County, Colorado District 50—Lee Hill School Census Records 1887–1900: An Annotated Index
    ISBN 978-1-68224-162-2 $9.95 + $4.00 S&H

Boulder County, Colorado District 51—Sunset School Census Records 1888–1900: An Annotated Index
    ISBN 978-1-68224-163-9 $9.95 + $4.00 S&H

Boulder County, Colorado District 52—Lafayette School Census Records 1888–1900: An Annotated Index
    ISBN 978-1-68224-164-6 $24.95 + $5.00 S&H

Boulder County, Colorado District 53—Noland School Census Records 1891–1900: An Annotated Index
    ISBN 978-1-68224-165-3 $9.95 + $4.00 S&H

Boulder County, Colorado District 54—Eggleston School Census Records 1892–1900: An Annotated Index
    ISBN 978-1-68224-166-0 $9.95 + $4.00 &H

Boulder County, Colorado District 55—Stony Lake School Census Records 1893–1900: An Annotated Index
    ISBN 978-1-68224-167-7 $9.95 + $4.00 S&H

Boulder County, Colorado District 56—Eldora School Census Records 1896–1900: An Annotated Index
    ISBN 978-1-8224-168-4 $9.95 + $4.00 S&H

Boulder County, Colorado District 57—Pine Cliff School Census Records 1896–1900: An Annotated Index
    ISBN 978-1-68224-169-1 $9.95 + $4.00 S&H

Boulder County, Colorado District 58—Pine Glade School Census Records 1897–1900: An Annotated Index
    ISBN 978-1-8224-170-7 $9.95 + $4.00 S&H

Boulder County, Colorado District 59—Allenspark School Census Records 1897–1900: An Annotated Index
    ISBN 978-1-68224-171-4 $9.95 & $4.00 S&H

Additional Boulder County Titles

Boulder County, Colorado Payments, Accounts, Burial Permits and Licenses, 1879-1893: An Annotated Index
    ISBN 978-1-68224-185-1 $11.95 + $5.00 S&H

Boulder County, Colorado Specialized Land Grants, 1857-1909, Agricultural Scrip Patents, Military Warrant Patents, State Volume Patents & Timber Culture Patents: An Annotated Index
    ISBN 978-1-68224-194-3 $13.95 + $5.00 S&H

Boulder County, Colorado Probate Case Files Index: 1862–1978
    ISBN 978-1-68224-112-7 $49.95 + $6.00 S&H

Boulder County, Colorado Lodged Wills and Inheritance Tax Waivers, 1899-1975: An Annotated Index
    ISBN 978-1-68224-109-7 $11.95 + $4.00 S&H

Boulder County, Colorado School Census 1877: An Annotated Index
    ISBN 978-1-68224-035-9 $15.95 + $4.00 S&H

Boulder County, Colorado, District Court, Petit Jury Lists, 1883-1910: An Annotated Index
    ISBN 978-1-68224-034-2 $11.95 + $4.00 S&H

Boulder County, Colorado District Court, Petit Jury Records, 1867-1936: An Annotated Index
    ISBN 978-1-68224-031-1 $24.95 + $5.00 S&H

Boulder County, Colorado District Court, Grand Jury Records, 1867-1922: An Annotated Index
    ISBN 978-1-68224-032-8 $11.95 + $4.00 S&H

Boulder County, Colorado Surveys and Mineral Claims at the General Land Office, 1859-1876: An Annotated Index
    ISBN 978-1-68224-030-4 $15.95 + $4.00 S&H

Boulder County, Colorado Clerk & Recorder, Loose Papers Box 1, 1861-1878: An Annotated Index
    ISBN 978-1-68224-029-8 $21.95 + $5.00 S&H

Boulder County, Colorado Clerk & Recorder, Loose Papers Box 2, 1861-1878: An Annotated Index
    ISBN 978-1-68224-028-1 $21.95 + $5.00 S&H

Boulder County, Colorado District Court Judge's Docket, Vol 1, 1867-1871: An Annotated Index
    ISBN 978-1-68224-026-7 $15.95 + $4.00 S&H

Boulder County, Colorado District Court Record, June 1862 to March 1866: An Annotated Transcription
    ISBN 978-1-68224-024-3 $11.95 + $4.00 S&H

Boulder County, Colorado Treasurer, Register of Accounts, 1867-1880: An Annotated Index
    ISBN 978-1-68224-023-6 $19.95 + $5.00 S&H

Boulder County, Colorado County Court Index Book I, Plaintiffs and Defendants: An Annotated Index
    ISBN 978-1-68224-021-2 $34.95 + $5.00

Minutes of the Board of Trustees of the University of Colorado, 1870-1876: An Annotated Index
    ISBN 978-1-68224-020-5 $11.95 + $4.00 S&H

Boulder County, Colorado District Court Civil Appearance Docket, 1878-1882: An Annotated Index
    ISBN 978-1-68224-019-9 $19.95 + $5.00 S&H

Boulder County, Colorado County Court Will Record, Volume A, 1875-1889: An Annotated Index
ISBN 978-1-68224-018-2 $11.95 + $4.00 S&H

Boulder County, Colorado, County Court Probate Record, Vol 1, 1875-1884: An Annotated Index
ISBN 978-1-68224-017-5 $11.95 + $4.00 S&H

Early Land Owners Along the St. Vrain Creek, Colorado Territory, 1860-1861: An Annotated Index
ISBN 978-1-68224-006-9 $11.95 + $4.00 S&H

Boulder County, Colorado District Court Widow's Relinquishment, Volumes 1 & 2, 1889–1937: An Annotated Index
ISBN 978-1-68224-009-0 $11.95 + $4.00 S&H

Boulder County, Colorado, District Court Guardians Bonds, Vol. A, 1876-1902: An Annotated Index
ISBN 978-1-879579-78-1 $11.95 + $4.00 S&H

Boulder County, Colorado Probate Court Fee Book, 1874-1890: An Annotated Index
ISBN 978-1-879579-88-0 $11.95 + $4.00 S&H

Boulder City Town Company Lot Sales 1859-1864: An Annotated Map Guide
ISBN 978-1-879579-87-3 $15.95 + $5.00 S&H

Brainard's Hotel Register, Boulder, Colorado, 1880: An Annotated Index
ISBN 978-1-879579-86-6 $15.95 + $5.00 S&H

Boulder County Commissioners Journal, 1861-1871: An Annotated Transcription
ISBN 978-1-879579-77-4 $45.99 + $5.00 S&H

Boulder County Commissioners Journal, 1871-1874: An Annotated Transcription
ISBN 978-1-879579-91-0 $39.95 + $5.00 S&H

Boulder, Colorado Teachers, 1878-1900: An Annotated Index
ISBN 978-1-879579-93-4 $11.95 + $4.00 S&H

Boulder County, Colorado District Court Execution Docket, 1875-1885: An Annotated Index
ISBN 978-1-879579-94-1 $11.95 + $4.00 S&H

Boulder, Colorado Births 1892–1906: An Annotated Index
ISBN 978-1-879579-79-8 $11.95 + $4.00 S&H

Boulder County Probate Court Appraisement Record A, 1875-1888: An Annotated Index
ISBN 978-1-879579-72-9 $11.95 + $4.00 S&H

Boulder County Assessor's Tax List, 1875: An Annotated Index
ISBN 978-1-879579-55-2 $11.95 + $4.00 S&H

Boulder County Assessor's Tax List, 1876: An Annotated Index
ISBN 978-1-879579-56-9 $11.95 + $4.00 S&H

Boulder Valley Presbyterian Church Records, 1863-1900: An Annotated Index
ISBN 978-1-879579-58-3 $11.95 + $4.00 S&H

Boulder's Masonic Pioneers, 1867-1886: Members of Columbia Lodge No. 14, Boulder County, Colorado Territory
ISBN 978-1-879579-57-6 $15.95 + $4.00 S&H

Map: Boulder City Town Company 1859 Original Survey Map
ISBN 978-1-68224-000-7 $24.95 (PAPER) + $7.00 S&H
ISBN 978-1-68224-001-4 $74.95 (MYLAR) + $7.00 S&H

Map: Boulder City Town Company, 11 Aug 1859 Land Lottery Map Showing Lot Purchases
ISBN 978-1-68224-002-1 $24.95 (PAPER) + $7.00 S&H
ISBN 978-1-68224-003-8 $74.95 (MYLAR) + $7.00 S&H

Map: Boulder City Town Company 20 Sept 1859 Map Showing Stock Certificates Issued by Lot
ISBN 978-1-68224-004-5 $24.95 (PAPER) + $7.00 S&H
ISBN 978-1-68224-005-2 $74.95 (MYLAR) + $7.00 S&H

Additional Titles from Around Colorado

Inventors in the Colorado Territory and their U.S. Patents, 1861-1876: An Annotated Index
    ISBN 978-1-68224-022-9 $54.95 + $5.00 S&H

Colorado Territorial Penitentiary, Board of Managers Reports, 1871-1877: An Annotated Index of Marshals, Wardens, Guards, Board Members, Prisoners, and Local Businesses
    ISBN 978-1-68224-039-7 $11.95 + $4.00 S&H

Colorado's Territorial Masons: An Annotated Index of the Proceedings of the Grand Lodge of Colorado, 1861–1876
    ISBN 978-1-879579-85-9 $29.95 + $5.00 S&H

Denver, Colorado Territory Wagon Sales & Repair Ledger 1867-1870: An Annotated Index
    ISBN 978-1-68224-040-3 $12.95 + $4.00 S&H

Denver, Colorado Police Force Record, 1879-1903: An Annotated Index
    ISBN 978-1-879579-81-1 $11.95 + $4.00 S&H

Arapahoe County, Colorado Territory Criminal Court Index, 1862-1879: An Annotated Index
    ISBN 978-1-879579-70-5 $11.95 + $4.00 S&H

General Research Titles

Map Your U.S. Research: A Workbook for Genealogists
    ISBN 978-1-68224-041-0 $27.95 + $5.00 S&H

Make the Most of Your Genealogical Research Trip: Battle Plan—Washington, D.C.
    ISBN 978-1-68224-027-4   eBook $5.95
    ISBN 978-1-68224-38-0   print $12.95 + $4.00

These titles are also available through Ingram.

Directory of Genealogical and Historical Societies, Libraries and Archives in the US and Canada 2022 (2 Vols)
    Vol 1, ISBN 978-1-68224-178-3 $125.00 + $10.00 S&H
    Vol 2, ISBN 978-1-68224-179-0 $125.00 + $10.00 S&H

Publishing Titles

If you would like to order one of these books, please send a check or money order to: Iron Gate Publishing, P.O. Box 999, Niwot, CO 80544. Our books are available online to institutions through Ingram, to individuals at Amazon.com and on our website:

www.irongate.com

Publish Your Family History: A Step-by-Step Guide to Writing the Stories of Your Ancestors
    ISBN 978-1-879579-63-7 $24.95 + $5.00 S&H

Publish Your Genealogy: A Step-by-Step Guide for Preserving Your Research for the Next Generation
    ISBN 978-1-879579-62-0 $24.95 + $5.00 S&H

Set Yourself Up to Self-Publish: A Genealogist's Guide
    ISBN 978-1-879579-99-6 $19.95 + $5.00 S&H

Set Yourself Up to Self-Publish: A Local Historian's Guide
    ISBN 978-1-879579-98-9 $19.95 + $5.00

Publish a Local History: A Step-by-Step Guide from Finding the Right Project to Finished Book
    ISBN 978-1-879579-64-4 $24.95 + $5.00 S&H

Publish a Memoir: A Step-by-Step Guide to Saving Your Memories for Future Generations
    ISBN 978-1-879579-65-1 $24.95 + $5.00 S&H

Publish a Biography: A Step-by-Step Guide to Capturing the Life and Times of an Ancestor or a Generation
    ISBN 978-1-879579-66-8 $24.95 + $5.00 S&H

Publish a Photo Book: A Step-by-Step Guide for Transforming Your Genealogical Research into a Stunning Family Heirloom
    ISBN 978-1-879579-67-5 $24.95 + $5.00 S&H

Publish a Source Index: A Step-by-Step Guide to Creating a Genealogically Useful Index, Abstract or Transcription
    ISBN 978-1-879579-68-2 $24.95 + $5.00 S&H

Publish Your Specialty: A Step-by-Step Guide for Imparting Your Research Expertise to Others
    ISBN 978-1-879579-76-7 $24.95 + $5.00 S&H

www.ingramcontent.com/pod-product-compliance
Lightning Source LLC
Chambersburg PA
CBHW081920170426
43200CB00014B/2784